Pride and Pe

Pride and Perjury

JONATHAN AITKEN

continuum
LONDON • NEW YORK

Continuum

The Tower Building   15 East 26th Street
11 York Road   New York 10010
London SE1 7NX   USA

www.continuumbooks.com

First published in Great Britain in 2000
by HarperCollins*Publishers*
Reprinted by Continuum in 2003

Scripture quotations identified KJV are taken from
the King James Version of the Bible

Scripture quotations identified NIV are taken from the
HOLY BIBLE, NEW INTERNATIONAL VERSION.
Copyright © 1973, 1978, 1984 by International Bible Society.

Scripture quotations identified CEV are taken from the
Contemporary English Version, copyright © 1997 British and
Foreign Bible Society; New Testament © 1991, 1992, 1995
American Bible Society

The private letters from Charles W. Colson on pages 257, 263, 274,
318 and 346 are quoted with his kind permission

A catalogue record for this book is
available from the British Library

ISBN 0 8264 7274 5

Printed and bound in Great Britain by
Creative Print and Design (Wales), Ebbw Vale

To Victoria

Contents

CHAPTER ONE

Riding High

SUMMONED TO SEE THE Prime Minister on 20 July 1994, the morning of the Cabinet reshuffle, I double-checked my appearance in the mirror of the bathroom I shared with the Chief of the Defence Staff, puffed up my chest like a pouter pigeon, and strode proudly across Whitehall in the direction of Downing Street.

Approaching the front door of No. 10, the elixir of imminent promotion put a spring in my step as a chaos of cameras flashed, clicked and rolled in my direction. This elation evaporated within seconds of my arrival inside No. 10, where I was greeted by a flustered private secretary saying, 'Oh dear, didn't you get the message that we don't want you?'

Totally deflated by this apparent cancellation of my appointment with the Prime Minister, I gradually recovered after being told that it had merely been postponed because of hitches over the timings of other ministerial comings and goings. These required me to cool my heels for the best part of an hour in an upstairs study, and even when I was eventually ushered into the Cabinet room for my moment of destiny the postponement syndrome continued.

John Major was the epitome of warmth in his greeting, yet he seemed curiously reluctant to come to the point. He began with some gracious compliments about my work over the last two years as Minister of State for Defence. Then he consulted his notes and gave me detailed instructions about the timing of my appointment with the Queen for the swearing-in ceremony as a new member of the Privy Council. Delighted as I was to be elevated to the rank of a Right Honourable Gentleman, the office accompanying the title remained tantalizingly veiled in obscurity for a few more minutes as the Prime Minister embarked on some discursive comments about the challenges facing his reshaped Government, particularly on the key battlefield of public expenditure control. This topic eventually proved to be the cue to the line I was longing to hear as the Prime Minister concluded, 'So I would like you to join the Cabinet as Chief Secretary to the Treasury.'

Later that morning I heard the tale of how Nicholas Soames had been so overcome on hearing the news of his promotion to the post he had coveted of Minister of State for the Armed Forces that he had said to his benefactor, 'Oh, *darling* Prime Minister – I think I'm going to blub.'

I know just how he felt. For my cup too was overflowing with emotions, perhaps almost tears, of political joy. Not only was I coming into the Cabinet after 20 years in the House of Commons: I was being given one of the most fascinating and powerful jobs in government, for the Chief Secretary to the Treasury is the controller of Britain's £300 billion public expenditure budget with a remit of responsibility that extends across all Whitehall departments, agencies and committees.

John Major, who had been a recent Chief Secretary himself, waxed lyrical about the opportunities that lay before me in deciding the priorities of the current spending round. As we talked, I began to appreciate that I had been dealt a hand that would do much more than enable me to *be somebody* in politics: I would have a real opportunity to *do something* in government – something, I hoped, that would be of enduring and important public service. With such thoughts burning in my brain, I walked away from No. 10 that morning suffused with a warm glow of exhilaration.

The rest of the day passed in a haze of happiness. Telling the family was the first joy. My wife Lolicia and our twin 14-year-old daughters Alexandra and Victoria received the news with sound-bites of ecstasy that would have been appropriate for acclaiming the winner of an Olympic gold medal. Son William, aged 11, was more cautious. 'But are you good enough at maths, Daddy?' he inquired, recalling that I had not always been an omniscient source of accuracy when assisting him with his homework. These filial doubts were swept away in the general family rejoicings, which reminded me of a good line of Disraeli's to the effect that political fame was 'quite useless, except perhaps as an offering of homage to those that one loves'.[1]

Those with whom I would be working were my next priority. My first call after seeing the Prime Minister was on the Chancellor of the Exchequer, Ken Clarke, since I was about to be coupled with him in the closest of Cabinet harnesses at the Treasury.

'Just what I wanted: a good, strong Eurosceptic,' he said with a breezy enthusiasm which was subsequently undermined by his reluctance to listen to my less than Europhile views on the single currency and EMU. Yet on that first day Ken could not have given me a heartier welcome, nor a better back-of-the-envelope overview of the battles we were to fight so successfully together in the public expenditure arena.

After greetings from other Treasury ministers and mandarins, I returned to the Ministry of Defence for an afternoon of festive farewells. All three junior ministers at the MOD – Robert Cranborne, Jeremy Hanley and I – were promoted to the Cabinet on that same day, so the champagne corks were popping like pom-pom guns on our ministerial floor, occasionally accompanied by some *sotto voce* warning shots fired by the Chiefs of Staff across the bows of the new Chief Secretary: 'We can count on you not to carry out any Treasury raids on the Defence budget in the next spending round, can't we?' They could.

My general feeling of floating on cloud nine on that glorious Cabinet promotion day was soon enhanced by the warmth of the congratulations that avalanched in from colleagues, constituents and friends, as well as by the favourable tone of the media comments on my appointment. Perhaps I was getting swept away on a tide of excessive hubris, but after a political career that had consisted of 18 years on the backbenches and only two years as a junior minister, it would have been inhuman of me not to feel a sense of elation at having so suddenly and unexpectedly arrived as a serious player at the top table of British politics.

Serious was the right word to describe the workload of the Chief Secretary. Instead of the single red box of government papers that I had intermittently taken home as a Defence Minister, the Treasury routinely sent round four or five of them each night, all crammed with briefs that seemed daunting in their complexity. Mastering the small print of the 30 or so Whitehall budgets under my command was a tough assignment, but I quickly discovered that strong political determination, combined with the intellectual discipline of burning midnight oil on the detail, could enable a Chief Secretary to win interesting battles – as the episode of the intelligence service budgets demonstrated.

It was Treasury custom and practice that the Chief Secretary should wield his axe early in the spending round on a handful of relatively low-spending agency budgets such as the Forestry Commission and the Arts Council, for which there was no direct ministerial responsibility. The most interesting items on this non-ministerial agenda, however, were the three principal intelligence service budgets belonging to the Government Communications Headquarters (GCHQ), the Security Service (MI5) and the Secret Intelligence Service (SIS).

Until 1994 these budgets had been lumped together under the mysterious heading of 'The Secret Vote', whose spending limits were ruled upon even more mysteriously by a Secret Vote Committee under the chairmanship of the Prime Minister, which according to Whitehall folklore was so secret that it never actually met.

The Treasury had cavilled at this arrangement for years and had won a turf war victory on it shortly before my appointment. This meant that I was the first Chief Secretary in history to be given the power to fix separate spending limits on each of the intelligence budgets, and to negotiate them in face-to-face bilaterals with the Chiefs of these services.

Annual public spending on the intelligence community in 1994 totalled around £1.1 billion, of which GCHQ accounted for some £850 million, while MI5 and SIS took approximately £125 million apiece. My brief from the Treasury proposed that I should seek an across-the-board reduction of 10 per cent, or about £110 million, arguing that such a cut could safely be made now that we were living in the era of an IRA ceasefire and an increasingly benign post-Communist Russia.

Bureaucrats fight their spending-round battles far more cleverly than most ministers. So it was predictable that Sir David Spedding, the Chief (or 'C') of SIS, would present a convincing demonstration of how his networks of secret agents would be fatally compromised if I imposed a cut on his service of the magnitude envisaged.

Equally predictably, Dame Stella Rimmington and Stephen Lander, respectively the Director and Deputy Director of MI5, were able to show me impressive evidence to prove that the IRA were busily re-arming and re-equipping their terrorist cells in anticipation of a breakdown in the current ceasefire. A large cut in the MI5 budget today, it was argued, would be a grievous blow to Britain's ability to fight the next and more dangerous round in the war against terrorism tomorrow. No Chief Secretary would want to make life easier for the IRA bombers, would he? This was the unspoken question left floating in the air over my lunch at Thames House with the divisional heads of the Security Service.

Over at GCHQ the arguments moved into the stratosphere of technical incomprehensibility. The Director, Sir John Adye, and his team of electronic eavesdroppers, while not actually speaking in code, nevertheless produced such bewildering countermeasures against the Treasury proposals that I was left appropriately jammed and baffled – though whether by chaff or by wheat it was at first difficult to judge.

After my initial rounds of bilaterals with the espionage establishment, I was discouraged. I was making no discernible progress towards my target of a 10 per cent cut in their budgets. To make matters worse in the eyes of my Treasury minders, this wimp of a Chief Secretary actually admitted to having been convinced by some of the arguments against cuts put forward by the spooks – at least so far as MI5 and SIS were concerned. On the other hand, the more I studied GCHQ, the more I suspected that it was suffering from out-of-date methods of management and out-of-date methods for assessing priorities. Devoting huge SIGINT (Signals Intelligence) resources to capabilities such as the monitoring of communications between Russian tank commanders in Chechnya undoubtedly resulted in a dazzling technical achievement, but what was the real value of such intercepts to our national interest? And who was guiding the Cheltenham-based boffins of GCHQ on how the Government perceived the changing priorities of national security in a post-Communist world? The more I asked such questions, the less satisfactory were the answers I received.

It occurred to me that the old saying, 'Who shall guard the guards themselves?' could profitably be amended to 'The guards shall cut the guards' budgets themselves.' If the best and brightest minds in the Whitehall intelligence community could be allowed to review the costings and strategies of GCHQ, I was confident that they would sharpen the organization's focus and save large sums of money annually. After some argument, the Foreign Secretary and the Cabinet Secretary agreed to my proposal. A review of GCHQ went ahead, chaired jointly at ministerial level by Douglas Hurd and myself, but effectively conducted by a working committee whose manoeuvrings were wondrous to behold. The key to this working committee's eventual success was my insistence that it should be presided over by an outside chairman – eventually agreed to be Roger Hurn, the Chairman of Smiths Industries[2] – and that it should include some of the radical and lateral thinkers from the elite group of civil servants I had led in a much bigger but similar costs review, known as Front Line First, of the Ministry of Defence's budget. The two outstanding members of this group were Alice Perkins (a.k.a. Mrs Jack Straw) of the Treasury and David Omand, a fearlessly outspoken Deputy Secretary at the MOD.

I followed the progress of the Hurn Committee closely, giving the lateral thinkers my full support and seeing some of the key players, particularly Roger Hurn, at private briefing sessions. The end results of the review were impressive. They included savings of over £200 million a year in GCHQ's budget; a modernized agenda of targets and priorities; a new London office to liaise with Whitehall more effectively; and a new GCHQ director – David Omand.[3]

'I think it's been a case of game, set and match to the Chief Secretary,' purred one senior civil servant as we emerged from the final meeting at which most of these decisions were taken.

A taste of such power can be sweeter than honey. As I had a number of similarly victorious skirmishes across Whitehall in the next few weeks, within no time what Shakespeare called 'the insolence of office' went to my head. Although I was one of the most junior members of the Cabinet, I was soon punching above my weight, making good use of my wide mandate to dig deep into the workings of much more senior colleagues' departments. I began to speak out, usually with some influence, on the broader political issues of the day such as Northern Ireland and Bosnia, at meetings of the Cabinet and its committees. I built a good relationship with the Prime Minister. Soon after I had concluded a successful spending round which made ample room for tax cuts by lopping a record-breaking £15 billion off the forward expenditure totals, John Major let it be known that he regarded me as a strong candidate for future promotion.

These inspired leaks from No. 10 started a trickle of foolish parliamentary and media gossip to the effect that I was something of a Cabinet dark horse, moving up on the rails into an interesting position for the future Tory leadership stakes. Although I knew enough ex-future Prime Ministers to regard such tipster tattle as the kiss of death, in the feverish atmosphere of leadership speculation that prevailed in early 1995, it was impossible to cool all hotheads down. Even I myself did not know whether to be pleased or embarrassed when the *Mail on Sunday* ran a huge feature article under the banner headlines:

HESELTINE IS TOO OLD
CLARKE IS TOO CAVALIER
AND PORTILLO IS TOO RIDICULOUS
So who will succeed John Major?
STEP FORWARD JONATHAN AITKEN
…The only Cabinet minister who hasn't a single enemy.[4]

If I did not have a single enemy at that time, I soon acquired them after the publication of this article. My relations with Michael Heseltine became noticeably chilly and, as I was later to discover, some ancient enmities in media circles were resurrected by this prophecy of my future stardom. As events were to turn out, the prophet who wrote the article, Roy Hattersley, got almost everything wrong in it. However, he did make one perceptive observation which most *Mail on Sunday* readers must have dismissed as pure flannel: 'Jonathan Aitken behaves as if he does not really care whether or not he climbs to the top of the greasy pole.'[5]

I do not know what aspect of my behaviour gave Roy Hattersley this impression, but either by luck or by good judgement he had hit a bull's-eye. For in my heart of hearts I was aware that something was going seriously wrong with my hitherto vaulting ambition and my appetite for power. What that something wrong was, I did not know.

All I could tell was that the more my career prospered on the surface, the more my deeper feelings were signalling an emptiness and lack of fulfilment within. One evening after a good dinner I tried to articulate these deeper feelings to a close friend, who ironically had spent most of the meal urging me to gird up my political loins for a future leadership challenge. When I brushed his blandishments aside, saying I was too loyal to John Major and too hesitant about actually wanting the top job at all, he laughed and told me I was suffering from a temporary ailment which besets many successful people in mid-life when all is going well for them. He described this ailment as 'divine discontent'.

I knew what my friend meant, even if his terminology was too grandiose. Gnawing away inside me was a problem I could not describe, except by giving it psychobabble labels such as 'lack of inner peace', 'emptiness of feeling', 'hollowness of spirit', or more simply 'something missing'. It was as though, after spending a lifetime wanting to climb a particular mountain, I had unexpectedly reached the final approach to its summit only to discover that there was nothing there worth the effort of the ascent.

Explaining this to myself, let alone to other people, was almost impossible. As far as any external eye could see, I was a fulfilled and happy politician whose star was rising and whose cup was full. Against a background of family contentment and financial security, I was riding on the crest of an exciting career wave, which in a sea of tired Cabinet colleagues seemed likely to take me onwards and upwards to still more powerful positions. But for what purpose? The pursuit of power is a good and honourable activity only if it is guided by the vision of wanting to serve. My vision was becoming increasingly clouded, although why or in what way I could not tell. All I vaguely surmised was that something was troubling me in that interior province of life which religious people call 'the soul' or 'the spiritual dimension'.

The first person to diagnose these stirrings of inner restlessness on my part was Lolicia. In the early part of our married life she had shown no particular curiosity for matters of religion. In recent years, however, she had become deeply involved in her search for 'New Age' spirituality, a quest which had taken her all over the world to meetings with gurus and teachers of different faiths. One of these encounters was in progress when I joined the Cabinet. On that day some enterprising reporter doing an article on the new ministerial wives managed to discover that Lolicia was away from Westminster taking part in a Tibetan retreat in Dumfriesshire. A press cutting some months earlier had described how the novice monks at the Tibetan Centre in Eskdalemuir were trained to meditate by shutting themselves up in dark wooden boxes for several days at a time. The reporter who telephoned our home in Sandwich in pursuit of these matters asked our 14-year-old daughter Alexandra whether her mother might not have heard of my Cabinet promotion because she could be locked away in a wooden box, seeking nirvana from Tibetan meditation. 'That sounds like Mummy!' said Alexandra gaily, and a theory turned into a story.

At this disclosure, tabloid reporters tumbled over themselves in the rush north to interview the 'Buddhist wife' of the Chief Secretary to the Treasury. They missed her, but that did not stand in the way of some creative headlines about Lolicia's 'conversion' which rather surprised the Rector and congregation of our local parish church in Sandwich where she was, and remained, a regular communicant. Nevertheless, a Buddhist Lolicia she became in the tabloids, and a Buddhist she has remained to them ever since, thus demonstrating the accuracy of Evelyn Waugh's one-liner on 'that compendium of other journalists' mistakes which newspapers have the audacity to call a library'.

In fact, at about the time when Lolicia had, according to the gospel of the tabloids, become a Buddhist she had internally come to the conclusion that the teachings of the Christian Gospels were those that stirred her most deeply. Although critical of many aspects of the established churches, she nevertheless found herself devoting more and more time to prayer in various Christian holy places – Medjugorje, Iona, the Brompton Oratory and Canterbury Cathedral being among her favourites. At first I was mildly dismissive of these devotional enthusiasms, but the results from Lolicia's prayers were convincing. Having previously given an impression of being somewhat aimless in her direction, she was visibly becoming more centred, more contented and more peaceful.

One other manifestation of Lolicia's interest in matters spiritual was that she began to challenge my own traditional and perhaps rather complacent Christianity with pointed questions such as 'Do you have too much spiritual pride?' or 'Do you believe in God with your heart or just with your head?' These interrogations, sometimes carried out by my impulsive spouse in a piercing whisper in the middle of a church service, at least had the effect of irritating me to the point where I began to think more deeply about my own beliefs.

At the time that I moved to the forefront of British politics, I was one of those people who call themselves a Christian without actually being one. Externally I could almost be described as a pillar of the Church of England, for I had grown up loving its music as a school, village and occasional cathedral choirboy, and had been sufficiently inspired by its teachings as a teenage confirmand to remain a practising Anglican communicant throughout my adult life. As a family we went to church virtually every Sunday throughout the 1980s and early 1990s, either at St Clement's, Sandwich, or at St Margaret's, Westminster – where for some seven years I held minor ecclesiastical office, first as the Parliamentary Warden and then as the Rector's Warden. These Trollopian sinecures involved notional responsibilities such as arranging memorial services for the great and good, restraining the Rector from straying from the *Book of Common Prayer*, and worshipping in liturgical harmony with my stern, unbending Deputy Warden, Enoch Powell.

Yet for all this outward piety, I do not think I had fully appreciated that true religion is a predominantly internal activity. Even if my externalism was not quite as obnoxious as that of the churchgoing Pharisee in Chapter 18 of St Luke's Gospel, the humility of the publican was far removed from me.[6]

Frequently questioned by Lolicia on these and other spiritual matters in the early 1990s, I became sufficiently unsettled to start re-examining my relationship with God. At that time it was not unlike my relationship with my bank manager, for I spoke to him politely, visited his premises intermittently, occasionally asked him for a small favour or overdraft to get myself out of difficulty, thanked him condescendingly for his assistance, kept up the appearance of being one of his reasonably reliable customers, and maintained superficial contact with him on the grounds that one of these days he might come in useful. Having reached the conclusion that God deserved rather better treatment than this, I began thinking about ways of improving the relationship. Then out of the blue I heard about an initiative which was to start changing the direction of my life – the Parliamentary Prayer Retreat.

There is an old Westminster joke about the routine ceremony of Prayers which takes place at the start of each day's parliamentary proceedings. Its line is that the Speaker's Chaplain kneels down, takes a look at the MPs present in the Chamber, and then spends the next five minutes praying fervently for the state of the country. Whether or not such doubts about the efficacy of our daily parliamentary prayers had anything to do with the setting up of the first Parliamentary Prayer Retreat is unknown. But whatever the genesis of it may have been, the start of Lent 1995 saw a meeting in the Crypt Chapel of the House of Commons of some 25 MPs, peers and parliamentary staffers who had expressed interest in joining an interdenominational Christian retreat.

I attended the first meeting of this experimental gathering out of a sense of churchwarden's duty tempered with a healthy dose of scepticism. This last attitude was evidently shared by other parliamentary colleagues, since several of them walked out after the retreat leader, Father Gerard W. Hughes SJ, had explained how it would work. The gist of his plan was that we should each set aside our own extra prayer time and we would also be allocated to a spiritual tutor, who would see us individually for an hour every week. During these private sessions we would be asked to 'pray from the Scriptures', which seemed to mean reading a verse or two from the Bible over and over again to find out whether a phrase from it 'resonates in your subconscious mind'.

As this explanation continued I was tempted to join those who were making their excuses and leaving, for this methodology sounded suspiciously like one of Lolicia's New Age quick fixes, the more so when Father Hughes said he would like to try out his experiment with us as a group. He then handed around a sheet of scriptural texts. At first glance, the top one was an incoherent Old Testament ramble from the Book of Isaiah. Father Hughes read it aloud and asked us to pray that some phrase from it might enter our hearts and souls. I closed my eyes as much from embarrassment as from devotional duty and hoped that this group therapy session would finish as quickly as possible.

The passage was Isaiah 43:1–5 and in the version we had been given it ran as follows:

Thus says the Lord who formed you and created you.
Do not be afraid for I have redeemed you.
I have called you by your name, you are mine.
If you pass through the sea I will be with you.
If you go through rivers they will not swallow you up.
If you pass through the fire you will not be scorched and
*   the flames will not burn you.*
For I am the Lord Your God, the Holy One of Israel,
*   Your Saviour.*
Because you are precious in my eyes
Because you are honoured and because I love you
I will give men in exchange for you and peoples in return
*   for your life.*
So do not be afraid, for I am with you.

As Father Hughes' recitation of these verses in the Crypt Chapel rolled on, Isaiah's words suddenly spoke to me, evoking pictures of floods, fires, tempests and other upheavals which could only be endured with the help of God's loving protection. I was also struck by a physical sensation which an old schoolmaster once felicitously described as 'pringles' – a combination of prickles over the scalp and tingling on the neck which can come upon a listener who is moved by a great passage of music, poetry or prose. This combination of pictures and pringles was confusing, but also sufficiently stirring to persuade me to sign up for the retreat course which a few minutes earlier I had rejected.

I was assigned for my spiritual tutorials to the Reverend Lister Tonge, a former Anglican monk who had found a new vocation as a Church of England priest specializing in the leading of retreats. Although it was easy to strike up a good rapport with such a gentle, yet intellectually challenging mentor, nevertheless our meetings soon ran into both practical and spiritual difficulties.

The practical problems stemmed from the fact that the retreat coincided with an exceptionally busy phase of my ministerial life. As a result every imaginable obstacle cropped up to block my appointments with Lister. Emergency meetings of Cabinet committees; the collapse of Barings Bank; urgent requests for 'a word' (Whitehall parlance for an unscheduled mini-meeting) with the Prime Minister or Foreign Secretary; unavoidable changes in the visiting times to the Treasury of important foreign personages, and so on, all combined to create the impression that my retreat commitments were jinxed. In the wall-to-wall appointment schedules that civil servants invent for ministers, it was never going to be easy to find extra temporal space for spiritual refreshment. However, with infinite patience Lister arranged, rearranged and re-rearranged his own busy timetable so that in the end we always managed to get our sessions together.

Overcoming the practical obstacles was only half the problem. Our next difficulty was that we ran into a spiritual blockage. Lister had prepared about a dozen texts for meditation and prayer, with the intention that we should work on one or perhaps two of them each week. But I was reluctant to move away from Isaiah 43. At the end of week one I said I thought I was growing in contemplative thought as these verses struck me from different angles, so could I please stick with them? I said more or less the same at the end of weeks two, three and four.

By this time Lister was growing worried. As he explained later, 'I was rather overwhelmed by the whole business of conducting retreats in the Palace of Westminster anyway, and then I found I was glued to this one text with an obviously very important Cabinet minister who disconcerted me even more by the intensity of his study. I was so worried that I went off to take advice from my own religious supervisor. I explained the whole situation to him and asked him, "Is it going wrong?" After hearing all the details he said, "No it's going unusually right. Mr Aitken must be reaching out very far and very deep. Let him stay on Isaiah 43 for as long as he wants."'[7]

As it happened, I stayed with the passage for the whole of Lent. It had become stuck in my new and more prayerful consciousness like one of those needles in the old days of gramophones which refused to move on to the next track of the record and so jumped back to repeat the same music over and over again. But what was the music of Isaiah's words saying? I could not interpret it. Instinctively I felt that I had started on some sort of vital inner journey, but I had no idea where I was going. Disturbed and disconcerted, I prayed with impatience for travel guidance or a route map, but answer came there none.

At around this time I went to an unusual performance of Wagner's opera *Die Walküre* which seemed to symbolize my difficulty. The production was sung in English, but at short notice the artist performing the leading role of Wotan, King of the Gods, had to drop out because of a sore throat. The emergency replacement Wotan, who was substituted at the last moment, could only sing the part in German. As a result the performance went ahead with the unusual feature of the King of the Gods performing in his native German, but with all the rest of the cast singing in English. In the interval a friend of mine commented, 'How like real life! Man speaks to God, but God answers in an incomprehensible language.'

This was more or less what I felt after my first in-depth attempt to study Holy Scripture during the Parliamentary Retreat. Those dire warnings about passing through fires, flames and floods seemed to foreshadow tempestuous times ahead. Would they be for me? If so, could I rely on Isaiah's assurance that I would pass through them without harm? Evidently I did not have enough trust in the Prophet's final exhortation, 'do not be afraid', for in the dark watches of the night I was struck by forebodings and presentiments of fear.

In daylight, however, my common sense and logic told me not to be so silly. I had nothing of any significance in my life to be worried about. Every horizon I could see offered vistas of clear blue sky. Our family life was happy; my ministerial duties at the Treasury were fascinating; my political career appeared to be on an upward path; our material life was comfortable; and my health problems with asthma seemed to be improving with the onset of spring. On life's scorecard of blessings to be counted, everything was going splendidly. The only note of warning came from the ancient voice of Isaiah, but if his Old Testament meanderings meant anything, even they were promising that all would be fine in the end. So I shut off my inner fears, had a happy Easter and organized a late skiing holiday with the family high in the Swiss Alps, where the skies were equally blue and cloudless. It was the calm before the storm.

CHAPTER TWO

Under Attack

THE DAY AFTER I had been tipped as the next leader of the Conservative Party by Roy Hattersley in the *Mail on Sunday*, the first media shot was secretly fired in the war that was to lead to my destruction.

On 30 January 1995, David Leigh, a journalist working for Granada Television (and later for *Guardian* Newspapers Limited), sent his editor a confidential, three-page memo headed 'Subject: JACKSON'. Its opening paragraph ran:

Jackson's entire success in life, which now leads to him being talked of for the highest office in the land, has been paid for by one Saudi prince – Mohammed bin Fahd, the son of the present King. Mohammed's money has discreetly propelled Jackson into successive control over a health farm; a private bank; a TV company; and the British defence ministry. His wife was, before their wedding, a consort of the Saudis. His elegant family, his impressive home in Lord North St, and his Prime Ministerial ambitions – all rest on the Saudi connection, and on Jackson's willingness to perform services for some of the most corrupt and tyrannical rulers on earth.[1]

If I had read this memo at the time and been told that Jackson was a code name for Aitken, I hope I would have had sufficient sense of humour to burst out laughing. Most of the allegations contained in it were not merely wrong but so comical that it would have seemed unbelievable to me then that any objective individual or organization could have given them credence.

Central to the thesis of this memo was the claim that 'the services' performed for 'some of the most corrupt and tyrannical rulers on earth' included pimping. 'Jackson started his lucrative career by providing houses, maids, cars and prostitutes for Prince Mohammed,' wrote David Leigh, identifying a brothel in Paddington and an escort agency in Kensington where these activities had allegedly taken place.[2]

After some extremely vague and false assertions about bribes and payoffs, Leigh's memo stated that I had been receiving commission payments on arms contracts: 'On the Al Yamamah arms deal it is said that Jackson got some commission. It is also said that his patron, Prince Mohammed, did too.'[3]

Having demonstrated his objectivity towards the Saudi royal family with acerbic comments on Prince Mohammed ('notorious in Saudi Arabia for his flagrant corruption') and the King ('a fat compulsive gambler called Fahd'), David Leigh brought his 'Jackson' memo to this conclusion:

Jackson was made a minister immediately post-1992 election. Immediately pre-1992 polling, Major struck a public – and electorally helpful – deal with King Fahd, who promised to buy lots more British arms. It looks as though the quid pro quo was to appoint the Saudis' man to supervise the huge Al Yamamah arms sales, to the Saudis themselves. Conflict of interest or what?

All this puts in a rather explicable light Jackson's anxiety when revealed to have been hob-nobbing with Ayas and co at the Paris Ritz. He was probably there to take instructions from Prince Mohammed.[4]

I will hold back the answers to these allegations until later chapters. All that needs to be said at this point is that David Leigh's charges were taken seriously at Granada Television and the *Guardian* (where his brother-in-law Alan Rusbridger had recently been appointed Editor), for they became the basis of the newspaper articles and the television programme that burst on the world four months later. On Monday 10 April 1995, the front page of the *Guardian* carried the banner headline: 'AITKEN "TRIED TO ARRANGE GIRLS" FOR SAUDI FRIENDS'. This sensational story was a trailer for the Granada *World in Action* programme, 'Jonathan of Arabia', which was to be broadcast later that day.

As in the Leigh memo, the most dramatic allegation was one of pimping, although the venue for this activity had now shifted from London to Berkshire. The only episode cited came from an interview with Josephine Lambert, the former Matron of the Berkshire Health Hydro, Inglewood, of which I had been a director from 1981 to 1992. Lambert described a telephone call allegedly made by me 13 years earlier, on the eve of a visit to Inglewood by Prince Mohammed in 1982, and was quoted by the *Guardian* as saying: 'He [Jonathan Aitken] rang back and said was it possible to get any girls for the Arabs? I said no, I don't know any girls; if you need girls, you bring them yourself.'[5] These words, it appeared, were the *Guardian*'s justification for its dramatic headline and pimping charge.

On its second page the *Guardian* carried two further Aitken stories, one headlined 'AITKEN CONNECTION TO SECOND ARMS DEALER DISCLOSED', the other 'NEW LIGHT SHED ON WHO PAID WHAT AT THE RITZ IN PARIS'.[6]

The first of these articles seemed to contain an allegation of improper ministerial conduct and business dealings between myself and two Lebanese brothers, Fouad and Ziad Makhzoumi. I had held a nonexecutive directorship in their company, FMS Limited, from 1985 to 1992. Although the *Guardian*'s article was opaque in its meaning, it appeared to suggest that there had been something improper about meetings I had held with Mr Fouad Makhzoumi in 1993 and 1994 while I was a Defence Minister, when we had undertaken preliminary discussions about the sale of British security

Pride and Perjury

equipment to the Lebanese police and security forces.

The second story was a follow-up to an earlier *Guardian* article about a weekend visit I had made to the Ritz Hotel in Paris in September 1993. The *Guardian*'s line was that I had improperly accepted hospitality by getting my hotel bill for 8,010 francs (approximately £900) paid for me by Said Ayas, an old friend of mine since 1973 and a long-standing associate of Prince Mohammed. The article was sceptical about my earlier 'convoluted explanation' about the payment of this bill, which I had claimed was paid by my wife. There were also some dark hints to the effect that my visit to the Ritz that weekend had been for some unspecified business purposes, implying that I might have been meeting various named Saudis in addition to Said Ayas, such as Prince Mohammed, Wafic Said, Sheikh Essam Darwish and Fahad Somait. All were prominent Saudi Arabian figures in the worlds of government and business, but (apart from Said Ayas) I had seen none of them in the Ritz Hotel in Paris.

I received the *Guardian* articles by fax in Switzerland just after midnight on 10 April. To say that I was upset would be an understatement. I saw these stories as the latest and most vicious instalment in a long-running campaign of previous articles by the *Guardian* designed to denigrate me, and I exploded with self-righteous indignation. My pride and sense of honour were particularly wounded by the pimping charge. It enraged me to be falsely branded in this way on the front page of a serious newspaper (which had made no effort to contact me in advance of publication), and I felt deeply humiliated because I knew these pimping allegations were completely and utterly untrue.

The other two articles on the inside pages were in a different category. The Makhzoumi story read so confusingly that it was far from clear what the *Guardian* was actually alleging. Most of it was what used to be called 'Mikado journalism' after Pooh-Bah's line in the Gilbert and Sullivan operetta: 'Merely corroborative detail, intended to give artistic verisimilitude to an otherwise bald and unconvincing narrative.'

The Makhzoumi allegations, as complex as any opera plot when related by *Guardian* reporter David Pallister, were long on the minutiae of what the company secretary of FMS Limited had or had not filed in its annual returns of the 1980s, but conspicuously short on evidence that the company had dealt in arms – something it had never done, being in the business of ceramic pipes. The revelation of a previous business connection between the Makhzoumis and myself looked rather less exciting by the time the reader moved from the article's headline to its seventh paragraph, because this contained a statement issued some weeks earlier by the Treasury press office, making it clear that my past merchant-banking connections with the Makhzoumis had been fully disclosed to Ministry of Defence officials in 1992. Moreover, I was confident that there was no merit to Pallister's innuendoes of impropriety because all my discussions with Fouad Makhzoumi about defence equipment sales to Lebanon had either been attended by or fully reported to government officials.

As for the Ritz story, I was far more nervous about this because I knew I was vulnerable to attack, both on the issue of having accepted hospitality while a minister and on the issue of whether my response to that attack – a claim that my wife had paid the bill – was true or false.[7]

With the wisdom of hindsight, I now recognize that the most sensible strategy in the face of the attack mounted by the *Guardian* would have been to issue a dignified statement rejecting the pimping charges and to have left it there. Unfortunately, however, my blood was boiling over the pimping allegations and over another aspect underlying the saga, namely the collaboration between the *Guardian* and Mohamed al Fayed, the owner of Harrods and of the Paris Ritz.

Mohamed al Fayed was pursuing a political vendetta of his own in the mid 1990s. He was nurturing a grudge against the British Government because the Home Office had refused to grant him citizenship. The first time I learned in detail of the lengths to which he was prepared to go in order to redress his grievance was when Sir

Robin Butler, the Cabinet Secretary, asked me to come and see him in his Whitehall office on 5 October 1994.[8] I had no idea why I was being asked to call on the Cabinet Secretary, and nothing could possibly have prepared me for the astonishing revelations that were made in this meeting.

Sir Robin Butler began by saying that, at the Prime Minister's request, he had to ask me about some serious allegations reported by Mohamed al Fayed via his emissary Brian Hitchen.[9] At a meeting between Mr Hitchen and John Major on 31 August 1994, the message had been delivered that Mohamed al Fayed was so incensed over the refusal of his citizenship application that he had decided to expose four Ministers of the Crown for corruption unless he was given British citizenship after all. One of the ministers who would be exposed was me.

Reading from the note of the 31 August meeting taken by the Prime Minister's Private Secretary Alex Allan, Sir Robin said that there were three principal allegations made against me by Mohamed al Fayed. The first was that I was the owner of two brothels or escort agencies, one in London and one in Paris, at which I arranged whores for Arabs. The second allegation was that Mohamed al Fayed claimed to have proof that I had met Wafic Said and Mark Thatcher in the Ritz Hotel in Paris on 19 September 1993, where we split the proceeds of a £1 billion arms deal, taking away our respective shares in cash. Brian Hitchen told the Prime Minister that Mohamed al Fayed had a tape recording of this transaction. The third allegation was that my bill at the Ritz Hotel had been paid by 'another notorious arms dealer'.[10]

The first two allegations struck me as so absurd that in any other context they could be shrugged off as lunatic fringe territory. Nevertheless, I was required to deny them in writing. On the third allegation the position in regard to the Ritz bill payment was more complex, but as this story had been exposed in the *Guardian* some months earlier with extensive help from Mohamed al Fayed, and as Sir Robin Butler had at that time accepted my explanation for the booking and billing of my hotel account to Said Ayas, there was no disposition on the part of the Cabinet Secretary or the Prime Minister to re-examine this episode.

One possible reason why there was such a light touch by No. 10 and the Cabinet Office when it came to the Ritz bill affair was because in this period there was a mood of strong anger among senior politicians and civil servants towards Mohamed al Fayed and his journalistic collaborators. John Major was so incensed by the message he received from Mohamed al Fayed on 31 August 1994 that he interpreted it as an attempt at blackmail and reported it as such to the Crown Prosecution Service for consideration. When the Cabinet discussed the al Fayed threats, the reaction was one of sombre outrage. The general feeling was that here was a man with a political agenda doing his best to destabilize Her Majesty's Government by feeding the most anti-Conservative newspapers of the day with viciously false rumours. Yet, however preposterous it might seem to members of the Cabinet to hear reports that the Home Secretary took bribes and that the Chief Secretary owned brothels, some journalists believed these exotic fabrications, so the media rumour mill continued to grind away.

The political climate of the 1994–5 winter was a bitter one. Seasoned observers of Westminster, Whitehall and Fleet Street could not remember a time of greater enmity between certain newspapers and an elected government. 'Tory Sleaze', with its subtitle of 'Cash for Questions', was the hottest issue on the agenda of papers like the *Guardian*, the *Observer* and the *Daily Mirror*, closely followed by the swirl of rumours surrounding Lord Justice Scott's impending report on British arms exports to Iraq during the Iran–Iraq war. The Scott Report was widely forecast by some journalists as due to bring down the Conservative Government, on the grounds that it would condemn several ministers for abusing their powers by signing Public Interest Immunity certificates in order to withhold evidence favourable to the defendants in the Matrix Churchill Case.[11] This fermenting brew of allegations involving sleaze, arms deals and ministerial wrongdoing created a poisonous atmosphere in which almost any anti-government gossip could gain an audience.

I was aware of Westminster rumours that my own resignation was being predicted on the grounds that Mohamed al Fayed had some exciting revelations to make about me. Thanks to the Cabinet Secretary's questions, at least I knew what those revelations were. In some ways this reassured me, for I simply did not believe that any fair-minded person would ever think of me as a pimp or as a corrupt pocketer of arms-deal commissions. Subsequent events were to prove how naive I was in taking this sanguine view.

After I had read the *Guardian* articles in Switzerland that April night, one of my immediate reactions was that the hand of Mohamed al Fayed must be behind them. This made my mood even more incendiary. So after a sleepless night (never the best background for good judgement) I made the decision to defend myself with an attack.

As dawn was breaking over the Alps, I drafted the text of what became known as 'the Sword of Truth speech' and flew back with it to London on an early morning flight from Geneva. When I reached Lord North Street, I found my front door surrounded by a crowd of reporters asking questions such as 'Are you a pimp, Mr Aitken?' 'Can you answer the *Guardian*'s allegations that you tried to procure prostitutes for Saudi princes?' These interrogations did not improve my temper; nor, when I reached the other side of the front door, did the discovery that Lolicia and the children were upset at having had to run a similar gauntlet of journalists shouting insulting questions about my alleged secret life as a pimp and procurer.

I tried out the Sword of Truth speech on an assembled group of civil servants and lawyers at a meeting in the Treasury, and on my family at home. Both these rehearsal audiences gave me strong encouragement. The Treasury group burst into a round of spontaneous applause as I ended my trial rendition of the speech, while at home Lolicia and Victoria were so emotionally supportive of it that they begged to be allowed to accompany me to my televised press conference at Conservative Central Office. 'Please let me come, Daddy,' said a passionate Victoria. 'I want everyone to know that I love you and that I'm proud of my father.'

Getting to Central Office was quite a task, for the 75-yard journey of three Aitkens across Smith Square was impeded by a morass of excitable paparazzi and television camera crews. A path had to be cleared for us by my loyal Treasury Private Secretary Paul Raynes, assisted by my special adviser John Bercow,[12] and eventually I reached the podium inside the packed conference hall.

The main thrust of my seven-minute speech was to announce that I was suing the *Guardian* for libel. I followed this with a strong denial of the newspaper's main charges against me and concluded with this more generalized passage:

I would like to make it clear that I am taking legal action not simply to clear my own name and reputation of the deeply damaging slurs that have been cast upon me.

For there are greater public interest issues at stake here, far more important than my own position.

Here in Britain we have both the best media in the world and the worst media in the world.

That small latter element is spreading a cancer in our society today, which I will call the cancer of bent and twisted journalism.

The malignant cells of that bent and twisted journalistic cancer includes those who engage in forgeries or other instruments of deceit to obtain information for the purposes of a smear story.

They include those who hold grievances or grudges of their own and are prepared to give false testimony about others to further their own bitter agendas.

Above all they include those who try to abuse media power to destroy or denigrate honourable institutions and individuals who have done nothing seriously wrong.[13]

The reference to forgeries in this passage related to the mock-up by a *Guardian* journalist of a letter on purloined House of Commons notepaper purporting to be signed by my Private Secretary at the Ministry of Defence, Jeremy Wright. This forgery, organized between Mohamed al Fayed and the Editor of the *Guardian*, Peter Preston, had been used as a device to obtain a copy of my Ritz bill by deceit. The manoeuvre had been exposed some months earlier and had caused the *Guardian* great embarrassment.

The reference to 'those who hold grievances or grudges' related to certain individuals who had been dismissed by me from their jobs many years before, and who had now reappeared in the role of informants to the *Guardian* and Granada. One of these was the former Matron of Inglewood who, as I revealed earlier in the speech, had been dismissed from Inglewood following her arrest by the police on suspicion of theft. Criminal charges against this Matron had not been pressed following the return of a large quantity of missing property. As this lady was the source of the pimping allegation in the *Guardian*'s lead story, it seemed right to me at that time that the public should be told about the background to her dismissal back in 1982.

My press conference ended with these words:

I have certainly made my fair share of mistakes in 30 odd years of life as a writer, businessman, parliamentarian and Minister, but I am prepared to stand on my record as a decent and honourable one – in Saudi Arabia and elsewhere – and to defend it not only before the jury of the courts but before the wider jury of all fair minded people.

If it falls to me to start a fight to cut out the cancer of bent and twisted journalism in our country with the simple sword of truth and the trusty shield of British fair play, so be it. I am ready for the fight. The fight against falsehood and those who peddle it.

My fight begins today.[14]

Although badly delivered because of my inexperience with the Central Office autocue, which gave me the look of a half-demented maniac staring into the wrong camera with bulging eyes, the immediate impact of the statement was massive. All the evening news bulletins led with lengthy televised extracts from it and the story continued to be front-page news in the national press the following morning. Telephone calls and messages of support flooded in. One of the warmest and earliest of these was from John Major who telephoned from No. 10 Downing Street. Other supportive callers in the next few hours included Margaret Thatcher, several Cabinet colleagues and numerous MPs. The general theme that came across from these early well-wishers, and from the avalanche of mail that followed in their wake, was along the lines of 'Thank heavens that at last someone has had the guts to take on al Fayed and the *Guardian*.'

It all sounded wonderfully exhilarating. A knight armed with the sword of truth and the trusty shield of British fair play was riding out to do battle with the dark dragons from the *Guardian* and Harrods. Yet from the very first moments after the press conference had ended I was always a hesitant hero, feeling as nervous in my inner thoughts as I had looked bombastic on the television screen. I knew there were vulnerabilities on my side, even though I believed they were limited in comparison to those of the *Guardian*. I also knew from experience that libel is always a lottery and that big court cases are both unpredictable and debilitating. After watching the news programmes on the evening of 10 April, I observed to my solicitor Richard Sykes, 'It looks good tonight, but you and I know what an ordeal lies ahead for us.'

CHAPTER THREE

On the Rack

ANY HOPES THAT MY Sword of Truth speech might have turned the tide of investigative and tabloid journalism away from interest in my alleged activities as a pimp and arms dealer were soon disappointed.

On the evening of 10 April Granada broadcast its *World in Action* programme 'Jonathan of Arabia'. I watched it in the Treasury with a team of civil servants and libel lawyers. The old cliché about not knowing whether to laugh or cry was a fair description of the gathering's reactions to this bizarre production. The tone was set by its opening sequence, which portrayed me riding across a desert landscape on a camel wearing flowing Bedouin robes over a City pinstripe suit. In later 'faction' sequences, all played by actors, I was pictured still dressed in this comic combination of Arabian and Savile Row costumes, sitting in a tent exchanging sinister handshakes with anonymous Saudi businessmen played as pantomime villains. Other surreal touches included 'reconstructions' of shady Arabian arms dealers in tribal dress shimmering in and out of the front door of 8 Lord North Street, and further appearances by the camel – later revealed to be Topsy of Chipperfield's Circus, hired by Granada for a day's filming on Blackpool beach.

The principal interviewees on the programme were the two Inglewood employees who had been dismissed in 1982, and my former secretary Valerie Scott (played by a speaking-part actress). The allegations from these sources were neither recent (being between 21 and 13 years old) nor unbiased, but this did not worry the producer David Leigh, who responded to internal anxieties within Granada about his witnesses by saying, 'Of course they have a grudge! That's why they're talking!'[1]

Although it was easy for me to rubbish 'Jonathan of Arabia' on grounds of factual errors, personal bias and theatrical absurdity, the thrust of *World in Action*'s allegations was clear and damaging. Based on what Valerie Scott had allegedly told the programme makers, they had constructed a thesis that I was a corrupt placeman of Prince Mohammed, who had helped me to buy my house in Lord North Street, showered me with personal gifts including a Jaguar car, and cut me in on improper business deals. The pimping charges by the Inglewood employees, as trailed by the *Guardian*, were repeated on screen. So the viewer was left with the overall impression that I had been involved in sleazy, immoral and corrupt activities with Saudi princes who had made me extremely rich in the process.

On the advice of my legal team, I issued a second libel writ against Granada and then attempted to resume normal ministerial duties. This proved more difficult than expected. It is one of the more disagreeable features of the political jungle that, once a public figure has been wounded by an attack and is visibly limping, he is likely to be so aggressively pursued by journalistic predators that it will only be a matter of time before he is eaten alive.

I discovered this law of the jungle the hard way. One of our first problems was coping with the pressures of the paparazzi on the family. 'Are these guys going to bug us for ever?' inquired William wearily after he and his schoolfriends had been chased and snapped during one of the early sieges. It was a good question, for although the army of cameramen which had surged around Lord North Street on the first day of the *Guardian*–Granada onslaught quickly reduced in size to a platoon, and then to just one or two persistent snipers, the media stakeouts of our family homes in London and in my Kent constituency continued at varying levels of intensity on many of the next 86 days until my resignation from the Cabinet on 5 July 1995.

The pattern of these stakeouts was that the early birds would arrive in Lord North Street and station themselves on or near our doorstep at around 6 a.m. Having established their 'pitch', they would open thermoses of coffee, eat food, chuck litter in the street and chat noisily among themselves as other cameramen, radio microphone holders and reporters arrived to join them. By 7 a.m. the congregation might be about 15 strong. It could easily double or treble if the day was a rough one in terms of news or rumoured news about 'the beleaguered minister'.

This media activity, which was amusing at first, quickly became a source of harassment for our family and for our neighbours. It would wake us up at dawn, for Lord North Street is a small row of Georgian terraced houses whose acoustics magnify all sound. If we managed to sleep through the journalists' early comings and goings, we could be aroused any time after 7 a.m., either by calls from mobile telephones in Lord North Street asking if so-and-so could have a doorstep interview, or by similar demands over our doorbell intercom.

When I came out of the house there would be an oppressive crush as I struggled to get into my government car against a background of shouts such as 'Hold it for today's picture!' or 'Are you going to make a statement on story x?' or 'Will you comment on reports that you did y?' I was sufficiently well disciplined to remain silent in the face of these pavement provocations, but that did not deter the paparazzi from chasing my car, which was often slowed down in rush-hour traffic. Their flashbulbs popped at me while my government driver Peter Beaumont ground his teeth and muttered through this regular ritual in his none too *sotto voce*, 'Bloody animals, they are! Bloody animals!'

There was not much peace from these media pressures at weekends, for the Sunday papers were often investigating some new 'Aitken revelation' on Saturdays which the Monday papers would feel obliged to follow up with further inquiries and photographs on Sundays. So our home in Sandwich Bay in my constituency became another regular siege location. At first the family bore up well under the strain of these unwelcome attentions, but the tension gradually started to take its toll, particularly after occasional episodes which ended in tears, such as the time when Alexandra's pony shied and reared up in the face of popping flashbulbs, or when William's friends refused to come round to play tennis on the grounds that they were 'too scared' of the photographers.

In the face of such pressures, we became something of a stay-at-home family, simply because it was no fun to go out shopping or walking if that meant getting hassled by frenetic lensmen hunting us down in search of 'today's picture'. Lolicia, however, was adamantly courageous in her refusal to make concessions to our tormentors, making her exits and her entrances at will, and overruling on more than one occasion the majority vote among the children for not attending our paparazzi-patrolled local church on Sundays. These sieges at St Clement's, Sandwich, added a new dimension of ecclesiastical responsibility to the duties of the Rector, the Reverend Mark Roberts, who became adept at shooing reporters and photographers out of his graveyard. Others might have preferred them to stay there!

What was all this media activity about? The answer was that large numbers of journalists were pursuing 'leads' from the initial onslaught by the *Guardian* and Granada, particularly in the areas of pimping, Arabian business deals and arms dealing.

The hunt for the evidence that I had been a pimp took several strange turns. One tabloid newspaper sent its reporters round the red-light districts of King's Cross and Amsterdam, carrying my photograph in the hope that some ladies of the night would identify their alleged former procurer who had turned into a Cabinet minister. Various dating agencies (including the escort businesses named in David Leigh's memo of 30 January 1995) were similarly approached, among them an impeccably respectable Anglo-American introductions

company operating from Broadstairs in my constituency, whose proprietor ejected her interrogators in contemptuous fury.

Disappointed with the lack of results from these investigations,
the tabloids turned their attention from my pimping life to my private life. This was a more fruitful field of activity for them, but
although I was unsettled by the intensity with which old girlfriends
from 15 or 20 years earlier were being approached with inducements
to talk, I believed (wrongly as things turned out) that any skeletons
which existed in my cupboard were of such antique vintage that they
could hardly stand up as journalistic scoops.

Perhaps I should have been warned by the spate of inquiries on
the theme of 'Aitken's Love Child' that tabloid reporters and their
informants recognize few frontiers. One of the first manifestations
of the quest for illegitimate Aitken children was the arrival of two
journalists at the Suffolk home of a married lady who had worked in
my office in the early 1980s. They suggested to her that they had
'firm evidence' that I was the father of her offspring. This respectable
lady called into the kitchen, 'Darling, there are two reporters
here from the *Daily Mirror* who say that Jonathan Aitken is the father
of our children!' She added to her uninvited guests, 'My husband
used to be in the SAS.' The reporters made their excuses and left
rather hurriedly.

A more sinister example of these activities came when a tabloid
reporter visited the former part-time butler (I will call him Mr C)
who had worked for us at Lord North Street in the 1980s. The
reporter claimed that his paper had 'proof' that I was the father of the
illegitimate son of a well-known lady and that this child had been
born in a flat near Victoria Station owned by Mr C, but lent by him
to me for romantic trysts and subsequent maternity arrangements.

Mr C laughed at this absurd nonsense and asked why on earth the
newspaper believed it. 'We are out to bring him [Aitken] down,'
replied the reporter. 'If you will give me the story, we will give you
£30,000.'[2]

Mr C told the reporter to get lost and that the story was completely untrue. 'Mr Aitken has never been inside my flat during all the years I worked for him,' he said emphatically.[3] This denial did not stop the reporter from trying to persuade Mr C to confirm the untrue story, nor from reoffering the £30,000 fee. Mr C was so angered by the nature of this 'bribe', as he called it, that he promptly telephoned me from his retirement home and later gave my solicitor a full statement on the incident.

Although it should have been possible to laugh off such 'cash for scandals' antics by Fleet Street's finest, the sheer frequency of these offers (which one newshound kept describing as 'a king's ransom', in return for 'all the dirty stories you know about Mr and Mrs Aitken') made them unamusing and eventually oppressive.

The reporters investigating my private life seemed to be equalled in number by the reporters investigating my business life. Although several stories on this subject found their way into print (usually in the *Guardian*, its sister paper the *Observer*, or *Private Eye*), they were neither important nor damaging, even though they seemed to be written mainly by conspiracy theorists who believed that all my past business links with Arabs were ipso facto suspicious. I was made well aware from media fishing expeditions that all manner of stories about Middle East clients of Aitken Hume (the small merchant bank of which I had been Chairman) were in circulation. They included drug dealing, money laundering and the trading of stolen art, to name just three occupations falsely ascribed to innocent and honourable former associates of mine, whose only fault seemed to be that they were Arabs. These tales came to newspapers as a result of 'information received' from sources whose lack of veracity was eventually demonstrated by the complete absence of column inches given to their tip-offs. Nonetheless, handling these weird inquiries was a dispiriting chore at the time.

The only line of journalistic investigation into my past business career which eventually caused trouble for me was the suggestion that I had been an arms dealer – and an illegal one. This allegation, which originated from a single source, had first hit the headlines on 30 March 1995, when the front page of the *Independent* screamed, 'NEW EVIDENCE ON AITKEN ARMS LINK – PRESSURE GROWS FOR MINISTER TO QUIT OVER DIRECTORSHIP OF FIRM THAT SOLD GUNS TO IRAN'.

The *Independent* claimed that when I had been a nonexecutive director of the Lincolnshire ammunition manufacturing company BMARC some seven years earlier, I had participated in boardroom discussions on a contract to export 140 naval guns worth £15 million to Iran – an illegal destination under the UN and British government embargoes in force at that time. As the *Independent*'s story explained, the former Chairman of BMARC, Mr Gerald James, was alleging that on 2 November 1988 I and the other directors of BMARC had discussed a contract described as 'Project Lisi' knowing of its Iranian end use. Mr James said that I must have been 'blind and deaf' if I was claiming not to know about these illegal exports, which he said were 'quite clearly going to Iran'.[4] When I denied any such knowledge, the *Independent* attacked me in a fierce editorial for my 'incorrigible ignorance' of these matters, saying, 'We contend that Mr Aitken is hiding behind a cloak of ignorance and non-recollection for which he does not apologise and which will not satisfy the British public.'[5]

I was astonished by the journalistic recklessness of such attacks because I was so utterly confident that I was in the clear. I was innocent of Gerald James' charges of having condoned illegal arms exporting to Iran. As I shall make plain in a later chapter, I was also innocent of all charges of arms dealing, for never in my life have I earned any commission or any other financial reward from an arms deal. This accusation of my being 'an arms dealer', so often reported by inference and innuendo but without factual backing, has from start to finish been a product of the media's imagination. Its only claim to truth is the number of times it has been repeated.

In the early days of Aitken arms-dealing stories, the specific false-hood about my involvement in an arms-to-Iran scandal by the *Independent* was not followed up with any great conviction by the rest of the media, or by the Opposition in Parliament.

There were good reasons for this caution, of which the most important was the identity of my accuser. Mr Gerald James, who had been dismissed from the chairmanship of BMARC's parent company Astra Holdings plc, and had been savagely criticized in a Department of Trade and Industry (DTI) Inspector's Report on that company, was widely regarded as an unreliable conspiracy theorist who bore a grudge against his former colleagues and the Government. Gerald James had been peddling a variety of sinister stories on Astra and BMARC for years. The gist of them was that his commercial misfor-tunes had been caused not by his failings as Chairman of the com-pany, but by a group of anti-James plotters from the Security Services, the City of London, Whitehall and 'The Establishment', whose main objective was to suppress the real truth about Astra's ille-gal exports.[6]

The widely held doubts about the credibility of Gerald James did not deter a small handful of journalists from believing him and fol-lowing up his stories with a new wave of investigations now that a Cabinet minister had been 'linked' to illegal arms dealing. This sub-ject was already the flavour of the season for quite different reasons, namely the expectation that Lord Justice Scott's impending report on arms exports to Iraq in the 1980s would cause ministerial resignations and bring down the Government. This scenario created a wild cli-mate in which rumours and innuendoes flourished. Inevitably I was dragged into them, even though I knew, and was later able to prove, that Gerald James' claims were nonsense.

President Harry S. Truman once said, 'If you can't stand the heat, get out of the kitchen.' It is good advice to politicians, who must expect to be unfairly attacked, criticized and even lied about at many stages of their careers. I had the Truman doctrine in mind during the spring and early summer of 1995, realizing that I had become something of a lightning conductor both for political grievances against the tottering Government, and for more personalized grievances by those who wished to settle old scores. I stood the heat and by the beginning of June it looked as though I had survived it. Two months after the broadsides fired by the *Independent* and the *Guardian*, it appeared that the frenzied journalistic searches for evidence that would corroborate the rumours of my alleged pimping, arms dealing and corrupt business activities were yielding a remarkably thin harvest. Leaving aside *Private Eye*, whose journalists worshipped Gerald James with the uncritical devotion of mediaeval believers in holy relics, no serious or substantive stories on these heavily investigated themes had appeared since the screening of 'Jonathan of Arabia'. Moreover, I was hearing from one or two friendly inside sources that the high command at the *Guardian* was getting anxious as it began to recognize that serious difficulties lay ahead when it came to proving the truth of the damaging allegations the paper had published on 10 April. If true, this was encouraging news.

Whatever comfort I derived from such straws in the wind, I cannot pretend that the 10-week period after the *Guardian*'s initial attack was anything other than an uneasy and unhappy time for me. Nevertheless, buoyed up by an inflated carapace of false pride and bravado, as well as by the steadfast loyalty of Lolicia and our children, I felt I had weathered the worst blasts of the storm. It was a feeling soon to be shattered by the intervention of a fellow Cabinet minister.

CHAPTER FOUR

Stabbed in the Back

ON THE MORNING OF Sunday 10 June 1995 the Permanent Secretary of the Treasury, Sir Terence Burns, telephoned me at home to ask if he could come and see me as soon as possible on a matter of urgent importance.

When he arrived some 20 minutes later the Permanent Secretary was not his usual genial self. As we sat down to coffee he bore the demeanour of a lugubrious provincial undertaker reporting unforeseen difficulties in the arrangements for a family funeral. He began by saying that the Cabinet Secretary had asked him to call on me personally to break some unwelcome news. This was that Michael Heseltine, then the President of the Board of Trade, had decided to make a statement to the House of Commons on Wednesday 13 June about BMARC. The statement would be an announcement that the Government was ordering a criminal investigation by HM Customs and Excise into allegations that BMARC had illegally exported naval guns to Iran. Heseltine would also be inviting the House of Commons Select Committee for Trade and Industry to hold its own parliamentary investigation into these same allegations with reference to possible breaches of the Export Licensing System.

As Terence Burns delivered this thunderbolt, the drawing room of my home in Lord North Street seemed to be whirling and spinning around my head as if I was taking part in one of those fairground horror rides with names like 'Doomtrack'. At first hearing, the news I had been given seemed incredible and incomprehensible. All I could see clearly was that such a statement must mean the end of my ministerial career. To protest that I was innocent of any knowledge of or involvement in arms exports to Iran would be almost an irrelevancy alongside the media storm that I knew would erupt as soon as the two major inquiries into BMARC were announced. Despite the requisite small-print qualifications about not prejudging the outcome of the inquiries, I felt sure that the headlines alone would create a lynch-mob atmosphere of predetermined guilt in which the prevailing tone would closely resemble the dictum of the Red Queen in *Alice in Wonderland*: 'Sentence first – verdict afterwards.'

If my first reaction was to accept the inevitability of my own political demise, the second thought to trouble my bewildered brain was: 'Why on earth is Michael Heseltine doing this?'

There had been no serious pressure on the Government from any quarter to set up a BMARC inquiry. The *Independent*'s story some eight weeks earlier had fizzled out and now looked like a damp squib, largely because there appeared to be no evidence, apart from the uncorroborated allegations of Gerald James, to suggest that there had been wrongdoing by me or by anyone else connected with the company. So the proposed statement was not a reaction to recent events: instead it had the look of a pre-emptive strike. But against whom? Or to prevent what? Michael Heseltine must surely have good reasons for making such a dramatic announcement, but what were they? I thought that the least I should do before resigning would be to get a full political understanding of the background to the ministerial statement so that I could prepare my own resignation statement accordingly.

'I must get Michael on the telephone at once,' I declared.

Sir Terence coughed nervously. 'That would not be appropriate,' he said, going on to explain that he had been sent round to my house as the Government's official emissary to break the news of the

BMARC statement because Michael Heseltine had decreed that it would be improper for him to have any direct dialogue with me on the subject.

'So if you do pick up the phone and try and speak to Michael he will refuse to take your call,' the Permanent Secretary continued, adding that the decision to make the statement was a *fait accompli*. 'The President of the Board of Trade has already secured the agreement of the Chancellor and the Prime Minister.'[1]

I was handed the draft text of Michael Heseltine's statement, which left me even more mystified. The gist of what he intended to say was that his Department had been investigating the weaknesses in the arms export licensing system of the 1980s; that BMARC had a better record of complying with the system than most defence manufacturing companies, but nevertheless some of its products might have slipped through the export licensing net and reached Iran via Singapore; that there might have been some indications of this in the intelligence reports on Iran at the time, although none of those reports had mentioned BMARC; that Gerald James had made serious allegations about BMARC exporting to Iran; and that therefore he (Michael Heseltine) had decided to set up the two inquiries by HM Customs and by the Trade and Industry Select Committee.

The more I re-read this draft statement, the more I felt that I was being stitched up. Michael Heseltine's decision to announce the inquiries was based on the slender foundations of uncorroborated allegations from Gerald James, unconfirmed rumours that BMARC's legitimate exports to a company owned by the Government of Singapore might have ended up in Iran, and unsubstantiated intelligence reports which made no mention of BMARC. I had myself read a summary of those intelligence reports in the Treasury a few days after the *Independent*'s story had appeared. I knew they were so vague and inconclusive that they could not possibly be construed as casting any reflections on me or on BMARC. Moreover, the transmission of these intelligence reports on Iran and the signing of the BMARC contract with Singapore both predated my arrival on the board of BMARC as a nonexecutive director by more than two years. The inevitable pillorying of me as the central figure under investigation for illegal arms exporting was therefore going to be based not on facts but on rumours, on a timetable which prima facie suggested my innocence, and on uncorroborated allegations of virtually incredible boardroom discussions made by the notoriously unreliable Gerald James.

There is no point complaining about bad luck in politics. Napoleon used to say, 'Give me a lucky General,' and the same aspiration could just as well apply to Cabinet ministers. My luck had run out. However unbelievable and unfair it might seem to me to have been portrayed by the *Guardian* as an Arabian pimp and by the *Independent* as an Iranian gunrunner, this was now going to be the public perception of me until the result of my libel case and the Heseltine inquiries set the record straight. As neither judgement would be given for at least a year, I felt I would have to depart from the ministerial stage in the wake of the Heseltine statement.

These thoughts, pounding through my brain on that Sunday afternoon after Sir Terence Burns had departed, made me utterly miserable. I felt I had been stabbed in the back by Michael Heseltine, deserted by the fates that decide political destinies, and badly let down by the God to whom I had been praying with increasing frequency and intensity ever since my experiences on the Parliamentary Retreat earlier in the year. That Isaiah 43 passage was turning out to be painfully accurate in terms of its prophecies of floods and flames, but woefully inaccurate in its reassurances that I would not be swallowed up or scorched by them. As far as I could see, I was about to be swept off the ministerial map by the Heseltine tempest. It would be better to bow out beforehand, proclaiming my innocence of these nonsensical claims of involvement in an arms-to-Iran scandal, rather than waiting to be blown away during the storm when no one would be listening to what I was saying.

In that dispirited but angry state of mind I sat down, without consulting anyone, to write my letter of resignation to the Prime Minister. The letter I drafted ran as follows:

Dear Prime Minister,

As a result of Michael Heseltine's statement to Parliament today [Wednesday] I am writing to offer my resignation from the Government.

I regard Michael's statement as an extraordinary attempt not only to undermine me personally, but much more significantly to destabilize the Government as a whole. Cabinet government cannot operate in such circumstances, and I cannot continue to work with a Cabinet colleague who behaves in this way.

On a personal level I have nothing to hide or fear from an investigation into the allegations about BMARC. Indeed I shall welcome the opportunity to give evidence to the Trade and Industry Select Committee's Inquiry foreshadowed in Michael's final paragraph.

As I made clear in a well-received statement to the House on March 30th, I was not given any indication or information while I was a non-executive director of BMARC that the company's contract with Singapore might subsequently result in components being shipped to Iran.

On a Ministerial level I would have welcomed any sensible move to give Parliament the full facts about what the Department of Trade and Industry or any other part of the Government knew about BMARC's export contracts. However I cannot accept that Michael's oral statement was the appropriate way of doing this. I will not be alone in detecting a personal hidden agenda behind the statement which will have profound implications for the Government as a whole.

I am sure you will recognise, perhaps with some fellow feeling, that I have been put in an impossible position by Michael's actions. That is why I feel it right to resign. I am extremely sorry to be departing in such bizarre circumstances, but would like to place on record my gratitude to you for giving me the honour and privilege of serving in your Government since April 1992.

Yours sincerely,

Jonathan Aitken[2]

Although this draft letter was an accurate reflection of my feelings at the time when I wrote it, I subsequently came to recognize that some parts of it were over the top. Indeed, I was persuaded of this the following day. When I arrived in the Treasury the following morning, complete with my resignation letter, my Private Secretary Paul Raynes hit the panic button. Within minutes Sir Terence Burns was in my office pleading with me not to send the letter and not to leave the Government. His argument was that my departure in this way would be interpreted as an admission of guilt. He also thought that my resignation would turn a drama into a crisis, for the sharp criticisms of Michael Heseltine contained in my letter would be a serious blow to a Government already reeling from splits over Europe, scandals over sleaze and growing fears about the contents of the soon-to-be-published Scott Report.

Burns said that he thought he could get some parts of the proposed Heseltine statement cut out or at least toned down. He went out and returned to my office surprisingly quickly having accomplished this. He then advised that my wisest stance should initially be one of 'dignified silence'; that I should sit impassively on the front bench while Michael Heseltine delivered his BMARC statement; and that I should soon afterwards issue a personal statement of my own promising my full co-operation with the two inquiries and reaffirming my innocence and ignorance of illegal arms exporting to Iran. After much soul-searching I eventually accepted this advice.

Although I inevitably had an unpleasant hour sitting on the government front bench on the afternoon of Wednesday 13 June as Michael Heseltine delivered his BMARC statement, the experience was not nearly as bad as I had feared. My prediction was that the statement would be greeted with a parliamentary uproar and with Opposition demands for my resignation, but I was wrong. In fact, the response of the House of Commons both at the time of the statement and in the emergency debate that followed it was surprisingly muted. The general tone of the exchanges in the House was restrained and fair.

As for Michael Heseltine, the best and wittiest portrait of his performance at the dispatch box came from my least favourite newspaper, the *Guardian*, whose reporting team wrote of him:

He was extremely sad, his demeanour made plain. Heseltine, who was on the left wing of the Tory Party, had reason to suspect Aitken might one day soon make a right-wing challenge for the Party leadership. He was mournful, too, as he explained that HM Customs were beginning a criminal investigation, and that the All-Party Trade Committee, if they wished to begin a similar investigation into his ministerial colleague, would have every co-operation from him. His dolour reminded one of the emotions of the oyster-eating protagonist in Lewis Carroll's 'The Walrus and Carpenter':

> '*I weep for you,*' *the Walrus said:*
> '*I deeply sympathise.*'
> *With sobs and tears he sorted out*
> *Those of the largest size.*[3]

Having seen me sorted out and cut down to size in this way by my Cabinet colleague, the House of Commons itself was in a more merciful mood. The prevailing view from all points on the political compass was that judgement should be suspended until the Select Committee had reached its verdict.

If the parliamentary reaction had been matched in its fairness by the media reaction, it is just possible that I might have survived in office. But the media approach was far more hostile, and in some cases hysterical. The Heseltine statement, in the view of many journalists, confirmed that there had been a major illegal arms-dealing scandal by BMARC and that I had been in the thick of it. Headlines to this effect exploded in all directions. Thereafter the disagreeable media pressures which had troubled me in the spring of 1995, from open harassment to undercover investigations and big money payment offers to potential sources, all surged up again with intensified vengeance in the second half of June.

As the wild speculation about my secret life as an Iranian arms dealer mounted, for the first time in the saga I started to ask myself, 'Is public life worth living if it goes on like this?'

By chance I discussed this question at some length and depth with Diana, Princess of Wales on the evening of 20 June. We were the guests of Douglas Hurd, who was giving a small, private dinner party in honour of Henry Kissinger. I knew the Princess from several previous encounters, but I was unprepared for the humour of her initial greeting – 'Thank you so much for taking me off the front pages in the last few days'⁴ – and for the intensity with which she wanted to talk when we sat down next to each other at dinner. We discussed our respective sons – two Williams, both heading for Eton – and the impact of media headlines on them. Princess Diana's theme was that young teenage children outwardly try to be supportive of a parent under attack, but inwardly shrink into protective emotional armour.

'They become so shell-shocked that they create shells of their own to hide in,' she said with feeling, adding that there were times when she and her sons seemed to be living through 'one long bad media dream'. The antidotes to these pressures were privacy and parental love, 'but it isn't that easy to give them that love when you, as a parent, become obsessed with fending off photographers and reporters,' she said.[5]

Although there could be no serious comparison between what the Wales and Aitken families had to put up with on this score, nevertheless this conversation with Princess Diana preyed on my mind during the month of June, particularly when we began to find our family life increasingly spoiled by the pressures of the paparazzi. In addition to their dawn assemblies outside Lord North Street, we now had to endure chases by them on visits to friends' houses, shops and restaurants. When Lolicia went for a get-away-from-it-all weekend visit to my mother's farmhouse in Ibiza, tabloid reporters arrived on the island in hot pursuit. Our children, back for half term, started to get jumpy whenever they came in and out of their home and found themselves jostled and photographed. I myself grew increasingly tense under these siege conditions, which were exacerbated by the steady flow of telephone calls from friends and acquaintances of the past telling us that they had been contacted by journalists anxious to investigate this or that rumour about our family, business or private lives.

One of the telephone callers in this difficult period was Paula Strudwick. She was an ex-girlfriend with whom I had a brief and much regretted relationship in 1980, a year after my marriage to Lolicia. I had not seen Paula for approximately 14 years, but as so many friends, girlfriends and business contacts of mine from the 1970s and 1980s were being bothered by journalists in these febrile days, it did not seem particularly odd that she should have been approached in this way too.

Paula, when I knew her, had been an attractive young woman working as a marketing executive for a property company. We were introduced to each other by a mutual friend, Dr Christine Pickard, at a lunch in an Islington restaurant and impulsively started a relationship that afternoon. Paula, as I remembered her, was a warmhearted, amusing and hedonistic lady whose only observable problem was her admitted dependency on amphetamine pills.[6] Our relationship ended in an uncomplicated parting of the ways after a few months.

So when a Miss Strudwick left a message at my office in mid-June with a cri de coeur for my help in dealing with journalists, I believed she was a bona fide ex-girlfriend under pressure and returned her call. When we spoke, her main plea was to have a meeting with me in order to discuss her problems of being pursued by reporters. The insistence of this request seemed suspicious, so the telephone conversation was a cautious one. Since it was being recorded by tabloid journalists, however, it was enough to seal my fate, for it confirmed the crucial information that Paula and I knew each other and had once had a relationship.

A day or so after this telephone conversation, two disturbing items of further information relating to Paula Strudwick hit me.

The first came from a young PR executive, Patrick Robertson, who worked closely with Sir Tim Bell's Communications Group. He had discovered from sources in the twilight world of exposé journalism that Gloria Stewart, a well-known agent in this field, was asking £150,000 from the *News of the World* for a big story about 'a prostitute called Paula and Jonathan Aitken'. Although the Paula I had known was not to the best of my belief a prostitute, the coincidence of her name and the suspicious telephone call from her made me realize that I might now be heading towards the dirty waters of unpleasant Sunday tabloid revelations about my past private life.

The second blow fell when a lawyer acting for Dr Christine Pickard telephoned my solicitor to report an extraordinary entrapment story. Christine Pickard, who in 1995 was a North London GP and police surgeon, had become a friend of mine in the 1960s when we worked together as young journalists on the *Evening Standard*. It was she who had introduced me to Paula Strudwick in 1980. The solicitor said that Paula Strudwick had recently invited Christine Pickard to dinner in her flat. With the wine flowing freely, the conversation had turned to reminiscences about me and, in the intimate girls' talk that followed, some embarrassing revelations had come out. To Christine Pickard's horror, the dinner turned out to be a set-up. Every word of the conversation had been recorded and was now in the process of being sold by Paula Strudwick's agent to the *News of the World*.

The *News of the World* is not noted for its restraint, but it rejected the Paula Strudwick story. The paper's executives were not satisfied that she was being truthful in some of the tales she was telling about her relationship with me, nor were they happy with the entrapment aspects of her revelations and their 15-year-old vintage. So the torch of muck-raking was passed to the *Mirror* Group, whose reporters had been openly telling the world of their political agenda, summarized by one of them with the words, 'We are out to bring him [Aitken] down.'[7]

This was a mission they shared with leading journalists from the *Guardian*–Granada team who were in touch with Gloria Stewart, Paula Strudwick and the *Sunday Mirror* Editor Paul Connew. When I realized the extent of the operation that was being orchestrated within this cabal of hostile journalists determined to expose me, my despair touched new depths. I decided that the time had come to tell the Prime Minister of my troubles and to seek his guidance on my future.

John Major has had a bad press as a Prime Minister, but as a human being of real warmth and kindness he deserves a five-star rating. Over a tête-à-tête drink in the Cabinet room on the evening of 16 June, his reaction to my tabloid and BMARC torments was one of heartfelt sympathy and support. He did not believe that my position, however difficult it felt, had yet become untenable. In his view the fallout from Michael Heseltine's BMARC *démarche* was painful but not lethal, since all the available facts pointed to my innocence. The tabloids had so far revealed nothing about my private life indiscretions in 1980, and what – if anything – they eventually published in 1995 might turn out to be a 48-hour wonder and nothing more. John Major said he hated the thought of a good Cabinet minister being driven out of office by press hounding of this kind. So the conclusion of the conversation was a robust 'Jonathan, hang in there.'

This prime-ministerial advice was accompanied by some ambiguous comments about the consideration he was giving to his own position, which at this time of midsummer madness was under constant attack from snipers, plotters and talk of future leadership challenges within the Conservative Party. So preoccupied was I with my own troubles that I did not correctly interpret the private signals John Major was giving me at the time, but six days later I understood what he had been hinting at when I received advance notice of the news that on 5 July there would be a surprise election for the leadership of the Conservative Party.

CHAPTER FIVE

Resignation

'NEVER RESIGN: WAIT UNTIL you are fired' was a famous piece of political advice given by Winston Churchill to my great uncle Lord Beaverbrook during the Conservative Party upheavals of the 1920s. It resonated in my mind during the final days of June 1995, but in the end I rejected it and arranged my own departure from the Government for reasons that were practical, personal and perhaps just a touch mystical.

The practical reasons were that I was beginning to recognize the impossibility of carrying the autumn spending-round workload of the Chief Secretary to the Treasury at the same time as preparing for the two BMARC inquiries and my libel action against the *Guardian*. Quite apart from these extraneous pressures, I knew that a Chief Secretary can only bargain effectively with his fellow ministers for reductions in their departmental budgets if he is in a position of political authority. The media charges against me had left me in the category of damaged goods. Instead of being perceived as one of the heavyweight fighters of the Cabinet, I had become one of its walking wounded. If I was going to be a liability to the Government in this way, it would be far better for me and for the nation's finances if I bowed out quickly before the spending round gathered momentum.

On top of these calculations, I had to factor in an assessment of the outcome of the leadership election which was thundering around

Westminster like the Battle of the Somme. During the last 10 days of June, Lord North Street began to resemble the trenches as rival camera crews, leadership contenders and spin-doctors slugged it out around Alastair Goodlad's house (No. 14), an outstation of the Major re-election team; beside Teresa Gorman's home (No. 15), a Redwood recruiting post; and beneath the pavements adjoining Greville Howard's residence (No. 4), where a large number of new underground telephone lines had been indiscreetly installed in preparation for becoming the headquarters of the abortive Michael Portillo campaign.[1] My own contribution from No. 8 to the goings-on in what one newspaper headline dubbed 'the street of intrigue' was to mount a persuasion offensive towards some nine or ten carefully targeted Eurosceptic MPs, most of whom eventually decided to stick with John Major rather than defecting to John Redwood.

Although the Major re-election campaign managers were confident of their number counts when it came to beating Redwood, they were worried about the damaging potential of a high abstention figure. At one stage there were strong rumours that Michael Heseltine's supporters intended to abstain *en bloc*. Intrigued by these reports and curious to know how Michael's mind was working, I decided to talk to him not only about the leadership drama, but also about my own drama, for I still could not understand why he had chosen to drop me in such deep difficulties with his manoeuvres over BMARC. Since the inquiries had now been announced, there was no reason why I should not lift the 'don't speak to me' embargo which Michael had imposed prior to his House of Commons statement, so I asked if I could talk to him privately at the conclusion of a Cabinet committee we were both attending.

When we were alone together in the Cabinet Office conference room, I put to him the blunt question, 'Do you think I should resign?'

After a disconcertingly long pause Michael Heseltine leaned forward, looked me straight in the eye and said, 'No you should not.

My judgement is that you would never have joined the board of BMARC if you'd suspected anything about shipments to Iran and I know of no evidence to suggest that you did. So I am sure you will be cleared. Of course if you did know, then when the inquiries report it will be a case of good night nurse, so you might as well go now, but if you did not know, then you should definitely not resign.'[2]

The tones of Heseltinian sincerity with which this homily was delivered were so transparently bogus that I knew at once I must take the opposite course of action. In any case, there were clearer signposts pointing to the door marked 'Exit'. On the media front I was asking myself rhetorical questions such as 'How much more garbage are the *Guardian* going to print in their efforts to make my Arab friendships and business connections look sinister?' 'Am I going to get done over in the Sunday tabloids with a kiss'n'tell story based on the reminiscences of Paula Strudwick?' 'How many more attacks can I bear?'

In this context I was disturbed to hear that the *Guardian*–Granada team of journalists who had been responsible for the 'Jonathan of Arabia' programme were now planning a second major collaboration assault, this time with articles and a documentary programme on my alleged arms-dealing activities. I also became aware that a two-man unit of reporters was following me around the clock – a worrying sign that a new, big Aitken story might be in preparation by some newspaper or another.

It was perhaps not surprising in this period of intense strain that I should have turned to God with the prayers and meditations I had begun to learn during the Parliamentary Retreat in Lent. The selfishness of my heavenly petitions at this time now makes me cringe with embarrassment, but at the time they were heartfelt almost to the point of becoming hysterical, as the episode of the visit to my father's grave perhaps indicates.

In the course of an exceptionally restless night in late June I had strange dreams about my father, who had died in 1964 when I was 21.

To me my father was a romantic hero, the quintessence of honour, integrity and courage in adversity. Born and bred in Canada, he so idolized the British Empire that in 1938, when he heard the 'Mother Country' was in peril from Hitler, he wrote from Toronto volunteering his amateur pilot skills to the RAF and was accepted by post a few weeks later for one of the first Spitfire squadrons.

Like his friend Richard Hilary (who made many complimentary mentions of Bill Aitken in his wartime classic *The Last Enemy*), my father suffered horrific burns and injuries from enemy action and spent his post-Battle of Britain years as one of the earliest guinea pigs of the plastic surgeon Sir Archibald McIndoe at East Grinstead Hospital. Emerging from that experience with a rebuilt face and walking on two sticks, my father was promptly offered a seat in Parliament, for those were the days when gallant 'sons of the Empire' from Australia, New Zealand, South Africa and Canada were enthusiastically welcomed as candidates and MPs by the Conservative Party.

Although my father's Canadian accent was so broad that some of his constituents had difficulty understanding what he was saying, he was elected as an MP and served in Parliament until he died in harness at the age of 56, from a heart attack which his doctors said originated from his wartime injuries.

Waking in Lord North Street from dreaming about my father, I observed from a bedroom window that the two reporters who were shadowing me had fallen asleep in their car. This understandable somnolence at 5 a.m. on a Saturday morning allowed me to give them the slip. Escaping by a back entrance, I decided on impulse to make an early morning pilgrimage to my father's grave, so I drove for 100 miles or so into the East Suffolk countryside, until I reached the village churchyard of Playford.

Although I had not been back there for over a quarter of a century, within seconds I located the weathered gravestone inscribed 'Sir William Traven Aitken KBE Member of Parliament for Bury St Edmunds. Died Playford Hall January 10th 1964' and sank down on my knees. After a few minutes of prayer and filial communion, I began to cry as I contrasted my father's honourable life of courage in war and unblemished public service in peace with the smear-ridden reputation which I had now acquired. As my mind reeled with the pimping and arms-dealing headlines of the past weeks and the tabloid exposés that lay ahead, my silent tears surged into racking sobs. 'Father forgive me' was the theme of my confused and emotional supplications as I begged my long-deceased parent to understand how sorry I was to have ruined the family name. I also wanted him to know that I had been unjustly accused of many of the sins and crimes for which I was now being pilloried.

As I prayed in the dappled sunshine of that glorious June morning in Playford churchyard, my mood slowly changed from one of tormented despair to a growing stillness and peace. Gradually I was calmed by the sights and sounds of natural beauty around me. The azure skies, the larks and blackbirds singing in them, the golden cornfields, the gentle breeze whispering through the overgrown grasses of the churchyard, and the sparkle of the sunlight as it danced across the rooftiles of Anna Airy's nearby cottage,[3] all combined to lull me into a mood of serenity which made my troubles feel small and unimportant in relation to the wonders of nature that were unfurled that morning in the glories of the Suffolk landscape.

One of my father's greatest pleasures in life had been weekend riding in those parts of rural East Anglia which are known as 'Constable country'. When he was really happy he used to sing in the saddle what my sister Maria and I called his 'Canadian boy scout songs' – muscular transatlantic ditties such as 'The Bear Went Over The Mountain', 'The Sons Of The Prophet', and 'Waffles And Bacon For Breakfast'. One of those songs suddenly tumbled out of the attic of my memory. It was about a rodeo rider who had terrible falls from his horse, but every time he fell he struggled to his feet, singing the refrain:

Gotta pick yerself up
Dust yerself down
And start all over again.

As I knelt beside the paternal grave, I somehow thought I could hear my father's cheerful twang booming out these lyrics which I had last heard from his lips well over 30 years earlier. They made me laugh and look at life in a different perspective. After some final prayers I drove back to London in much more cheerful spirits.

The mood of temporary optimism I had derived from Playford churchyard did not last. During the next few days we learned that certain investigative reporters had now trained their sights on Lolicia, grilling old friends with questions about the preposterous allegation, hinted at in David Leigh's internal memorandum of 30 January 1995, that she had been a prostitute for Saudi Arabian clients before our marriage. Having obtained confirmation that sums of money were being offered by a tabloid journalist to former associates and employees of ours if they would corroborate this and other ludicrous stories, we briefly considered publicly confronting the newspaper concerned with the record of these propositions. The idea was abandoned but not, alas, forgotten because of a burlesque farce involving a misdirected fax.

What happened was that Patrick Robertson, the PR executive who had been intelligence-gathering on my behalf in tabloid circles, reported the not unexpected information that the *Sunday Mirror* was digging away into my private life of 15 or 20 years earlier and had come up with 'some pretty dreadful stuff, far worse than any extra-marital affair'. He dispatched this cheerful news via fax, but unfortunately pressed the wrong digit on his fax machine, thus transmitting the message not to me but to a London arts producer who promptly circulated it to his friends in the left-wing press.

I learned of this slip of the fax button from a gaggle of reporters and photographers who accosted Lolicia and myself as we emerged from St Clement's Church in Sandwich on the morning of Sunday 18 June. The *Guardian* carried a prominent churchyard picture the next day of the Aitkens at bay, and the rest of the media pack soon followed with waves of vague but titillating speculation on imminent tabloid revelations about the beleaguered Chief Secretary.

Despite these advance warnings, such revelations were conspicuous by their absence in the next Sunday's papers. I learned that the *Sunday Mirror* had broken off negotiations with Paula Strudwick for reasons that included the exorbitant six-figure price demands from her agent and the unwillingness of Paula herself to supply suitably lurid details and pillow talk from our past encounters. This reprieve, which I correctly suspected was merely a temporary one, at least gave me a little more breathing space in which to ponder on the resignation question.

At this time I discussed my future with my closest friends in the House of Commons and with the leaders of my constituency association. Both groups were of the 'hang in there' school of political survival. So far as my South Thanet constituents were concerned, no minister under fire could have had better support, particularly from my Chairman, John Thomas, who regularly and articulately appeared on the media voicing total loyalty. So my home base looked secure, although in my heart of hearts I knew that neither it nor I could withstand a new round of dramatic media attacks.

The last straw that broke the Aitken camel's back on the issue of resignation was another episode involving photographers, journalists and a church – this time St Peter's Church, Hammersmith. By coincidence of timing, I had agreed many months earlier to give an address on the occasion of the church's patronal festival on Sunday 25 June. Preaching sermons was not my speciality at the best of times, so when I knew I was in imminent peril of tabloid exposé I telephoned the vicar to withdraw from my commitment. 'But even if you are attacked on that very Sunday morning, you should still come,' was his unexpected response. 'Everyone will have sympathy for you, for we are all sinners and as Christians we all believe in the forgiveness of sins.'[4]

I was touched by this doctrinally correct, if politically unworldly advice, so I duly showed up at the appointed hour with my St Peter's Day sermon in my pocket. Although the tabloids were quiescent, the *Guardian*–Granada team were not. Sitting prominently in the third or fourth pew of the church were about half a dozen of the journalists who had led the original 'Jonathan of Arabia' attack on me in April, including David Leigh, David Pallister and Quentin McDermott.

It seemed unlikely that this group were regular worshippers at St Peter's, an impression that was confirmed by their ostentatious walkout in the middle of the service, just after I had delivered my address. They also engaged in a churchyard stakeout with cameras after the Eucharist. The purpose of this activity, as I saw it, was to increase the pressure on me. In this objective the *Guardian*–Granada team were entirely successful, keeping up the heat by publishing a report which managed to sneer at both the author and the subject of the sermon. The paper's diarist Matthew Norman wrote:

Congregants at St Peter's in Hammersmith were electrified on Sunday by a guest preacher ... Mr Aitken visited the church (which stands a few doors from the house in which Stephen Milligan, his PPS, so bizarrely met his maker)[5] to sermonise about St Peter...

It was Peter who, in comic history's first recorded Frankie Howerd impression said, 'Nay, nay, and thrice nay' when asked if he knew Christ ... Whether Mr Aitken sees himself as a latter day St Peter is unclear. Against the thesis is the disciple's charmless opinion on women, for whom he counselled submissiveness. In favour, though, is his drawing of the trusty sword against soldiers come to arrest Jesus. 'A man of impulse and aggressive energy' according to a biblical guide book, St Peter also had many contacts in the Middle East.[6]

When I read these feline barbs, I said to Lolicia in tones of sorrow rather than anger, 'These boys can't even leave us alone in church and I don't think they'll ever leave me alone until they've destroyed me completely.' The thought fermented in my mind for the next few hours, until at about 7.00 p.m. that same evening I walked round to the Pimlico home of the Government Chief Whip, Richard Ryder, and told him that I wanted to resign from the Government as soon as possible. We both agreed that the natural break and reshuffle period which would follow the leadership election would provide a convenient opportunity for my departure.

After that it was all over bar the farewell audiences. These were surprisingly moving occasions. My leave-taking of John Major occurred when he was on tenterhooks of political suspense, for we met just days before the leadership election result, whose outcome would decide whether or not he too would be departing into political oblivion. Yet despite his own worries he was kindness personified. 'I've had many resignations but none so sad or so unfair as yours,' he said dolefully.[7] My response was that life is often unfair but that I would be behaving unfairly to him if I struggled on in the Cabinet as a wounded beast of the political jungle. The reality was that I had become a target for a small group of journalists and I would remain their target until I either resigned or cleared my name. John Major shook his head, but did not disagree with my diagnosis.

We moved on to talk about some of the Cabinet dramas we had fought together, particularly on Bosnia and public spending. He told me he would take a lot of trouble over writing his reply to my formal letter of resignation. 'I want everyone to know what an outstanding minister you've been, and that I expect to bring you back into the Cabinet once this nonsense is over,' he said in an angry tone of voice, later reflecting these thoughts in the official resignation correspondence.

I was touched by his warmth although, for my part, I was sure we were not just bidding *au revoir* to each other as Cabinet colleagues. But he seemed to believe otherwise, for his voice was choking as he put his arm round my shoulder and walked me to the door with a final hug and the words, 'As the Scots say, haste ye back!'

But haste ye back to what? In the next few days, as a victorious John Major reshaped his Cabinet, the political world rolled on without me and the tabloid tanks rolled on towards me, the *Sunday Mirror* opening fire with the front-page headline 'AITKEN'S FLING WITH VICE GIRL'.

Although the reader had to study the small print before discovering that the fling had taken place 15 years earlier and that Paula Strudwick denied ever having passed on to me the information that she had become a vice girl, nevertheless it was the sort of sordid exposé which made me hide myself away in shame, hoping that the world would just disappear under my feet.

The world of court protocol had certainly not disappeared, because a day or so later I received the message: 'The Queen wants to see you at 12 noon on Thursday at Buckingham Palace.'

So bruised were my nerves by this time that I made an attempt to disobey this royal command. The courtier whose help I tried to enlist as an intermediary for this avoidance manoeuvre sounded horrified. 'No, no, you can't possibly get out of it. The Queen *always* gives a farewell audience to her outgoing Cabinet ministers, whatever the reasons for their departure. It's an important tradition. You hand over your seals of office and she thanks you for your work for her Government. It won't take more than five minutes.'

My suggestion that these courtesies could just as well be exchanged by correspondence, since the Chief Secretary to the Treasury has no ancient seals of office to return, was rebuffed in even more pained tones. 'Absolutely out of the question. You can't possibly snub the Monarch just because the press have been giving you a hard time.'[8]

These blunt words brought me to my senses, so at the appointed hour on the following Thursday I presented myself at Buckingham Palace. After being escorted through various red-carpeted corridors and gilded anterooms by a succession of pages and equerries, I was ushered into a surprisingly intimate green-and-white sitting room and left alone with the Queen.

The next 25 minutes consisted of one of the kindest, most sympathetic and enchantingly warm encounters I have ever had with another human being. As with all royal audiences, it must remain private, but suffice it to say that anyone who believes media reports to the effect that the Queen is a cold or unfeeling lady would have reversed their opinion totally had they been a fly on the wall at this conversation. Perhaps the warmth had something to do with the fact that the royal family bear their own scars from tabloid attacks, but whatever the reasons, I came away from Buckingham Palace that afternoon feeling that a rare and healing balm had been poured into my wounds by a hand with a uniquely compassionate touch of kindness.

There was something so final about this leave-taking that I decided to go for a reflective walk around Green Park. It was a humid afternoon, without a breath of wind, and even the leaves on the plane trees seemed to be wilting in the sultry heat. My own spirits were wilting too. I entered a downbeat mood of introspection and began an uncharacteristically negative self-interrogation.

Should I leave public life completely, stand down at the next election and try to start a new career in business or as an author?

If not, could I really afford the prohibitively expensive financial costs of fighting my media adversaries in the courts of law? One legal practitioner had advised me that my libel actions against the *Guardian* and Granada Television could cost as much as £2 million if they went the full distance and ended in defeat. Such a loss at the notorious casino called libel would virtually bankrupt me. Was it worth it?

Could I answer all the charges that had been hurled against me, not only in the courts but also in the criminal investigation that had been started by HM Customs into my alleged arms-dealing activities, and before the House of Commons Select Committee of Inquiry into the same allegations? This last body consisted of six Labour and six

Conservative MPs with a Labour Chairman. Surely it was much too political a tribunal to give me the unequivocal 'not guilty' verdict I was seeking?

Was I being too proud, too full of hubris to care so much about the attacks that had been made against me?

Would it not be an easier option just to shrug them off, and to sail away quietly into the sunset of early retirement?

Agonizing over these questions as I meandered in the direction of Hyde Park Corner, an asthma attack struck me. This was not an unknown experience. I had suffered from mild asthma for years and although my symptoms had become more acute in recent months, they were normally containable by the usual medical devices such as pills and puffers.

Unfortunately, this particular asthma attack was the worst I had ever encountered and I had no means of controlling it. In my anxiety to be impeccably groomed and punctual for my meeting with the Queen, I had forgotten to put the vital Ventolin puffer in my suit pocket. So with my breathing becoming shallower and shallower, I subsided onto a park bench desperately gasping for air.

After a few minutes of this misery, a stranger sat down beside me and asked, 'Do you need help? Can I get you a doctor?'

Between wheezes and expectorations of catarrh, I explained that I was having an asthma attack but that I knew from experience it would ease off in a few minutes.

The stranger peered at me. 'Aren't you Jeremy Hanley?' he asked.

Wondering whether this misidentification should be attributed to the fleeting nature of political celebrity or to the physical effects of asthma, I denied being the ex-Chairman of the Conservative Party, who tips the scales at least 40 pounds above my average weight.

'Oh sorry, I've got you – Jonathan Aitken – yes, you have had a rough time. It may be the cause of your asthma. Did you know that stress can bring on asthma?'

'I know about that theory,' I wheezed.

'My daughter used to be an asthmatic,' continued the stranger, 'but then she healed herself when she became a born-again Christian. By the way, I saw you on television the other day coming out of church with your family. Have you been saved?'

This inquisition was becoming more than I could bear. I resisted the temptation to curtail it by repeating Alec Douglas-Home's anecdote about a man who, after being pressed by a lady salvationist on the same question, reluctantly answered in the affirmative only to get the supplementary question, 'Then why are you not dancing in the streets and singing aloud praises to God?'

'Because, Madam,' he said, 'I consider it to be such a close-run thing that I thought I had better keep quiet about it!'

Far from keeping quiet himself, my companion embarked on a sermon about the advantages of born-again Christian worship. I tried to cut him short by rather pompously volunteering the information that I was a Churchwarden at St Margaret's, Westminster. Unfortunately this disclosure encouraged him to new flights of fervour.

As the sermon gathered momentum, my annoyance at being held captive by a passing religious zealot had the beneficial effect of releasing a surge of adrenalin which reopened my bronchial tubes. As soon as I realized I was breathing more normally, I made my excuses and left. Disentangling myself from the park-bench preacher required a degree of abruptness on my part which bordered on rudeness. I regretted this afterwards, particularly as the last words of his exhortation stuck in my mind for longer than I had anticipated. 'The answer to your problem is in your pain,' he said. 'And your pain can be cured by your faith.'[9]

At the time I was so irritated by my evangelical interlocutor that I did not take in his message. A day or two later, however, it came back to me with some force when I read a similar theme in the pages of *God of Surprises*, a best-selling work of spiritual guidance by Father Gerard Hughes SJ – the leader of the Parliamentary Retreat which had made such an impact on me several months earlier. The passage from *God of Surprises* that caught my eye was this:

What may appear to us as a reason for despair – some failure, loss of job, reputation, disgrace ... can become a moment of grace and the beginning of a new life if only we can acknowledge our failure and turn trustingly to God. The answer is in the pain and no human state is ever hopeless.[10]

Mulling over Gerry Hughes' words as I did time and again in the summer of 1995, I found myself entering strange moods of introspection and retrospection. Little by little my subconscious mind began to throw up ancient flashbacks of memory involving pain and faith. By their knocking insistence, these memories somehow became relevant to my present personal predicament and to the inner journey that had now begun in earnest.

CHAPTER SIX

Prayers and Pleadings

AN INNER JOURNEY OF the soul cannot easily detach itself from the outer journey of real life. When I first started to test the waters of prayer and meditation, the adventure was confused by the enormous pressures of my ministerial workload. Even in the months after my resignation, when I had stepped off the treadmill of government, there was still so much to do as a busy Member of Parliament and as an even busier libel plaintiff, that my inner journey kept being delayed and sometimes derailed by the demands of politics and litigation.

When I issued my writs against the *Guardian* and Granada, I had very little idea what a leviathan I was challenging. The magnitude of the battle ahead of me gradually revealed itself as my opponents filed their 'pleadings' – a legal term for the outline of their arguments and allegations. These pleadings eventually ran to over 500 pages and amounted to a war of attrition on almost every aspect of my life in the past 20 years which had directly or indirectly been connected with the Arab world.

When the first wave of the defendants' pleadings landed on my desk, I did not know whether to be overwhelmed with gloom at the immensity of the struggle ahead of me or overjoyed with delight at the scale of the mistakes in the information provided by the *Guardian*'s journalists and their sources.

The opening paragraph of the defence set out the lines of battle. According to the *Guardian*, for over two decades in the House of

Commons I had been unable 'to take a fully independent line as a Parliamentarian and Minister' because 'the plaintiff's business career and fortune has depended on his connection to the Saudi royal family, which runs a corrupt and repressive regime'.[1]

The specifications for this astonishing charge were set out in flamboyant language and detail. According to the pleadings I had, with the demeanour of a servant towards a master, become 'the factotum' of Prince Mohammed bin Fahd of Saudi Arabia in about 1975, assisting him in a number of contracts and business ventures, as a result of which my position had 'essentially been one of dependency on Prince Mohammed'.[2]

The pleadings went on to say that, in my role as the Prince's dependent factotum, I had helped him to win two huge commercial projects in Saudi Arabia – the Philips-Ericsson-Bell contract for the telephone network of the Kingdom, and the GEC-Philips street-lighting contract for the city of Riyadh – making myself extremely rich in the process. I had also helped him to buy Inglewood Health Hydro, an establishment at which I had allegedly sought to persuade the Matron to procure call girls for visiting Arabs. Among many other exotic but false claims, the pleadings asserted that in 1977 I recruited stewardesses to work on Prince Mohammed's BAC 1-11 aircraft as prostitutes.

Moving on to arms dealing, I had apparently conducted myself corruptly as a director of BMARC, 'having been hired for his Saudi connections on the footing that he would supplement his salary as a director by participating in the commission taken by his Saudi connections'.[3] I had also concealed these connections from my constituents, the electorate and the public generally, particularly my connection with Prince Mohammed.

As soon as I read these opening attacks in the pleadings, I realized that the onslaught which the defendants had launched was going to consume vast quantities of my time and energy, even though every one of the above quoted allegations was untrue.

In the end I was able to obtain proof that, for example, I had taken no part in the Philips-Ericsson-Bell bid for the Saudi telephone contract (witness statement of the Chairman of Philips), which in any case had been signed two years before I joined the board of Prince Mohammed's company; that there had never been a GEC-Philips bid or contract for the street lighting of Riyadh (witness statements of executives from both companies); that Prince Mohammed had not been involved in the purchase of Inglewood (company records); and that the only stewardess I had ever recruited for the BAC 1-11 aircraft was a lady of impeccable respectability who later married a partner in a leading London firm of solicitors (statements of BCAL captains and cabin crew).[4]

On the arms-dealing front, Gerald James' allegations that I was a corrupt pocketer of commissions from both sides looked unseaworthy even by his standards when it was proved that BMARC had never won any contracts in Saudi Arabia and had never paid any commissions there. As for the concealment charge, the defendants seemed initially to be ignorant of the details of the rules governing the Register of MPs' interests while I was a backbencher, since it emerged that I had in fact registered all my Saudi interests there correctly. Nor did they appear to realize that my business connection with Prince Mohammed had been well publicized in the financial press in the early 1980s and had lasted from 1979 to 1984, ending when the Prince resigned from his companies in Britain and Saudi Arabia following his appointment as Governor of the Eastern Province.

How these facts could possibly be squared with the defendants' principal allegation of dependency was a bewildering mystery. I would be the last person to disagree with any sensible claim to the effect that my connection with Prince Mohammed, as a director of his former UK company, had been a source of commercial strength and status to me during my early years in business. But to suggest that this had created a lifelong dependency was ridiculous, as my bank statements and tax returns (which the defendants later compelled me to produce) clearly demonstrated. Although comfortably off by most people's standards, I was not rich by the standards of big business, having an income of around £100,000 a year and a net worth, including our family home, of around £2–3 million.

I had last done a business deal with Prince Mohammed in 1982. Since then I had enjoyed an interesting and individualistic career in Parliament as an independent-minded backbencher. I had achieved some success on both sides of the Atlantic as an author. I had helped, as a public company chairman, to build a tiny City of London merchant bank into a sizeable US-led investment management group in which the small shareholding Prince Mohammed had bought in 1982 (140,000 shares out of 33 million shares in issue) was insignificant. Moreover, far from being some sort of corrupt Saudi placeman in Parliament as the *Guardian*'s pleadings insinuated, I had actually made no speeches and asked no parliamentary questions in the House of Commons about Saudi Arabia during all my years as a director of a Saudi company. On what basis, therefore, could anyone seriously allege that my Saudi connections had created, in the words of the pleadings, a 'resulting inability to take a fully independent line as a Parliamentarian and Minister in matters relating to Saudi interests'?[5] It was an absurdity – but it was an absurdity I had to disprove.

If this account of the early manoeuvres in the pleadings makes it sound as though I was in an upbeat and confident mood as a plaintiff, it is giving a wrong impression for three reasons.

Firstly I was daunted, and at times downcast, by the volume and expense of the work needed to disprove the *Guardian*'s main allegations. To give just one example: it was a Herculean task to trace the British Caledonian Airways captains and crew who had operated Prince Mohammed's BAC 1-11 in the late 1970s. They were all retired from flying, they now lived in different parts of the world, and in the case of the stewardesses they now had, because of marriages, different names from the time when I had known them. Finding them, explaining the pimping or prostitution allegations against me (and by implication them) and persuading them to co-operate by giving witness statements to my lawyers was an exhausting assignment – and it was only one of many such challenges I had to meet in order to answer the pleadings.

Secondly, although I felt indignant at many of the wild allegations made in the legal documentation, like most libel suits the case was not always a simple, black-and-white affair in every particular. There were one or two uncomfortable areas (such as the well-publicized Saudi investment in 1980 in Aitken Telecommunications and TV-am) and one dangerous area. This was the matter of the payment of my bill at the Ritz Hotel in Paris in 1993. With the help of extensive inside information given to them by their collaborator Mr Mohamed al Fayed, the *Guardian*'s journalists had pieced together some circumstantial evidence to suggest that my public explanations on this subject were untrue. They were right.

I recognized from the outset that this was a vulnerable area in the pleadings, but for reasons of pride and stupidity I completely underestimated the potential of the Ritz bill cover-up to explode and destroy all the rest of my case. The way I saw it in those early days was that the *Guardian* and Granada had published massive falsehoods about me in the areas of pimping, arms dealing and corrupt dependency on Prince Mohammed. In defending myself with much prideful anger against this onslaught of very serious allegations, I needed to present a seamless web of rebuttal. If that meant telling a lie about the relatively unimportant matter of who paid my £900 Ritz Hotel bill, it seemed to me to be a necessary small one in self-defence against much greater falsehoods.

I therefore rode roughshod over all those rules and axioms about how the end does not justify the means; how two wrongs do not make a right; and how the truth is absolute. Although dimly recognizing that the Ritz bill might have the potential to be my Achilles heel, I was stupid enough to believe, on the basis of the available evidence, that my opponents had neither the arrows of proof nor the shooting skills to hit me fatally in this one weak place. In any event, I could not drop this part of the argument once it had been made central in the pleadings to my opponents' plea of justification. So, like a commanding general who has to fight on five or six battlefields simultaneously, I continued to hold the line on the Ritz, in the pleadings, in public, and in private with my own lawyers, even though I knew in my heart that I had neither the offensive nor the defensive weapons for the task. This was to prove a supreme act of folly.

The third feature of my troubled mood at this time was that the legal retrospection into my past activities in the world of Mammon had coincided with a parallel retrospection into my past relationship with the world of God. One of the most interesting features of my spiritual tutorials with the Reverend Lister Tonge during the Parliamentary Retreat had been our discussions on the gateway to this world – prayer.

Now that I had the time and inclination to focus on this subject more deeply, I found myself entering a supernatural world of conscious and subconscious flashbacks to those times in the past when my prayers had received a response. Amongst all these memories, none was more vivid than the one I sometimes called 'the miracle of Victoria'. It was a story of pain and prayer which began on the day when our family doubled in size – the most thrilling, terrifying and ultimately thankful episode of my life.

On the morning of 14 June 1980, Lolicia gave birth to our identical twin daughters Alexandra and Victoria. Their arrival in this world was immediately preceded by what turned out to be the connected event of a paramilitary spectacle which could have come straight from a Hollywood movie. A few minutes after Lolicia entered the operating theatre, the courtyard of her hospital was invaded by a cavalcade consisting of six armed police motorcyclists, a jeep full of soldiers, several police cars with sirens blazing, a Red Cross ambulance and a running posse of tough-looking young men barking commands into their walkie-talkie radios. By the time this noisy militia drew to a halt, every window in the hospital had been flung open as wide-eyed staff and patients looked out in wonder. Had there been a *coup d'état*? A terrorist bombing? An assassination? Since we were in Switzerland, these scenarios seemed improbable, but no more so than what happened next.

When the ambulance doors were flung open, all it contained was an enormous bouquet of flowers. These turned out to be addressed to Mrs Jonathan Aitken. They were delivered to the back door of the hospital with crisp military efficiency and the cavalcade then roared away. Before I could make any further inquiries as to why or by whom these extraordinary arrangements had been made for sending a bunch of flowers to my wife, a beaming gynaecologist emerged from the operating theatre saying, 'Congratulations, Monsieur Aitken. Say hello to your very pretty daughters!'

To their proud father these tiny babies (birth weight 1.6 kilogrammes, or 3 pounds 2 ounces), with their exquisite features and delicate limbs, looked like the most beautiful human souls in all creation. Lolicia, although sleeping off her anaesthetic (the delivery had been by Caesarean), also resembled an idyllic picture of beauty and contentment. I do not think I have ever felt such soaring joy and rapture as I did when I gazed on these three visions on that most marvellous of summer mornings.

By nightfall those early rejoicings had turned to ashes. After a day of medical disasters the doctors felt it necessary to warn me that all three ladies in my life were on the danger list and that one of them was likely to die.

Coping with this crisis had been the most testing experience of my adulthood. Now that I was facing another form of crisis and testing 15 years later, I found myself constantly revisiting that past maternity drama in my mind, searching perhaps for clues or lessons which might help me to cope with the coming libel case drama.

The maternity drama had unfolded in Lausanne because Lolicia had developed acute gynaecological problems on a visit there during the last three months of her pregnancy. She had to be rushed into the nearest hospital, the Clinique Cécile, and immobilized until the births – which on first assessment were entirely satisfactory.

After receiving upbeat post-natal reports from the surgeon and making more adoring inspections of my new family, I set out for a celebration lunch. My host was the former US President Richard Nixon, whom I had come to know well in the years following his resignation after Watergate.[6]

'Did my flowers arrive OK?' he asked.

I thanked the thirty-seventh President of the United States for his generosity, but when I described the spectacular arrival of his floral tribute he was astonished. Further investigations revealed that his secret service detail had decided that a hospital delivery job afforded them the opportunity to rehearse with the Swiss authorities the procedures to be followed when a visiting head of state gets shot. 'It's probably an omen that your daughters will often be surrounded by excitement and young men,' said Nixon cheerfully. So far in their lives this has turned out to be a rather accurate prediction.

President Nixon was staying at Lausanne's premier hotel Le Beau Rivage with his old friends Bebe Rebozo and Bob Abplanalp. This triumvirate certainly knew how to make a happy father feel happier. All I can remember about their hospitality is that the food and wines were superb and that President Nixon gave a toast to our newborn babies in which he spoke touchingly about his bonds with his own two daughters Tricia and Julie. He added wistfully that, looking back on his career, he wished he had been able to spend far more time with his children in their childhood and teenage years.

The late lunch had expanded into early evening cocktails before I remembered that spending more time with our daughters should now form part of my agenda. After wending my way back to the Clinique Cécile, I was told that Alexandra and Victoria had developed some breathing problems and it had been thought wise to move them to Lausanne's much larger Hospital Cantonal where special oxygenated incubators were available. As this was presented as the sort of precautionary measure that was almost routine for prematurely born twins, I set off across the city to the hospital with no sense of foreboding.

The first sign that I was entering a world of life-threatening medical crises came when I reached the intensive care unit of the Hospital Cantonal. Prematurely born twins often have breathing difficulties in the first hours of their lives, and I had already been told to expect that Alexandra and Victoria would need to spend a day or two in an incubator. However, I was utterly unprepared for the scene that greeted me. Both babies were strapped down and wired up as if they were undergoing some high-tech electronic torture combined with mechanical force feeding. At several points on their bodies electrodes had been stuck to their skin, with wires leading off to a computerized console of dials and indicators. Needles were protruding from veins in their arms and legs, with more tubes and wires leading off to other monitoring equipment. Drip tubes were stuck up their nostrils, and a clamp held their heads in place at an awkward angle. The centrepieces of the medical equipment in and around each of their incubators were the contraptions inserted above their mouths which resembled automatic bicycle pumps. About every five seconds these pumps would whirr upwards and then thrust a downward burst of air into the babies' mouths, causing their upper bodies to quake and quiver like tiny animals shuddering in a storm.

I was devastated by this spectacle, which at first glance could only mean that Alexandra and Victoria were in acute pain and critically ill. I listened with growing concern to the doctor's technical explanations of the cardiovascular crises that were endangering their lives, and I asked the vital question. 'What are their chances? Please give it to me straight.'

'It is too early to tell,' came the reply. 'Both babies are in serious difficulty. But if I had to give you a prognosis I would say that

Alexandra has a 50–50 chance of pulling through. She was weakening a few hours ago but now she is holding her own. For Victoria the prognosis is not favourable. She was more feeble than Alexandra when she came in here and she has been slowly sinking ever since. She is in a fragile condition now, so her chances do not look good.'

Shattered by this news, I stood with tear-filled eyes gazing at our daughters' heartbreakingly minuscule bodies, so frail and helpless under the pounding of their air pumps and the glare of the arc lights around their incubators. Forbidden to make physical contact with my flesh-and-blood offspring for fear of increasing the risk of infection, I had to use telepathy instead of touch to transmit parental love. I think I would have collapsed completely during the early hours of my vigil had it not been for the kindness of the nurses who tutored me in the scientific readings from the monitoring equipment whose changing signals were the harbingers of life or death.

By about 9 p.m. I realized that, emotionally exhausted though I was, I must go back to see Lolicia. The question of how much or how little to tell her about the cliffhanging nature of the ordeal our daughters were suffering became academic when I was met in her ward by a sombre reception committee. The doctor in charge told me, 'I regret to have to inform you that Madame has developed a pulmonary embolism.' He explained that a potentially lethal blood clot was moving around Lolicia's lower body. If it reached her lungs it would kill her. The next 48 hours would be crucial. While massive doses of anticoagulant drugs were being used to dissolve the embolism she would be kept under sedation and should not be disturbed or upset.

Faced with the prospect of losing my entire family, I went down on my knees that night to say prayers of burning intensity. The chance of having them answered seemed low for spiritual as well as medical reasons. I felt I was in a weak position from which to start asking the Almighty for favours; indeed, I hardly knew where to begin when it came to the serious business of imploring God for his help and compassion. Yet at various stages of my life I had been given lessons in how to pray by, among others, Sister Mary Finbar, the Irish nun who had nursed me through three years of tuberculosis in a Dublin hospital; Ralph Sadleir, the inspirational Eton priest who had prepared me for confirmation; John Gilling, my Oxford college chaplain; and Canon Keith de Berry, the Rector of St Aldate's, Oxford. Some of their teachings flickered from the rusty memory cells of my brain as I struggled on that dark night of three souls to communicate with the only power I felt could save them.

As the days passed it seemed that my prayers were being answered. Lolicia's embolism crisis receded, Alexandra's lungs gathered strength, and Victoria remained stable although still in a critical condition. But then the infections started to appear. Both daughters had intestinal problems. Alexandra recovered from hers with the help of antibiotics, but Victoria's grew worse. Then Victoria developed hepatitis, which turned her pale skin a jaundiced yellow. She weakened but hung on. More days passed. I returned to London for a 24-hour trip to take the chair at an important Aitken Hume board meeting. Halfway through it an urgent message was brought in from the paediatrician in Lausanne to say that Victoria had taken a turn for the worse and that I should return as soon as possible. My cousin and business partner Timothy Aitken said he had never seen anyone turn as pale as I did when I read that note.

'I'm afraid it's nature's destiny. The younger of gorilla twins always dies,' said my over-candid friend John Aspinall the zoologist, who happened to see me just after I received the bad news. With this discouraging wisdom from the animal kingdom ringing in my ears, I caught the next plane to Switzerland.

When I arrived back at the Hospital Cantonal, the news was grim. Victoria had developed a serious new infection of the blood. She was not expected to last the night. Hope was fading to such an extent that the medical team relaxed the sterilization rules and allowed me for the first time to make skin-to-skin contact with my daughter. 'Even if you do give her another infection it cannot make it any worse,' said a well-meaning nurse, lifting aside one of the panels of the incubator.

Removing my surgical gloves, I gratefully stroked Victoria's fragile cheeks and arms and put my finger in the palm of her hand. This was the first time in Victoria's short life that human contact had been made with her body to do anything other than stick a needle into her. She seemed instinctively to recognize the difference between the medical touch and the paternal touch, for she responded by gripping my index finger with a power that stirred me to the depths of my being. Throughout that night I hung over Victoria's incubator, stroking her, touching her, praying for her, and above all rejoicing in wonder at the amazing feeling of that tiny hand reaching out for and clasping her father's finger. For the rest of my life there will be no memories as powerful as the memories of that night; no touches like those touches; no bonding like that bonding; and no prayers like those prayers.

When the consultant came in early the next morning he seemed astonished that Victoria was still alive. 'I have a proposal,' he said. 'It is risky but in rare cases it works. If you consent I shall change all Victoria's blood.'

What happened next was the most spine-chilling spectacle I have ever witnessed. Two huge hypodermic needles with bulky syringes attached to them were inserted into Victoria's lowest veins and the doctors swiftly suctioned every drop of blood out of her. As the syringes filled up, the crying baby suddenly became silent, bloodless, breathless and immobile. It was as if Victoria had become a lifeless rag doll instead of a living human being. Then, quick as a flash, the suctioning stopped, the needles were whipped away, and a transfusion from two bags of new blood started to be pumped back into her upper veins. The rag doll stirred, re-inflated, coughed up an alarming quantity of blood mixed with vomit, started breathing again, and finally gave a loud cry. Victoria Aitken was back in business. As the nurses cleaned up the incubator, the former veteran war correspondent of

Vietnamese, Biafran and Middle East battlefields could watch no longer.[7] I went outside, threw up and wept uncontrollably.

For the next four hours all went well. Victoria did not reject the new blood and there were no signs of re-infection. But just as I was dozing off under a blanket in one corner of the intensive care unit, the alarm bleeper above Victoria's incubator gave its scream of danger. It was the dreaded signal that she had stopped breathing.

By good fortune one of the doctors was standing alongside the incubator when this thunderbolt struck. He started shouting instructions. Nurses and other doctors came running, one of them bearing yet another ferocious-looking hypodermic needle which was plunged into Victoria's chest.

'What's happened?' I cried.

'Cardiac arrest!'

Victoria's heart had stopped. She was technically dead from a heart attack, and she remained dead for the next two minutes or so while the medical team fought to save her. I saw the fear in the nurses' eyes and the beads of sweat on the doctor's forehead as they performed the emergency resuscitation routines. As they struggled I surrendered. In a low voice I heard myself saying, 'Holy Mary, mother of God, pray for Victoria now and at her hour of death, Amen.'

I had not said the 'Hail Mary' for over 30 years, when I was taught to say it every night by Sister Mary Finbar in my Dublin TB hospital, but somehow it surged up through my subconscious memory in this hour of need. I repeated it perhaps a couple of dozen times until suddenly and unexpectedly the tension around the incubator eased. Victoria's heart had started beating again. She was alive.

Almost the first person to be sure that Victoria had rejoined the land of the living was her Serbian great-grandmother, Spasa Mojsilovic. As a result of having established squatter's rights at the incubator because of her almost round-the-clock attendance during Victoria's fight for life, Granny Spasa had a ringside seat at this most traumatic round of the battle and was swift to declare the result. 'Veektoria vive!' she yelled, distributing kisses to me, to the nurses, and to the duty paediatrician whom she tried to engage in a Slavonic jig. The Swiss doctor looked startled, though pleased, at this tribute to his medical skills, but after a few moments of indulging these Balkan celebration rituals he drew me aside to give me a disturbing professional warning.

'I am afraid I should tell you that this could happen again at any time,' he said. 'Victoria remains extremely vulnerable.' He added that a cardiac arrest of the length Victoria had just suffered might have caused brain damage. It would almost certainly have done so in the case of an adult, but for such a small baby brain damage under these conditions was less likely. However, one could not be certain of that one way or the other for two or three years.

The prospect of more heart attacks and possible brain damage for Victoria sent me into my deepest prayers yet. A sympathetic nurse who understood the depths of my agony asked if I would like her to call the head consultant of the unit. She thought he might offer a second opinion that was more reassuring on the subject of brain damage than the one given by his colleague.

'No thank you,' I heard myself replying, 'Victoria is in the hands of God.'

For me to be making so firm a declaration of trust in God at a time of such depressing medical prognosis was uncharacteristic, for in those days I prided myself on my intellectual rationality. Perhaps the adversity of the family drama in Lausanne, and the impassioned prayer with which I responded to it, caused me to cross a supernatural bridge and to enter a new world of faith in which I have believed ever since, however inadequately I may have practised it.

As for Victoria, she seemed to be crossing bridges of her own because, contrary to clinical expectations, she began a remarkable recovery. A mere 48 hours after her cardiac arrest she was so much stronger that she came off her breathing pump machine, and a week later she was out of her incubator. Thereafter her return to total good health was an unbroken triumph. She has not had a serious illness in her life since.

With all gratitude to the paediatricians and nurses in the Hospital Cantonal of Lausanne, I have always regarded Victoria's recovery as being influenced, if not granted, by the power of prayer. Agreeing as I do with Alfred, Lord Tennyson's famous line, 'More things are wrought by prayer than this world dreams of',[8] and continuing to feel that I was hearing some mysterious but still incomprehensible signals from the Isaiah 43 verses I had studied at the Parliamentary Retreat, I began to wonder if prayer could help me with the pleadings and with the new wave of legal and media attacks that hit me in the summer of 1995 on the subject of arms deals.

CHAPTER SEVEN

Arms Deals

ONE OF THE FUNNIER *Private Eye* covers when I was under fire as a Cabinet minister consisted of a photograph of the Rector of St Clement's Church, Sandwich, the Reverend Mark Roberts, standing with me and my family in the church porch after a service as a superimposed speech bubble proclaimed, 'IT'S AN ALMS DEAL!'[1]

The joke was a good one at the time, but it soon wore thin. For it emerged that a small number of journalists, whom I later characterized as 'the Gerald James Hallelujah chorus',[2] seriously believed that I really had been an arms dealer and that I had made huge sums of money from my arms-dealing activities in the Middle East. So to set the record straight: I have never in my life made a penny from an arms deal, either by way of commission or in any other way. The extraordinary labels that have been slapped on me by some sections of the media such as 'merchant of death', 'missile salesman', 'arms dealer', 'notorious arms dealer', and even 'illegal arms dealer', are quite simply false.

There is no great mystery about how these canards got into circulation. Almost every rumour which connected me to arms deals in Iran, Iraq, Saudi Arabia or anywhere else emanated from one individual, Gerald James, the former Chairman of Astra plc and BMARC Ltd.

To describe Gerald James as an oddball would be a libel on oddballs. In his days as a company director he did appear a little strange and he made some decidedly odd commercial judgements in his business life. But it was only some years after his dismissal from the Astra group of companies in 1990, following the harsh public criticisms that were made of him in a Department of Trade Report,[3] that he turned into an obsessive eccentric whose main activity in life seemed to be fuelling a credulous coterie of journalists with ever more fanciful arms-deals theories involving conspiracies by MI5, the SIS, Royal Ordnance, the DTI, the 'Establishment' of the City of London, the Foreign Office, No. 10 Downing Street, the SAS, GCHQ, an assortment of Arabs and Iranians he had never met, various British ministers he had never met either, and myself – whom, alas, he had met all too often.[4]

As a high-profile minister in a Tory Government which was rumoured to be tottering towards the precipice of Lord Justice Scott's 'Arms to Iraq' report, I was a juicy morsel of grist to the rumour mill which Gerald James and his journalistic collaborators were feeding. In an earlier merchant-banking phase of my life I had briefly been a nonexecutive director of Astra's Lincolnshire subsidiary, the British Manufacture and Research Company Ltd, or BMARC, which made naval guns and ammunition. Even earlier I had met and corresponded with James when a business consortium of which he was the leader bought a small firework company located in my constituency.

Some time after he and his colleagues had made this acquisition in 1982, James invited me to visit the company's premises near Sandwich. The occasion was rather more entertaining than the usual run-of-the-mill MP's factory visit for, after I had shaken hands with most of the 80-strong workforce, I was invited to test their latest wares. The company had just expanded its product line from fireworks to military training pyrotechnics, so the test devised for the local MP required me to put on combat fatigues and to trot along a path strewn with booby traps which ignited various rockets, smoke grenades, squibs, poppers, thunderflashes and other simulated battlefield training devices. When I had run the gauntlet of these noisy but harmless toys, the local newspaper recorded me as saying that I had enjoyed my exposure to 'bangers for grown-ups'.

Over a cup of tea afterwards with the company directors, they asked me if I could point them in the direction of any organization or individual who might help them to sell their products in the Middle East. So I wrote to Gerald James suggesting that he might like to get in touch with two contacts of mine who were trading in exports to the region. Nothing ever came of this letter. Little did I guess when I made this abortive effort to help a company in my constituency that, many years later, James would use the episode to explode a firework display under my seat in the Cabinet.

Gerald James launched two rocket attacks against me in 1995. The first was his widely reported allegation that I and all the other directors of BMARC had conspired in the illegal export of naval cannon to Iran via Singapore. The second, to which the *Guardian*–Granada team devoted many column inches and much of a television documentary, was the James-inspired suggestion that I had been the central figure in what the *Guardian* headlined as an 'Aitken arms to Iraq link' which had sought to do 'military deals with the Iraqi war machine' at a time when Iraq was 'covered by an arms embargo'.[5]

As far as the BMARC arms-to-Iran affair was concerned, although Michael Heseltine's original decision to set up investigations into Gerald James' allegations by both HM Customs and Excise and the House of Commons Select Committee for Trade and Industry had seemed a devastating blow to me at the time, at the end of the day the findings of these inquiries were to prove a great blessing.

The Customs and Excise investigation was a criminal matter. 'AITKEN IN NEW ARMS QUIZ ... YOU'RE UNDER CAUTION, THE DETECTIVES TOLD AITKEN' screamed the front page of the *Daily Mirror*[6] on the day after I had voluntarily submitted myself to an hour of professional questioning at the Customs headquarters on Lower Thames Street in the City. The investigators who interviewed me had already seen all the other relevant witnesses, including the BMARC directors and their former Chairman-turned-accuser. As Gerald James had been unable to produce a scrap of written or oral evidence to corroborate his exotic Iranian conspiracy allegations, the Customs officers left me with the impression that they thought my accuser was unreliable, if not unhinged. 'We accept everything you say,' they told me at the end of my session.

I took my chance to ask them whether they had found *any* evidence to prove that some of BMARC's cannon had in fact been illegally exported to Iran. 'We have found no evidence of the kind which we could begin to go to court on that BMARC's products went via Singapore to Iran,' replied senior investigator Derek Dubery.[7] After such an observation it did not come as a great surprise to be told some time later that the investigation by HM Customs had completely exonerated me and all my former BMARC colleagues.[8]

The Select Committee inquiry into BMARC was, in my preliminary judgement, unlikely to be as fair as the Customs investigation. It was a tribunal of politicians chaired by a Labour MP, appointed to report on an alleged arms scandal in an election year when scandals were high on the political agenda. At the very least I expected some noisy knockabout during the Committee hearings and in the media reporting surrounding them. These expectations were justified so far as the advance coverage by the *Guardian*–Granada team of journalists was concerned. They lionized Gerald James as a hero, devoting an entire *World in Action* programme to his assertions, which included the central claim that at BMARC board meetings the illegal smuggling of naval cannon to Iran via Singapore had been approved by all the directors including me. 'It was discussed quite openly that in fact the end destination was Iran,' said James, speaking from a mocked-up Granada set of the BMARC boardroom whose main and entirely fictitious feature was a large portrait of me hanging above the mantelpiece.[9]

This was not the only misleading visual device or statement to be screened by the producer David Leigh in that programme. As red fountains spouted up blood and a torch panned its way through darkened cobwebs to packing cases marked 'Iran', 'Iraq Sales', 'Arms Sales' and 'Secret Payments', the voice of the presenter intoned, 'This British company went all out to fuel the bloodiest war of the decade ... A British politician tried to set up a military deal to Iraq when government policy was to prevent them ... he felt confident enough to recommend an agent, his own business partner, for military deals with the Iraqi war machine.'[10]

All this was nonsense, as the *Guardian* and Granada eventually had to concede when 18 months later they withdrew their defence of justification to my claims for libel arising out of their programmes and articles on these alleged arms deals. The only way the producer David Leigh had been able to buttress Gerald James' thesis that I was illegally dealing in arms to Iran and Iraq was first by falsely asserting that the former Astra Fireworks company in my constituency manufactured 'arms' (a claim disproved not only by the facts of what Astra made, but also by the witness statement of the Government Explosives Inspector who licensed the Sandwich factory and visited it regularly[11]); secondly by wrongly asserting that there had been a government embargo in place which would have banned the export of Astra's pyrotechnical products (Foreign and Commonwealth Office documents showed this was untrue); and thirdly by selectively editing a letter I had written to Gerald James in 1985 to make it look as though my offer to introduce the company to a couple of Middle East export contacts had been a business partnership arrangement rather than an act of helpfulness by an MP to a company in his constituency.

What I had actually written in the letter was this: 'Once I have made the introductions I really wish to bow out of the picture as I am anxious not to mix up my Parliamentary and business roles with a company operating in my constituency.'[12] Both the *Guardian* and Granada chose to omit this important passage of my letter in their extensive reporting of it. They also failed to report that the suggested introductions never took place. As the journalists were eventually forced to concede, nobody from Astra ever contacted or met the two individuals I had thought might be useful to the Sandwich factory's export drive, and so no exports ever took place as a result of them.

So much for my activities as an arms dealer 'to fuel the bloodiest war of the decade' and to do 'military deals with the Iraqi war machine'.

Although these facts about the absence of arms deals with Iran and Iraq eventually emerged after months of painstaking research and legal work, at the time when the Select Committee hearings took place the truth was still largely unknown. Indeed, it was clear that some members of the Committee had been taken in by the *Guardian*'s barrage of insinuations suggesting that I was an experienced arms dealer, for I was asked a whole range of questions about my knowledge of the arms trade going back to my days as a reporter of the Nigeria–Biafra civil war 30 years earlier. By the time the two-and-a-half-hour session was coming to an end, however, I detected among all members of the Committee a groundswell of sympathy as one *Guardian*–James allegation after another had been weighed in the balance and found wanting. Sensing that the tide was turning in my favour I took my chance in the closing seconds to say this:

Could I say one final word to you, if I may, a personal word, as the session is ending. I am sure that all members of your Committee, whatever their political allegiance is, recognize in human terms what a serious crisis it is for anyone, perhaps particularly a Member of this House, suddenly to be accused with allegations of criminal wrongdoing, of the kind that I and others have had to face, from Mr Gerald James. In my case the effect of those allegations are pretty self-evident: enormous damage to reputation, intense pressure on family and, of course, end of a ministerial career. I am not looking for personal sympathy when I make these points, but what I am asking your Committee for is a fair, impartial and thorough assessment of the actual evidence that Gerald James and his journalistic supporters have given, because I suggest to you that there has been no credible evidence of any wrong-doing presented to you. I do not believe that Her Majesty's Customs have found any such credible evidence in their investigations so far. Indeed, there may well not be any credible evidence that BMARC's products ever went to Singapore via Iran in breach of export controls. So I think my suggestion to you is that on the basis of credible evidence so far you may have been led off into a wilderness of weird characters and rumours and lies, but at the end of the trail there is not a real scandal of wrongdoing but a phoney scandal in which there was no wrongdoing by anyone at BMARC and certainly no wrongdoing by me. My own conscience in this matter could not be clearer.[13]

Within hours of this conclusion, my appearance before the Committee received almost universally favourable media coverage. The only exception was the *Guardian*. Its negative report by David Pallister contained an illuminating example of the way the paper let its standards slip or bend when it came to Aitken stories. Pallister introduced into his piece an extract from the letter (which had not itself been quoted in the Committee proceedings) I had written to Gerald James in 1985 offering to introduce him to an export contact 'who seems to be able to produce excellent results in both Iraq and Saudi Arabia'.[14] Both countries were legal export destinations at that time. In Pallister's story, however, he had altered the last line of the letter to read 'in both Iraq and *Iran*', thus deleting a legal export destination and replacing it with an illegal one – which just happened to be the subject of the alleged BMARC scandal under investigation.

To my suspicious mind at the time, this looked like *Guardian* letter-doctoring taken a country too far. My lawyers agreed and swooped on it as a useful addition to our pleadings giving further and better particulars of the *Guardian*'s alleged bias against me.

As I look back on this reportorial transgression, which I saw at the time as a flagrant example of *Guardian* perfidy, I wonder in retrospective amazement what the fuss was about. Who cared whether Pallister erred, strayed from or even doctored the text of my letter? Who was bothered whether Saudi Arabia was deleted and Iran inserted? Who knew which country was a legal or illegal destination for exports of military pyrotechnics which were never ordered anyway? These sensible questions were not asked at the time because there was a war on. It was not the war between Iran and Iraq, but the war between a politician's pride and a newspaper's pride – a pride so strong that it could only result in the fall of one or other of the combatants.

In fact, the first fall in the saga of BMARC came to Gerald James. Contrary to my expectations, the Trade and Industry Select Committee came to a unanimous agreement and published a report which vilified him and vindicated me. After a detailed and thorough examination of all the evidence, the Committee pronounced,

We find that Mr James's allegations are in general incredible. Had they been true, even taking into account the fact that some documents are missing, neither our inquiry nor Sir Richard Scott's could have failed to find at least some evidence to corroborate them … On the matters we have examined in detail Mr James has proved to be a highly unreliable witness and we do not believe any purpose would be served by investigating his allegations further.[15]

Turning to me, the Select Committee concluded that I had neither known, nor ought to have known, about James' Iranian conspiracy tales. They delivered this verdict: 'Our conclusion is that none of the allegations made against Mr Aitken have been substantiated.'[16]

As a consequence of the findings, I enjoyed a brief hour or two in the media sunshine which produced many favourable stories and one good laugh. By chance, on the morning when the BMARC Report was published, I had a long-standing engagement to see the Prime Minister's Ecclesiastical Appointments Secretary at No. 10 Downing Street. The purpose of my visit to this middle-ranking civil servant was to pass on the views of the Wardens and congregation of St Margaret's, Westminster about the merits of certain distinguished Church of England canons who were candidates under consideration for appointment to the Deanery of Westminster.

The BBC reporter who saw me entering No. 10 was understandably unsighted on the arcane nature of my business within. So, taking a somewhat reckless flier, he speculated on the lunchtime news that, in the wake of the Select Committee's report, the Prime Minister had invited me to rejoin the Cabinet. With frantic demands for a correction from the Downing Street press office coming over his earpiece before the bulletin ended, the BBC's political correspondent ended the story of my vindication by the Select Committee with the memorable line that I had been discussing BMARC at No. 10 Downing Street 'because he is also the Rector of St Margaret's, Westminster'. With this improbable news item encompassing an unholy alliance of guns and canons, here ended the Apocrypha of Gerald James.

CHAPTER EIGHT

A Retreat of Two Nuns

IT WAS NOT ENTIRELY inappropriate that my absolution by the BBC for arms dealing should have become confused with a matter of religion. It happened that much of the reporting of the 'Aitken in arms to Iran/Iraq/Saudi Arabia scandals' had coincided with my participation in the second Parliamentary Retreat, during Lent 1996.

My spiritual tutor throughout this second retreat was Sister Madeleine Prendergast, an Irish Catholic nun from the Sisters of the Holy Union in Dublin. 'And what would you be hoping to get out of our meetings together?' she asked me at the beginning of our first session.

'I'd like to learn how to pray,' was my reply.

'You can't learn that and I can't teach that,' she answered with a twinkle in her eye and a lilt in her voice that I came to know so well. 'But, as your prayer guide, maybe I can help you to get in touch with your inner feelings and to pass through the layers of your subconscious until you find a place where you will be listening to God and fulfilling his purposes for you.'

Listening to God? Passing through layers of the subconscious? Getting in touch with inner feelings? Fulfilling his purposes? This was not my idea of learning how to pray. At that stage I thought of prayer as a source of holy electrical energy which could be turned on to help achieve *my* purposes, if only I could learn how to find the right command switches. 'Ask', 'Seek', 'Knock', 'Win Libel Case',

'Rejoin Cabinet', 'Become Prime Minister', 'Win the National Lottery', and so on. I was not so frank as to label these dream switches by name to Sister Madeleine, but I think she more or less guessed what might have been going on in my proud and self-centred head. 'I saw you as someone who was searching for something very deep, but you wanted that something to fit in with your plans and your lifestyle,' she said to me three years later.' At the time she gently led me forwards and I reluctantly went along as we talked, meditated and prayed together in the general direction of inner feelings, layers of the subconscious and a listening God.

Slowly some strange things started to happen. For example, when doing meditations with Madeleine I began to feel tears welling up in my eyes. This happened occasionally at first and then quite often. After some early resistance I relaxed and let them flow. Deuced odd behaviour from a stiff-upper-lip Englishman – but perhaps it was all right to let the lip tremble on retreat with an Irish nun whose combined qualities of holiness and homeliness were leading me into deeper waters than I would ever have explored on my own.

Then some of my prayers began to be answered. On the eve of my appearance before the Select Committee's BMARC hearings, for which Madeleine and others had been praying, one of the parliamentary chaplains, the Reverend Francis Pym, came to visit me with a particularly fervent intercession based on the text, 'I will give you a mouth and wisdom, which all your adversaries shall not be able to gainsay nor resist' (Luke 21:15 KJV). That was more or less what happened. My adversaries had worked hard to ensure that my grilling by the Select Committee would be a disaster, but it was widely reported as a triumph. The journalists who had accused me of illegal arms dealing were in some disarray. Their ranks started to crumble. The *Sunday Telegraph* paid damages for their publication of a false arms-dealing story by Mark Watts, a Granada researcher close to Gerald James. The BBC gave me a handsome apology on the six o'clock and nine o'clock news for a similar story they had mistakenly broadcast on the basis of the *World in Action* arms-dealing allegations. I forgave them their press passes.

The strangest development was that some of the retreat texts we were studying led me into deep retrospection, particularly Psalm 139 which is all about the mystery of God's inescapable presence and sovereign providence. It begins:

> *O Lord, you have searched me and you know me.*
> *You know when I sit and when I rise;*
> *you perceive my thoughts from afar.*
> *You discern my going out and my lying down;*
> *you are familiar with all my ways.*

(VV. 1–3, NIV)

As the full implications of this all-seeing, all-controlling God sank into my mind during the retreat, I began to make journeys backwards into time, dimly recognizing those periods when 'the days ordained for me were written in your book before one of them came to be' (v. 16). These thoughts went so deep that Sister Madeleine was temporarily relegated to being the *second* most important Irish nun in my spiritual life. To my amazement in that Lent of 1996, I began to think about, talk about and pray about a remarkable but long-forgotten lady who had been an important figure in my early childhood around 1947. Her name was Sister Mary Finbar, and the story of our connection is worth retelling.

Sister Mary Finbar was a Roman Catholic nun who had been in charge of the nursing order of the Little Sisters of the Poor at Cappagh Hospital in Dublin in the 1940s. I was admitted into that hospital under her care as a four-year-old child with a severe case of tuberculosis.

Half a century ago TB was a killer disease, feared as much as cancer is today, if not more. My TB had been contracted from an

Irish nanny some 18 months earlier, but it had gone unnoticed because of the separations of wartime. My father was then an RAF fighter pilot recovering from burns and other plane-crash injuries. My mother divided most of her time between visiting my father in hospital and carrying out her duties as a WRVS (Women's Royal Voluntary Service) centre organizer in the East End of London during the days of the Blitz. Against the background of such pressures, it seemed sensible to leave me in the care of my grandparents in Dublin where my grandfather was Britain's Ambassador to Ireland, then a neutral country untroubled by the privations of war, such as food rationing.

Although it was vaguely observed that I was rather a sickly child prone to coughs and colds, the significance of these ailments was missed until I began losing weight and having difficulty walking. As these problems worsened, I was taken to see specialists in London, Liverpool and Dublin. From x-rays, tests and lumbar punctures it was established that I had an advanced case of TB which had spread across both lungs and into some of my bones, notably my pelvis and right hip. At the end of these examinations the optimistic diagnosis was, 'This child may live but he will never walk,' and the pessimistic diagnosis was, 'This child cannot live.'

The only dissenting voice from this medical consensus was Dr Macaulay, the consultant at Cappagh Hospital. His prescription was drastic but hopeful. According to Dr Macaulay, if I was immobilized completely for up to three years on what was called 'a frame', made out of steel struts, wooden base panels and plaster-of-Paris walls, there would be a fair chance of making a full recovery.

I duly settled into this three-year sentence, but five decades on I can remember little about Cappagh except for the pain, the Pope and Sister Mary Finbar.

The pain came mainly from my right hip, where to this day I carry some deep scars. Drainage tubes were pushed in and pulled out there; a nasty abscess developed on the femur bone which had to be operated on several times; and the general soreness chafed against the plaster walls of my frame whenever I coughed up blood – which was frequently.

Dr Macaulay's nephew, who seemed familiar with the details of my case when he was interviewed for a BBC radio profile of me in 1995, described my treatment as 'terribly traumatic'.² I suppose that description may be right in retrospect, but at the time I believe I regarded my life in the children's ward of Cappagh as extremely competitive rather than distressing. The high points of the day were the morning and afternoon 'wheel-outs' when the French windows of the ward were flung open and all the patients were wheeled onto a stone terrace and ordered to breathe deeply. Nowadays TB, although still a dangerous disease, is quite easily cured by antibiotics. These had not been invented in the mid-1940s, so the only treatment was fresh air. Taking longer and deeper breaths of Irish ozone than Paddy or Seamus or whoever was my next-door neighbour in the line of beds on the terrace was the name of the game. The nuns clapped if you did well and, as I enjoyed their applause, I strove mightily in the breathing stakes. This was just as well, because the real competition was not for breath but for life.

The life-threatening dimension of my Cappagh memories may have grown in the telling, but my recollection is that funerals were a regular occurrence in the children's ward. Certainly I can remember occasions when our beds were wheeled round into a circle and a priest would say Mass for the soul of poor little Bridget or Eamon, who had passed away to heaven in the night. Despite all the sales talk from the nuns about the joys of heaven, I was quite sure that I did not want to go there. But since my condition deteriorated during my early months in Cappagh, my confidence that I was going to dodge this celestial destination was not universally shared.

To this day my mother tells a story of how she came over from London to visit me and was so shattered by my further weight loss and pallor that she was certain my days were numbered. She burst into tears, sobbing despairingly to the doctor, 'He's going to die!'

Luckily I was feeling rather perky that morning and my arms and legs had been unstrapped from the frame in order to make a maternal embrace easier. So to everyone's astonishment I got off the frame (something I had not been able to do for weeks) and ran over to her, saying cheerfully as I gave her a hug, 'Don't cry, Mamma. I'm getting better. I'm not going to die.'

At this, an astonished junior nun crossed herself and, according to family folklore, declared over and over again that a blessed miracle had taken place until she was told, 'Stop blethering, you stupid gel!' by my staunchly Protestant grandmother.

My grandmother was a British Ambassadress in the imperial tradition. She took her religion seriously. Although she was herself an Anglo-Catholic, she was deeply suspicious of much Roman Catholic doctrine and had a particular aversion to the infallibility of the Pope. Her Victorian Anglicanism made it difficult for her to adjust to having her grandson nursed and taught by 'RCs' – an expression she delivered with much rolling of the r's. As a counterbalance to the Pope's influence, my grandmother tried to organize occasional religious instruction of her own. To help her in this task she recruited from the British Embassy my grandfather's press secretary, whom she described all her life as 'a pillar of the Church of England'. This bald-headed gentleman, whom I called Mr Benjamin, was a highly entertaining bedside visitor. I do not recall him saying a word about the Church of England, but I do remember that he kept me amused for hours by telling funny stories and reading poems, some of which he had written himself. It was not until some years after I had left Cappagh that I discovered his real name was John Betjeman. No wonder he is my favourite twentieth-century poet.

One day my grandmother thought she had scored a victory over the Pope. She was escorting me down to the operating theatre when my hospital trolley passed a large, illuminated portrait of Pope Pius

XII. When I saw the picture I exclaimed, 'Oh look, Gran, it's the King!' and started singing 'God Save Our Gracious King' at the top of my voice until we reached the anaesthetic room. My grandmother enjoyed retelling this tale well into her nineties, sometimes with elaborate embellishments about how the surgeons had dropped their scalpels in horror at hearing the national anthem sung in de Valera's Republican Ireland during wartime. 'You showed your true Protestant faith,' was her punchline to this much repeated anecdote.

Faith and faith-healing were central to the mission of the nuns at Cappagh Hospital, and especially to Sister Mary Finbar who nursed me day and night. What I remember most about her was her sense of humour, her skill as a teacher and her deep, still silences of prayer.

Sister Mary was great fun to be with, for she knew how to captivate a child's imagination with a joke, an imitation or a funny story. Fifty years on I find it impossible to recreate her humour, except for one performance which involved her doing an impression of a not very bright novice nun shouting to the ward full of comatose children, 'Wake up, begorrah, it's time to take your sleeping draughts!'

Humour was much used by Sister Mary when giving me my early reading lessons, which were conducted in slow motion because of the defects in our magic lantern. This antediluvian electrical device was essential for my tuition because, being flat on my back with my arms pinned down, everything had to be projected onto a screen above my head. One of the many inconveniences of the magic lantern was that it became overheated by its light bulbs. Sister Mary was none too skilful with her hands at the best of times and we got into great fits of giggles together as she tried to change the pages under the plates of the lantern, which gradually became as incandescent as burning coals. In cold print this hot activity does not look particularly amusing, but it created great merriment at the time as we counted the 'oh bothers' and the much more sinful 'oh drat its' for which Sister Mary claimed she had to say penances at Friday prayers.

Sister Mary's prayers made a great impression on me. At night-time when I was drifting off to sleep Sister Mary would kneel by my bed. Her stillness was astonishing. Often I would wake up and find her in exactly the same position as she had been when my eyes closed. So I had the impression that she had been in prayer for hours. Years later, I came across William Wordsworth's lines:

It is a beauteous evening, calm and free;
The holy time is quiet as a nun.

I thought this a perfect description of Sister Mary.

Her prayers, combined with Dr Macaulay's operations, helped me to beat the TB odds, for three years later I was able to leave Cappagh Hospital and have led a healthy life ever since. As far as I knew, my memories of this period had long been forgotten, but Sister Madeleine's spiritual tutorials mysteriously brought them all back, and with them two other poignant recollections of my first Irish nun.

In the months of convalescence after I left Cappagh, Sister Mary remained much in my mind. I saw her again on only two occasions. The scene of our initial reunion was the first big children's party I had been invited to since coming off my frame. It was held at Heveningham Hall in Suffolk, one of the stately homes of England, then owned by the Vanneck family whose children Margita and William were my contemporaries at Miss Ingate's school in the nearby town of Halesworth. My early days at this school had been dogged by some lingering after-effects of my illness. I was a bright little teacher's pet in the classroom but a weakling in the playground, unsteady on my feet and apt to fall over embarrassingly often. Some of the bigger boys, who spotted that I had the balance problems of an overgrown toddler, took it out on me for being Miss Ingate's favourite by pushing me over when no one was looking. Such experiences did not add to my self-confidence. So I set off for the Vanneck party in a mood of excitement and trepidation, the latter emotion being caused by a deep-seated fear that I would not be able to join in the games and the dancing like all the other children.

I can remember this party as vividly as any event of my childhood. The great Wyatt ballroom of Heveningham was festooned with paper chains and Christmas decorations. Tables were groaning with jelly, ice creams, cakes, sausage rolls and egg sandwiches – a lavish spread in that era of post-war austerity. The girls were in frilly frocks of all colours, making them seem far more grown up than the boys, who were dressed in drab brown school uniforms. There was a conjuror, a Punch-and-Judy show, then finally came the dancing.

Mrs Vanneck announced that we should take our partners for Strip the Willow. Shyly I asked the prettiest girl in our class, a blonde seven-year-old called Janice Bensley, to dance with me. We were talked through the steps, which consisted of whirling and twirling all along a line of the 50 or so children present, then holding hands to gallop up and down the length of the ballroom.

Miss Beverley, the school pianist, made the room ring with much crashing of introductory chords, and then we were off – stomping and clapping to the resonant rhythm of Sir Roger de Coverley. When it came to Janice's and my turn to weave our way down the line, all my physical fears and frailties vanished. We swung, swerved and galloped like two racehorses in the final furlong of a Newmarket classic, ending up with a wild circular spin which left us almost airborne with dizziness and happiness. What a moment! When the music finally stopped I went skipping away down the long corridors of Heveningham, singing and whooping in ecstasy, 'I can dance! I can dance!'

Suddenly, at the end of the corridor I saw Sister Mary Finbar. I rushed up to her, hugged her, and gave her the good news as if I was the town crier: 'I can dance! I can dance!' Sister Mary returned my hug and kissed me. Then she gave me her blessing in the words she had used so often at bedtime in Cappagh Hospital and walked away.

As we were driving home from Heveningham in our Hillman

Minx after the party, I told my mother that I had seen Sister Finbar. 'Don't be silly, darling,' she said. 'Sister Finbar is in Ireland. You've been eating too much ice cream.'

Well, maybe I had. Or maybe I hadn't.

The next and the last time I saw Sister Finbar was nearly 20 years later. By then I was a journalist reporting on the troubles in Northern Ireland. On the day of one particular departure from Belfast in 1967, all the British Airways flights to London were booked, so I routed myself home via Dublin on Aer Lingus. Driving through the outskirts of the city with two hours to spare before check-in time, I suddenly saw a large sign saying 'Cappagh Hospital'. On impulse I went in, found a nun and asked to see Sister Mary Finbar.

The Mother Superior of the order duly appeared and said she was terribly sorry, but Sister Mary would not be able to meet me because she was sick in the infirmary. Although disappointed, I was taken on a tour of the hospital which brought back many memories, particularly when I saw the terraces where the TB children had been wheeled out for our daily deep-breathing exercises.

Just as I was about to leave, Sister Mary made an unscheduled entrance. Apart from walking with a stick, she was exactly as I remembered her – serene, smiling and radiating strong energies of goodness and kindness. We hugged each other like long-lost friends and talked emotionally for half an hour or so, reminiscing about the overheating magic lantern, Dr Macaulay, my grandmother, John Betjeman and other Cappagh figures from our shared past.

What was marvellous about this conversation was the discovery that the bonds between us were still tremendously strong. Sister Mary was not some dreamed-up Florence Nightingale figure. She was the real living and loving lady I remembered so well. When the time came to say goodbye, I was overwhelmed by emotion, particularly when Sister Mary said she still prayed for me every night because she always knew I had been healed for some great purpose.

The Mother Superior walked out with me to my car, saying she could hardly believe what had just happened. She explained that Sister Mary had been bedridden with a serious illness for many weeks. The way she had got up and walked and talked with such vigour must be the work of the Lord, because only yesterday the doctors had thought she was close to death. Since the Sister Mary to whom I had just been talking was plainly full of life, I suspected a touch of Irish blarney. Yet the Mother Superior remained in the back of my mind and moved to the forefront of it a few days later when I was walking along Victoria Street in London. For some reason I began to worry about Sister Mary, so I did something I had never done before, which was to go into Westminster Cathedral and light a candle for her in one of the prayer chapels.

Two days later I received a letter from the Mother Superior of Cappagh telling me that Sister Mary had died, and that in her last hours she had spoken about the joy my unexpected visit had brought her. After I had read the letter I returned to Westminster Cathedral, lit another candle, and promised never to forget Sister Mary Finbar. It is a promise I am glad to have kept by writing this account of my memories of her.

As the Parliamentary Retreat came to its end at Easter 1996, I was conscious of feeling some deep debt of gratitude to both my Irish nuns, Sister Mary and Sister Madeleine. Between them they had given me a glimpse of a past and a future in which what really mattered was the power of God. Yet, for all the reassurance of Isaiah 43, I was living in a present where what really mattered to me was the power of the *Guardian*. It was under the growing pressure from the *Guardian*'s lawyers that I switched the focus of my thoughts from prayers to pleadings, and from Ireland to Arabia.

CHAPTER NINE

Arabia, their Arabia

SOME OF MY BEST friends are Arabs. They have been so for over 30 years and they remain so today, even though our friendships took a battering in the campaigns mounted by the *Guardian*–Granada team of journalists. In particular, the *World in Action* documentary 'Jonathan of Arabia' seemed offensive to many Middle East viewers (and to some British ones too) on account of its racial caricatures of Arabs as sleazy, sexually licentious Bedouins practising bribery and corruption in tents and sowing wild oats in Mayfair. Such visual images, reinforced by pejorative reporting in print, created an impression that my circle of Arab friends consisted largely of arms dealers, bribe takers, girl buyers, multimillionaires and tyrants. Those who think I am exaggerating may have cause to revise their opinions if they replay the videotapes of the relevant *World in Action* programmes and study the purple prose of the *Guardian*'s numerous articles during the saga.

Once a stereotype, always a stereotype. I do not expect this chapter to erase the mythology created by an ever-repetitive media. Yet because the truth is rather more interesting than the propaganda, I would like to set out a short account of how I became involved in the Arab world, what I did there, and why I remain proud of my friendships and (rather modest) achievements in it.

For my first eight years of visits to the Middle East I did not go to Saudi Arabia or know any Saudi Arabians. My early friendships were made in Jordan, Lebanon and in what were then called 'The Trucial

States', particularly Abu Dhabi, Dubai, Kuwait, Bahrain, Oman and Ras-al-Khaimah. I first went to them by accident, or rather by a mistake of news editor's geography comparable to one of the comic passages in Evelyn Waugh's *Scoop*.

Sitting in the bar of the Caravelle Hotel in Saigon in 1966, I received a telegram which began, 'Since you nearest Abu Dhabi move coupwards soonest...' This text may be a slight exaggeration, for I have lost the telegram in question. But that was the substance of it in the style of 1960s' Fleet Street communication to foreign correspondents in the field.

I had no idea where Abu Dhabi was, an ignorance evidently shared by the *Evening Standard* newsdesk, because perusal of an atlas showed that it was nowhere near Vietnam, nor was it even in Asia. Old Africa hands had not heard of it either. Finally an Australian war correspondent with a good memory for press cuttings said, 'Isn't that the oil place ruled by the bloke *Time* called Sheikh Jackpot?' And so it was. According to a yellowing copy of *Time* magazine, Abu Dhabi was a small island in the Persian Gulf headed by a sheikh named Shakbut who had 'hit the jackpot' by striking a couple of offshore oil wells. The news magazine story portrayed Shakbut as a miserly eccentric who hoarded the oil money under his bed in piles of banknotes which were being eaten by mice. Further inquiries revealed that while the mice of Abu Dhabi were getting fat, the natives were growing restless. Indeed, well before the *Evening Standard*'s intrepid reporter could organize his travel arrangements to the Gulf, Shakbut had been deposed in a coup de sheikhdom masterminded by the British political agent for the Trucial States, Colonel Hugh Boustead, installing a new ruler in his place, Sheikh Zayed.

Colonel Boustead was no great admirer of journalists, but as luck would have it he professed to admire my 'good bloodlines', as he called them, after discovering that he had served under my maternal grandfather, who had been Governor General of the Sudan at the time when Boustead was a subaltern in the Sudan Camel Corps in the 1920s. On the basis of these ancient connections I was given a *laissez passer* to Abu Dhabi and a promise of an interview with its new ruler.

Abu Dhabi today is a metropolis of glass skyscrapers, expressways and high-rise apartment blocks. In 1966 it was a collection of shanty-town huts and a mere handful of stone buildings, of which by far the largest was the Ruler's Fort – a castellated edifice straight out of *Beau Geste* or *The Seven Pillars of Wisdom*. There I interviewed Sheikh Zayed about his ambitions for his people. Fortunately this first-ever newspaper profile of the future President of the United Arab Emirates was a sympathetic one, even if it did contain the economically unpre-scient line, 'Some optimists believe Abu Dhabi's oil revenues could one day rise to $100 million a year.' In fact they exceeded $10 billion a year.

The last time I saw Sheikh Zayed, in 1994, he introduced me to members of his *majelis*, or court, with the words, 'This is the Englishman who came to see us when I was so poor that I could not afford pen and paper. I had to explain my plans to him by scratching in the sand with a stick.'[1] The last sentence was accurate, and even if Sheikh Zayed himself was never quite that impoverished, many of his fellow countrymen were living near the breadline in the 1960s. However, with the purse strings about to open, a small number of Western-educated students from Trucial State families were return-ing to Abu Dhabi. One of them became my friend. His name was Saif Ghobash and within six years of our first conversations in the Ruler's Fort of Abu Dhabi in 1966, he was appointed as his country's Foreign Minister.

Saif Ghobash was a sensitive, humorous man who combined deep Gulf roots with a wise understanding of Western culture. He taught me to enjoy the tribal customs of Bedouin society, and in return I gave him some insights into the tribal customs of British politics. Soon after I had been adopted as a parliamentary candidate for Thanet East, I took him on a tour of my prospective constituency.

Out of the blue he asked me if I could do him an 'enormous favour'. Could I get his two children into good English boarding schools?

The children were duly found places at prep schools in Broadstairs. They became my wards. I took my *in loco parentis* duties seriously because the Ghobashes were such an interesting family. No strings or business deals complicated our relationship. Saif and I enjoyed a genuine and disinterested friendship based on our shared passion for politics.

A year or so after I had been elected as an MP, an appalling tragedy occurred. Saif Ghobash was assassinated. Ironically, he was killed by mistake. A terrorist had climbed to the roof of Abu Dhabi airport with orders to murder the departing Foreign Minister of Syria. As this dignitary, Abdel Halim Khaddam, was giving his fraternal farewells and embracing his host, the gunman pulled the trigger and shot the wrong Foreign Minister.

A few hours later I had the deeply distressing task of collecting 8-year-old Adnan and 10-year-old Maysoune Ghobash from their schools, breaking the news of their father's death, and flying them home to their mother in Abu Dhabi. The episode was reported in a few column inches in the British press, but in the Gulf it was a huge news story. The poignant television pictures of the two children coming off the aircraft hand in hand with me made an emotional impact. The locals asked who on earth this English MP was who was so close to the Ghobash family that he had been trusted to bring the bereaved children home in their hour of tragedy. From that time on, all over the Gulf, I was not just another visiting businessman. I was a friend.

Friendships made in adversity can ripen in prosperity. By the mid 1970s I was working in the City of London for Slater Walker, whose commercial banking troubles were given a temporary respite by some sizeable property sales I achieved to the Abu Dhabi Investment Authority.

Although I had my successes as a merchant banker, the truth was that I was always more interested in the politics and the personalities of the Gulf than I was in making money from it. I did well, but a sharper businessman with my inside track of contacts and friendships would have done far better. This may be my financial epitaph, and it applied not only in Abu Dhabi (soon to become the capital of the United Arab Emirates) but also in the new marketplace I had begun to visit – Saudi Arabia.

Almost the first Saudi Arabian I ever met was Prince Mohammed bin Fahd at a lunch in Paris in 1973. He was an elegant, courteous and rather shy young man whose father was Minister of Education – and with no likelihood, so far as I was aware, of succeeding to the throne. Prince Mohammed invited me to come and visit him in Riyadh, which I did about six months later. We had some interesting conversations, but as a business trip my mission was a failure. Nobody I met in Saudi Arabia was remotely interested in Slater Walker's financial services. The country seemed to be one big chaotic building site, and few Saudi businessmen could look beyond the horizons of domestic land deals and construction contracts.

Just about the only person I met who seemed to have some grasp of Western financial institutions was Prince Mohammed's business manager, Said Ayas, a Lebanese-born medical student who had recently joined 'The Al Bilad Establishment for Fair Trading and Economy', as the Prince's fledgling company was called. In the long hours I spent in Riyadh waiting for the Prince (an activity requiring nocturnal stamina and patience in large quantities) I got to like and know Said Ayas rather well, but as he and everyone else at Al Bilad politely rejected all my offerings of UK share portfolios, unit trusts and property investments, I did not believe that our acquaintanceship would progress much further.

A few months after this visit to Saudi Arabia, Said Ayas telephoned me in a state of great distress. In a voice choking with tears he told me that his mother was critically ill, possibly dying, from renal failure and a kidney stone blockage. She had been put on an air ambulance plane which had just taken off from Taif in Saudi Arabia and would be landing in London in seven hours' time. Said Ayas' immediate problem was that he knew nobody in London except me. His sister was flying in from Switzerland, but she too had no contacts in the medical world here. Could I help her to arrange a doctor, a hospital, a kidney surgeon and an ambulance to meet the plane at Heathrow? This was quite a tall order in the middle of August, but here was a family in desperate trouble so I pulled out all the stops. My own GP, Dr Tony Greenborough, was in town and between us we arranged everything, including a room in the Wellington Hospital, a renal physician and top kidney surgeon Mr Turner Warwick. It was a close call, but after an emergency operation and several anxious days in intensive care, the life of Madame Fariah Ayas was saved.

Said Ayas was excessively grateful to me for the small part I had played in this drama. We became good friends. He introduced me to a Palestinian entrepreneur of vision and energy, Dr Ramzi Sanbar, who had recently opened up a civil engineering consultancy office in London. I became a director of his company. Within no time the Sanbar group was winning contracts all over Europe and the Middle East, recruiting British engineers, architects and surveyors by the dozen, and riding high on the crest of the construction boom wave. My work focused mainly on the United Arab Emirates where I won a major design contract for Sheikh Zayed's Presidential Court building, but we had Saudi clients too, of which the most important was Prince Mohammed bin Fahd.

I gradually came to know Prince Mohammed after several of his working visits to our London offices, and particularly after an episode which was to feature 20 years later with sinister overtones in my libel battles with the *Guardian*. This was Prince Mohammed's purchase of a BAC 1-11 aircraft.

Visiting France on business with Ramzi Sanbar in the summer of 1977, he and I received a casual invitation from Prince Mohammed to join him for lunch at the Paris air show. After lunch the Prince announced that he was interested in buying an executive jet. Never having been on this kind of shopping expedition before, I tagged along for the princely perambulation around the stands at the show, watching with mild amusement as aggressive salesmen from Boeing, Dassault, Aerospatiale, Learjet and goodness knows who else swooped on the Prince like piranhas scenting blood.

British aircraft company representatives were conspicuous by their absence throughout these hard-selling activities until, by chance, there hove into view the formidable figure of Sir Kenneth Keith, Chairman of Rolls-Royce.[2] I knew Sir Kenneth, having once stayed at his home in Norfolk for a dance, so I introduced him to Prince Mohammed. Instant combustion. Within seconds the virtues of air-craft powered by Rolls-Royce engines were being lauded to the skies as Sir Kenneth propelled the Prince towards a British BAC 1-11 air-liner laid out with a VIP executive fit.

It was a case of love at first flight. Fifteen minutes after going on board this luxuriously equipped aircraft, Prince Mohammed had negotiated a price of $3.5 million with its owner and signed a cheque for the down payment. 'It's a pleasure doing business with you, Mr Al Saud,' said the President of Omni Aircraft Inc., Mr Wayne Hilmer Jnr, who had never in his career made a quicker sale.

Impulse-buying of airliners can create problems. Sir Kenneth Keith having moved on to his next appointment, aviation expertise was sorely lacking in the Prince Mohammed entourage. When it came to resolving questions about contracts, spares, pilots, servicing, or even moving the plane out of Le Bourget, no one had a clue. 'Let Jonathan arrange it,' said the Prince, having somehow gained the impression that my social life with the Chairman of Rolls-Royce had endowed me with considerable aeronautical wisdom. In fact I had none. The best I could do on a Saturday evening was to contact a solicitor friend of mine, Mark Vere Nicoll, who in turn produced an aviation lawyer to ensure that the Prince at least had good title to his BAC 1-11. How to fly it was tomorrow's challenge.

Although I would have been hard pressed to tell the difference between a BAC 1-11 and a Boeing 727, I suddenly found myself taking decisions of the sort normally reserved for senior executives of airline companies. Did we want to buy a new INS? Yes, we'll have one of those, I said, after learning that the initials stood for Inertial Navigation System, and that the plane could not fly the Atlantic without it. How about a spare Rolls-Royce engine? After telephoning Sir Kenneth Keith, that sounded like a good idea too.

Pilots and servicing were the next and biggest problem. Omni Aircraft Inc. proposed a contract which would have cost over $1 million a year. I told the Prince he should get a rival quote from British Caledonian Airways who operated a fleet of BAC 1-11s out of Gatwick. BCAL came up with an offer of around $500,000 and with it two of the nicest and most professional aircraft captains you could ever hope to meet, Graham Kneath and Michael Cole. Between them they hammered out 'Operation Royal Flight', which was modelled on the RAF's Queen's Flight. With BCAL's help an engineer, a Gatwick-based ground maintenance team and two ex-BOAC stewardesses were recruited. Within weeks the aircraft was fully operational in Saudi Arabia, where the professionalism of its British aircrew was so much admired by senior members of the Saudi royal family that they often preferred to borrow Prince Mohammed's efficient BAC 1-11 in preference to the government planes provided by Saudia.

The administration of the BAC 1-11 quickly moved out of my hands as Captain Mike Cole took over the reins as full-time Managing Captain. Setting the operation up had been an interesting interlude for which I received no special reward or thanks at the time, although about 18 months later, when Prince Mohammed decided to open a London office, the trust I had built up with him over the aircraft may well have been the key factor in his decision to offer me the job of Managing Director of Al Bilad (UK) Limited. In the meantime, the BAC 1-11 continued to earn kudos for its owner and prestige for Britain generally by operating as a royal flight of faultless excellence. Despite the initial eccentricities of the purchasing process in Paris, the story of Prince Mohammed's aircraft reflected nothing but credit on all concerned with it.

It was therefore amazing to discover, nearly 20 years later, that the story I have just told was being rewritten to reflect maximum discredit on me, Prince Mohammed and members of his aircrew. The source of this discreditation exercise was an interview for Granada's *World in Action* with Valerie Scott, who had been my secretary in 1977. According to the transcript, she referred to the BAC 1-11 as 'a sort of flying knocking shop', accused me of taking a $2,000 commission on its $3.5 million purchase price, and vividly described the sleeping arrangements on board. 'I was ever so impressed that there was a bedroom on the aeroplane ... lots of sort of marble looking bedside cabinets and this enormous bed with an en suite bathroom,' she said.

After Valerie Scott had recounted how BCAL had supplied a shortlist of airline stewardesses for me to interview, the uncut transcript continued:

Interviewer: Why do you now feel you should have warned the girls what was in store for them?

Valerie Scott: Well I did try and warn them actually at the time. I felt really bad about it because these were professional airline stewardesses coming for what they believed to be a straightforward air stewardess's job. I knew that it wasn't going to be quite as straightforward as that because the members of Prince Mohammed's staff would expect the girls to do a bit more than serve them drinks and meals. It was, we thought of it as, a sort of flying knocking shop...

Interviewer: But did Aitken know what he was recruiting them for?

Valerie Scott: Oh yeah, he would have known. He knew what the Prince's entourage wanted.

Interviewer: Were there special requests about what type of girls?

Valerie Scott: Yes, you had to be blonde and beautiful.

Interviewer: Who told you that?

Valerie Scott: Aitken told me that, I don't know who told him.

Interviewer: So Aitken was quite deliberately recruiting blonde, beautiful girls that the Arabs would want to have sex with?

Valerie Scott: Well, yeah, I mean I don't think that was a pre-requisite … I think it would have been more honest if he had said because then that would have given the people the opportunity to say no.

In retrospect, it seems extraordinary that this heavily prompted interview should have been accepted by the *Guardian* and Granada lawyers as the basis for the very serious allegation in their clients' pleadings that in 1977 I had recruited stewardesses to work as prostitutes on Prince Mohammed's aircraft.

To make matters worse, not a word of was true. There was no bedroom on the BAC 1-11, no en suite bathroom, no $2,000 commission, no knocking shop, and the only stewardess ever recruited by me was a most respectable brunette. She was Jill Wales, an ex-BOAC stewardess from Yorkshire who subsequently enlisted another of her former BOAC colleagues, Angela Gale. It would have been hard to find two more level-headed, impeccably behaved and thoroughly professional air hostesses than Jill and Angela. When the *Guardian* and Granada produced their distasteful allegations against them in the pleadings, these by now matronly ladies were incensed, as were the BCAL captains who had commanded the Prince's aircraft. Someone in the *Guardian*–Granada camp eventually realized that they were in serious trouble with these false charges, because soon after the High Court hearings of my libel action had begun, the defendants' counsel George Carman QC withdrew the allegations, shortly before five members of the aircrew arrived to give their evidence in my defence. It was one of the more unpleasant episodes in the entire libel case saga.

My experience of Prince Mohammed and his 'entourage' was that they were rather reserved and cautious individuals with good brains and good manners. The more I got to know them, the more I liked them. When I became Managing Director of Al Bilad (UK) Limited in 1979, I had few difficulties in working alongside them as professional colleagues. Al Bilad (UK) itself was an operational success but a commercial disappointment. We were an efficient buying office, and we won a handful of small export contracts in the £2–10 million range for British companies selling products such as electricity generators, lifts and post office sorting equipment. But to my chagrin, the big export deals and the big money eluded us. Arms deals there were none. They were never even discussed by me and my colleagues at Al Bilad (UK).

In 1984 Prince Mohammed entered the Saudi Government, resigned the chairmanship of Al Bilad (UK) and severed his connections with the group. Al Bilad (UK) continued as a representative and buying office for its parent company, but with a staff of three and a much reduced level of activity.

Where my Saudi connections proved rather more interesting was in the field of inward investments and the outward visits I had to make to the Kingdom in connection with them. During the 1980s various Saudi associates of mine invested over £50 million in the UK. Their projects included a civil aviation factory in Northern Ireland, the Williams Formula One Grand Prix engineering company, the Aitken Hume merchant bank, a West End hotel, several property purchases, Inglewood Health Hydro, and TV-am. The last two items caused trouble for me in the libel case, although not in a way that I think would have had a dramatic effect on the ultimate result had the battle gone the full distance.

The TV-am issue was whether or not I had improperly concealed the £3 million non-voting Saudi interest in TV-am in the early 1980s. That it had been kept confidential at the investor's request was indisputable. Whether it was improper to maintain this confidentiality was a confusing matter of judgement which I probably got wrong. George Carman's line of cross-examination on the TV-am issues was somewhat undermined by the fact that the Saudis had been model passive investors, coming up with the rescue money that saved TV-am from insolvency in 1982 and never interfering with a single management or editorial decision. Despite all the huffing and puffing about the sinister nature of 'Saudi control' over such influential items as Roland Rat and the daily flow of early morning cartoons and sofa chit-chat, the truth is that no such control was ever exercised or attempted.

As for Inglewood – labelled 'Inglenookie' by the *Guardian*–Granada team of journalists, who luridly portrayed it as a den of sexual iniquity – this was a respectable and well-run Berkshire health hydro which an Arab investment consortium, headed by the Al Athel family of Riyadh, had purchased in 1981. For the next 14 years, Inglewood was managed professionally, successfully and uncontroversially. It employed a locally recruited staff, headed on the medical side by a doctor with a clinic unit of SRN and SEN nurses, and on the hotel-keeping side by a first-class team of dieticians and managers. Every week about 70 patients took up residence at Inglewood. The majority of them were middle-aged English ladies who came there for losing weight, reducing stress, and in some cases for convalescence after operations or illnesses. I was the nonexecutive Chairman of Inglewood, receiving monthly reports from the Managing Director and keeping a merchant banker's eye on the company's finances, but doing very little else because the organization ran so quietly and smoothly.

Almost the only trouble we ever had at Inglewood occurred in 1982 when the Newbury police arrested the then Matron and

General Manager Jo Wilson (as she was then called). The arrest followed an investigation into theft and fraud allegations which had been made by another senior member of the staff. A significant quantity of Inglewood's missing property was recovered after a police visit to the country house shared by Jo Wilson and Robin Kirk, a consulting osteopath to Inglewood. They gave their explanations to the police and no criminal charges were ever brought. Kirk and Wilson had their contracts terminated. A new General Manager was appointed and there was no further trouble.

For the next 13 years Inglewood continued to look after its patients well. The Arab owners were happy with the good dividends they received for their investment, which steadily multiplied in its value. They never interfered with the day-to-day management of the hydro. Their only contribution, apart from approving major items of capital expenditure, was to send some 30 or 40 patients a year from Saudi Arabia to lose weight. These patients were mainly women who kept themselves to themselves. There was never any whiff of scandalous or improper behaviour by Arabs at Inglewood until the *Guardian* launched their attack on 10 April 1995 under the headline 'AITKEN "TRIED TO ARRANGE GIRLS" FOR SAUDI FRIENDS'.

The genesis of this attack was David Leigh's interviews with the two dismissed Inglewood employees Robin Kirk and Jo Wilson (now Jo Lambert). As in the interview with Valerie Scott, there was a remarkable amount of audible prompting on the tape. In the uncut version of the filmed interview with Jo Lambert, it took no less than six interventions by David Leigh before he obtained from the former Matron the words which were actually broadcast on the programme 'Jonathan of Arabia'. It is worth reprinting these promptings directly from the Granada transcript, because this interviewing technique does raise important questions about journalistic ethics. The interview, which had obviously been extensively discussed in advance off camera, reaches the point at which the subject of my alleged 'pimping request' over the telephone to Jo Lambert in 1982 starts to be raised.

David Leigh: Just, erm, tell me again about the episode in which Jonathan rings up and says 'they're coming down' erm with a bit more detail really starting from, you know, the phone rings: it's Jonathan – just let's relive it a bit more.

Jo Lambert gives an answer which makes no mention of any pimping request on the telephone.

David Leigh: Let me just stop again. Tell me exactly what he said on the phone as near as you can remember and how the conversation went and what was involved.

Jo Lambert gives a second answer making no mention of any pimping request on the telephone. After another question from Leigh, at a third attempt, she adds:

Jo Lambert: He also said that he wanted, was there any women around, er could I get any women for them and that's when I had the conversation about saying no I couldn't and if he wanted women he could bring them from London.

David Leigh: Just take me through that bit about the women from beginning to end because we've told it in two halves now. That's a separate phone call is it?

Jo Lambert: Yes, the arrangements were one phone call and then he rang me up and asked me if I would arrange for women to go down to be there and that's when I had the conversation.

David Leigh: Right, let me just ask you about it in two halves. First of all when he rang up the first time and asked for these arrangements about the tennis court, the riding, and the fruit machines, this was all having to be done in a great hurry?

Jo Lambert: Yes, I think I had about four days and when I said to him but it's going to cost a fortune and who's going to do it, he said charge them double, they'll pay for it if they want it.

David Leigh: Now he then made a subsequent phone call to you and talked about women so tell me about that phone call from beginning to end.

It was only at this point in the interview that Jo Lambert, at what might be called the sixth time of asking, finally gave the answer (quoted in full in Chapter 2, page 19) which alleged that I had asked her if there was any possibility of 'getting girls for the Arabs'.

Others more detached from subsequent events than I can be must judge for themselves whether David Leigh's interventions and promptings amounted to fair journalistic interviewing or whether they set up a contrived performance designed to strike a blow against me in the *World in Action* programme. My own reaction after studying the transcripts and watching the mastertape of this interview was to say to my solicitor that Granada's *World in Action* programme should be renamed *World in Well-Rehearsed Action*. I also found it astonishing that the Editor of the *Guardian*, Alan Rusbridger, had summoned up the nerve to use this interview as the basis for the paper's front-page story on 10 April 1995.

It was equally astonishing that nobody at the *Guardian* or Granada seemed to have asked the question whether any girls or prostitutes had ever actually been procured at Inglewood during my 11 years as a director there, either at the time of this one and only visit in 1982 of Prince Mohammed for lunch, or on any other subsequent occasion.

The answer, as even Jo Lambert and her partner Robin Kirk had to admit, was no. Inglewood was a good business but it was never involved in monkey business. These allegations of pimping were false.

My Arabian business activities (Al Bilad, Inglewood and other small investment projects for Gulf clients) were not heavily time consuming, but they did give me an interesting and specialized merchant banker's insight into the Middle East. Compared to the US market where, as Chairman of Aitken Hume, I had to make at least six visits a year to attend board meetings of our New York subsidiary, which managed $6 billion of mutual funds, my responsibilities for looking after the investments of my Arab clients were relatively small. However, I enjoyed them disproportionately to their commercial value because I found the economic, cultural and political scene in the developing Gulf, particularly in Saudi Arabia, so fascinating.

Saudi Arabia is not to every Western visitor's taste. The sluggish pace of commercial life, the postponement of decisions, the politeness that has to cope with the unpunctuality of princes, the conflicts between puritans and progressives, the aggressive pieties of Islam such as the megaphone prayers that disturb sleep, and the harsh and sometimes arrogant certainty that Saudi society is superior to Western society – these are the superficial irritations that many foreigners find hard to accommodate.

Whenever I dispatched executives to Riyadh or Jeddah in search of business, I used to warn them of the apocryphal desert gravestone with the inscription, 'Here lies the Westerner who tried to hurry the Saudis', or of the no less apocryphal story about how the Riyadh office of IBM had been translated to mean Inshallah (as Allah wills) Bokhara (tomorrow) Mumkind (perhaps). To those who came back boasting about their inside track with this or that prince or their inside knowledge of the royal family, I would say, 'The wisest observers of the House of Saud only know how little they know.'

I knew as little as anyone for the first decade or so of my travels to Arabia. Yet gradually, as I came to like and understand my Saudi contemporaries more and more, and as I lived with them through the human ups and downs of their lives, I began to grasp the subtlety of their tribal confederations, their dynastic marriages and the simmering tensions between ancient religion and modern development in Saudi society. The latter point was brought home to me in an episode worthy of the Keystone Cops on the day I was arrested in Riyadh by the *mutawa*, or religious police.

Rising in my hotel room early one morning, I decided to go jogging – something I had done many times before in Saudi Arabia. Navigation was not easy in a city which was then largely without street names or house numbers, so I ran up and back one long road. When I was on the return leg of my journey, I was stopped by a posse of officious gentlemen carrying sticks whose leader addressed me with sanctimonious aggression.

'You are under arrest.'

'What for?'

'For wearing obscene Western clothing.'

I looked down at my rather baggy shorts and T-shirt. 'I am sorry if I have offended your customs, but I have jogged many times before in Riyadh without any problem.'

'But you have not worn them in this street before.'

'No, I don't think I have ever been in this street before.'

'That is your crime. You have shamed yourself in this street by running past a girls' school.'

I protested that I had no idea I was anywhere near a girls' school and that a visitor would have to possess expert local knowledge to be aware of what went on behind any of the anonymous high-walled houses in the street.

'You are lying. You have run past the girls' school – TWICE.'

Patiently I explained that I had passed every building twice, because I had run up and down the entire road. Far from exonerating me, this answer seemed to confirm my guilt. I was in double trouble.

'He has confessed,' said one of the religious policemen who were encircling me with their staves, giving the uncomfortable impression that they were about to perform the punishment meted out by the *lictores* of ancient Rome.

'Who are you? Why have you come to Saudi Arabia?'

It was time to pull a little rank. 'I am a British Member of Parliament.'

'Impossible. Not in those obscene clothes.'

Inwardly I had to agree that I looked an improbable parliamentary figure in my sweat-soaked running kit. Then I remembered that I had an appointment with my travelling companion Julian Amery to see the Saudi Minister of the Interior later that morning. I tried pulling a higher rank. 'I am here in Riyadh with the Rt Hon. Julian Amery MP, a former British Foreign Minister, who knew King Abdulaziz. We are to see Prince Naif, the Minister of the Interior, at 11 o'clock this morning,' I explained. 'I will be wearing a suit then.'

The religious policemen laughed, perhaps a little nervously, at these mentions of higher authority.

'Who arranged your meeting with Prince Naif?' asked their commander rather less aggressively.

'The appointment was made through Ibrahim Al Awaji and Abdullah Battal.'

The mention of these two Ministry of Information officials caused a thaw in the atmosphere. The sticks went down. After some internal discussions among the policemen, I was given a mere verbal beating in the form of a lecture on the wickedness of Western decadence as symbolized by my shorts, on the purity of Saudi womanhood, and on the importance of not polluting the latter with the former. To judge by the tone of the sermon, I might have been a streaker at the gates of Cheltenham Ladies' College, but no charges were to be preferred. I was bundled into a police car and driven back to my hotel.

'Do not offend our laws again,' was the police commander's parting shot.

When I relayed this story to my more sophisticated Saudi friends, they laughed so much that I felt I could have earned a good living in Riyadh as a comedian. 'You have learned the hard way two great truths about Saudi society,' said one of them. 'The first is that the *mutawa* are powerful but crazy. The second is that the leaders of the Al Saud are far more liberal than their followers.'

'Liberal' is not an adjective frequently applied to the royal family of Saudi Arabia, but in reality they do preside with relatively enlightened and outward-looking leadership over a traditionalist society where religious zealotry is constantly fomenting public opinion towards intolerance. Just as the Tudor monarchy had to reign over Puritanism, so the Saudi monarchy has to rule in harness with fundamentalism. Never were these forces in potentially greater conflict than at the time of the Gulf War of 1991.

When Saddam Hussein invaded Kuwait in 1990 and looked poised to strike next against Saudi Arabia, I had known Prince Mohammed bin Fahd for over 15 years. He was a key figure on the Saudi stage. As the son of King Fahd (who had succeeded to the throne in 1982) and as the Governor of the Eastern Province, Prince Mohammed found himself acting as the administrator in chief for the refugees fleeing from neighbouring Kuwait and as the civilian host to the half-million or so Western servicemen from the American, British and other coalition forces who made their base camp in his emirate. It was his appointment with destiny and he met it well, but there were times when he found himself in difficult and uncharted waters of international politics and public relations. I was flattered when he turned to me for advice on how he should handle these dimensions of the impending conflict.

Although I was only a backbench MP at the time, it did not require the mind of a master strategist to see how much was at stake for both the Arab and Western worlds in the run-up to the Gulf War. Both communities had serious problems in finding the political will to hold together the fragile coalition that eventually stood firm against the Iraqi dictator. The narrowness of the vote to go to war in the US Congress, the early criticisms by the media in Europe of the proposed Western commitment to Saudi Arabia and the barely suppressed opposition in Saudi society to the Western military presence on Islamic soil were all reminders that Operation Desert Storm, as Wellington said of the Battle of Waterloo, was 'a damned close-run thing' – politically if not militarily.

My contribution to the political battle to win over public opinion in the West during the build-up period to the Gulf War was to exercise an influence over two important men 6,000 miles apart from each other – Prince Mohammed bin Fahd and President Richard M. Nixon.[3]

Prince Mohammed listened to me when I advised him to seize the initiative with the foreign media in the Eastern Province and to explain to US and British television film crews how Saudi Arabians felt about Saddam's threat to their homes and way of life. What the international viewers wanted to see was not more silent pictures of the King holding audiences, but articulate, English-speaking Saudis giving interviews.

Under Prince Mohammed's leadership, therefore, some of the best and brightest young princes threw hierarchy to the winds and supplanted their fathers and uncles as spokesmen for the Kingdom. Some of them (starting with Prince Mohammed, Prince Abdullah Feisal Al Turki and Prince Fahd bin Salman) were extremely effective on camera, and so were a number of articulate Saudis from the armed forces, the universities and the business community who explained their society and its values to the global television audience. The concept of having young Saudis giving live interviews on television may not sound much of a breakthrough in the West but, in their deferential and closed Arabian society, it was a revolutionary change which did much to help swing international opinion behind the build-up to Operation Desert Storm.

On the stage of American opinion the former US President Richard Nixon had by 1991 moved out of the shadows of Watergate and was enjoying an indian summer as an elder statesman. I was hard at work on his biography, but when the Gulf conflict loomed I worked almost as hard at briefing him on the war politics of Arabia. He too listened and acted. When the Congressional votes drew near, Nixon swung into action as his country's most respected foreign policy expert. Reaching out to President Bush, to mighty editors and senators, down to obscure and recalcitrant first-term Congressmen, Nixon lobbied with passion to get America's Gulf War policy well planned and well supported. His *New York Times* article of 6 January 1991 (which I helped to draft) in support of the Bush administration's strategy, entitled simply 'Why?', was probably the single most influential piece of journalistic advocacy in the days before the crucial votes in the House and the Senate. Without Nixon's intervention those close votes might just have been lost.[4]

I may well be exaggerating my political influence in the Gulf War preparations. At best it was a minute one, akin to that of a very small cog in a huge complex of international machinery. Nonetheless, I was quietly proud of having helped to strengthen one or two significant bridges of Arab–Western understanding at a critical moment in the history of both civilizations. At that time I regarded it as the only meaningful contribution – modest though it was – that I had made towards the peace and stability of the Gulf. Yet that in its way was also a tiny contribution towards the stability of the West, for who knows what furies of global destabilization would have been unleashed if Saddam Hussein had triumphed by default.

Looking back on my business and political activities in the Middle East from 1966 to 1992, I have often wondered: What did I do that was so wrong that it triggered such waves of animosity among journalists, employed mainly by the *Guardian* and Granada, in 1995–7?

On the credit side of the balance sheet, there were some small but definite pluses in terms of jobs created, export contracts won, friendships made and influence exerted. On the debit side, the minuses have always seemed to me to be thinner than pulp fiction. There was never any involvement by me in pimping or procuring. I never earned a penny from an arms deal. I did not make a personal fortune from the modest commercial achievements I helped to accomplish. I was never engaged in any form of bribery or corruption. Although I earned a good income from my business links in the Middle East, I was neither dependent on Arab money nor did I become significantly rich from it. Despite frantic efforts to substantiate such assertions in their publications and their pleadings, none of my journalistic adversaries have even begun to prove that what I have just said in the previous few sentences, in court, and on many other occasions, is untrue.

The unhappy conclusion I have reached is that the attacks made on me for my Middle East friendships and business activities were not made because those connections were wrong, but because they were connections with Arabs. And I doubt whether these attacks would have been launched at all if I had not unexpectedly been made a minister in April 1992.

CHAPTER TEN

Defence Minister

ONE OF THE MOST agreeable surprises of my political career was to be appointed as Minister of State for Defence. After 18 years on the backbenches, many of them spent displaying an independence of mind and voting patterns which did not always commend me to the Whips, I was unexpectedly brought into the Government by John Major a few days after his own agreeable surprise of winning the April 1992 Election.

'Immerse yourself in the detail,' was the Prime Minister's advice when he offered me the job. 'You'll have one of the biggest budgets in Whitehall so you must keep an eagle eye on the purse strings in the department which can spend money faster than any other. You'll find yourself taking some difficult decisions. Like EFA. And do we need a fourth Trident submarine?'[1]

My mind reeled. I had no idea what EFA was. I knew nothing about Trident submarines. The largest budget I had ever handled was of the order of £10 million. I had no previous defence experience.

'Perfect qualifications!' drawled my outgoing predecessor Alan Clark. 'You'll do it bloody well and have a marvellous time. It's one of the best sub-Cabinet jobs in Government. You have enormous power because your decisions are so damn complicated that no one else really understands them.'[2]

It took a great deal of time and effort before I understood the complications of what my new job entailed. Bewildering acronyms were the first hurdle. Mine was MinDP (Minister for Defence Procurement), which meant that I was in charge of Britain's £9.5 billion a year purchasing budget for defence equipment, whose most urgent topics awaiting my attention were astonishingly expensive items in programmes known as EFA (European Fighter Aircraft), SSE (Trident Submarines), ROTHR (Radar Over The Horizon), SHS (Support Helicopter Systems), SDI (Strategic Defence Initiative) and Spearfish (Naval Torpedoes). Merely to be told about some of these subjects required me to be indoctrinated with codewords and security clearances by strange spirits called from the vasty deeps of the MOD with peculiar names such as 'Seedy' and 'Cissy' – respectively the Chief of Defence Intelligence (CDI) and the Chief of the Strategic Submarines Executive (CSSE).

In addition to being the Minister in charge of Defence Procurement, I was the Minister for Defence Exports (then running at £3.5 billion a year), the Minister for the Defence Research Agency (which was spending nearly £1 billion a year on research for tomorrow's weapons), and the sponsoring Minister for Britain's Defence Industries (which employed 500,000 people). Other hot potatoes which landed on my desk in the early weeks of my appointment were the future of nuclear submarine refitting at the Royal Dockyards, the Market Testing Initiative which might result in a large number of redundancies among MOD civilians, and a request to sign Public Interest Immunity Certificates in connection with the Matrix Churchill case – the slow-burning fuse which detonated the Scott Report. I was also told I must help out with ceremonial duties, such as travelling to Quito to represent the Queen at the inauguration of the President of Ecuador, and escorting the Princess of Wales to the launching of HMS *Vanguard*. Away from such royal diversions, there were heavy parliamentary pressures and an intriguing mixture of red-box paperwork, which ranged from the almost unreadable (budget figures on weapons programmes) to the almost unmentionable (classified intelligence reports).

With this sort of workload I never had a dull moment at the MOD. It was my good fortune to arrive there at a time of great strategic change and to be surrounded by exceptional colleagues – ministers, service chiefs and senior civil servants. Under Malcolm Rifkind as Secretary of State we were a happy ship, and one which I believe we navigated well in the uncharted policy waters we had entered in the world of defence.

For nearly half a century the defence policy of Britain and NATO had been based on the threat that 'the Soviets are coming'. Suddenly they weren't. In that belief, one of my first ministerial decisions was to reject a submission from the Royal Navy asking to spend some £750 million on torpedoes designed to destroy Russian submarines. 'Your grandchildren may regret your decision, Minister,' said a disappointed Admiral. It was a salutary thought, for with this and many other projects on my desk, a long-range vision was required to see whether or not the Russia of the early twenty-first century might revert to its old habits of imperialistic aggression.

Our short-range vision was focused on the Balkans and the Gulf. British forces were operational in both theatres. Bosnia was the more high profile because of the horrors of ethnic cleansing, but the horrors of the secret new 'weapons of mass destruction' which both Iran and Iraq were acquiring seemed even more worrying in strategic terms.

On the day that John Major made me a Defence Minister, he said to me in his study at No. 10 Downing Street, 'I think your knowledge of the Gulf will stand you in very good stead.'[3] Only after I had access to classified briefing material did I realize the full import of what he meant – for the weapons build-up by the Iranians and the Iraqis was an unreported menace in 1992, with the potential of bringing the Gulf and the whole world to the brink of a twenty-first-century Armageddon.

The MOD was short on Gulf specialists when I arrived there. So was the Secret Intelligence Service, although the Foreign Office had several first-class people. Assessing the threat was the first challenge. After a clandestine meeting with the Iranian Defence Minister, I was left under no illusions as to what his country might be planning in the fields of missile technology, naval warfare and terrorism. Saddam Hussein was bristling in his underground bunkers with even more sinister plans. Discussing these worries in Washington with every available expert from the Director of the CIA downwards, it was clear to me that the Western Alliance had to embark on a long-term strategy of containment if we were serious about preserving peace and stability in the Gulf. The most articulate exponent of such a containment policy was the pre-eminent US foreign policy expert whose biography I had finished on the day John Major called the 1992 Election – Richard Nixon.

'Nations only resort to aggression when they believe they will profit from it,' wrote Nixon in 1983. 'Conversely they will shrink from aggression if it appears in the long run it will cost them more than it benefits them. For this reason wars tend to break out when the aggressor is strong and his victim is weak. They are unlikely to happen if a sensible military balance of power exists between potential contestants. If there is no profit in war, aggression will be deterred and a practical liveable peace will be preserved.'[4]

Preserving a practical, liveable peace in the Middle East will never be easy, but the Nixon doctrine of creating a sensible military balance of power between the potential contestants looked the wisest route to it. The Gulf in the early 1990s bore an uncanny resemblance to Europe in the 1930s. Two ruthless dictatorships – Iraq and Iran – were greedily eyeing their smaller and weaker neighbours. Kuwait had been the first to fall. Even though it had been liberated, would it fall again? Who might be next on the dictator's hit list? The Tumbs Islands? The United Arab Emirates? Bahrain? Saudi Arabia? The leaders of these countries all thought they were vulnerable to their neighbouring predators and were doubtful of the resolve of the West to mount a second Operation Desert Storm. So the wisest course of action for them was the expansion, retraining and re-equipping of their armed forces, carefully co-ordinating these plans with the military powers of the West.

The re-equipping of the Gulf States' armed forces was a strategic necessity in the eyes of the Western alliance, but it was also a commercial opportunity for Western defence companies. I found myself at the centre of their activities as Britain's Minister for Defence Exports. Although the promotion of arms-sales contracts was a comparatively small part of my overall ministerial responsibilities, there were times when I and the Defence Export Sales Organization (DESO) – a branch of the MOD – had to go into overdrive to support British interests. One of the first of these episodes concerned the re-equipment of Kuwait's land forces.

Having been the scene of the mother of all battles, the State of Kuwait decided to hold the mother of all trials before placing its orders for tanks and armoured cars. Competition from American, French, Russian and German companies was fierce, but Britain had two strong contenders for these contracts: the Challenger Two tank made by Vickers in Leeds and the Warrior armoured vehicle made by GKN in Birmingham.

The principal trials were held in August 1992 when the summer heat in Kuwait was 120°F in the shade. The Challenger Two did not perform entirely in accordance with the glowing terms of its sales brochure. There were troubles with speed and with cornering manoeuvres. Post-trial rumours alleged that the tracks on one side of Vickers' demonstration tank had mysteriously been loosened during the hours of darkness before the test. Whether or not that tale was apocryphal, it was marginalized by the true story of the final salute of the Challenger Two at the end of the trial. Instead of coming to a stop at a respectful distance from the VIP enclosure, the Kuwaiti driver of the demonstration tank just managed to halt his roaring monster some 15 yards short of the Royal Box, and then pointed its gun barrel directly into the stomach of the visibly shaken Emir. After such a finale it was not a surprise to learn that Vickers were pipped to the post in this particular contract race by the American Abrahams Tank.

Britain did, however, win a valuable second prize in Kuwait, for GKN's Warrior armoured vehicle outscored all its rivals in terms of performance, quality and value for money. The Kuwait Ministry of Defence duly announced that the Warrior had won the competition and that a £1 billion order would be placed with GKN, subject to the finalization of the contract negotiations. Soon after this announcement the Crown Prince of Kuwait visited London and told various important personages, including Margaret Thatcher, how delighted he was with this result.

That should have been that, but in the slow-paced world of Arab administration the interlude between the announcement of an order and the signature of a contract can be such a long one that disappointed losers sometimes seize their moment to subvert the competition result by opportunistic rebids. This was exactly what happened when, some weeks after the contract announcement, the aggressive US Commerce Secretary Ron Brown descended on Kuwait with what he called 'a bargain-basement counterproposal' of two American armoured vehicles for the price of every one British Warrior. Even though the rival 'offers' were almost as different as chalk and cheese for reasons involving specifications, spares and capabilities, the Kuwaiti Government came under intense pressure not to sign its announced contract with Britain and to reopen the competition. This pressure came to its climax with a telephone call to the Crown Prince from the Vice President of the United States and a personal message to the Emir from President Clinton.

Although we continued to fight back with less exalted British representations through our own diplomatic channels, it became clear as more time passed that we were losing ground. Our slippage was confirmed when we learned that the Kuwaiti Cabinet or Council of Ministers had put on the agenda for its next meeting a discussion item proposing that the GKN contract negotiations should be suspended and that a new armoured vehicle competition should take place.

Faced with the loss of a £1 billion British export order, the MOD came under intense pressure 'to do something'. Malcolm Rifkind and I both did our utmost, making flying visits to Kuwait to see ministers and officials. Despite these endeavours, the prospects for getting the GKN order confirmed continued to weaken in the face of the American pressure.

What might have tipped the scales Britain's way was a personal telephone call from the Prime Minister to the Emir of Kuwait in the last 48 hours before the vital Council of Ministers' meeting took place. I tried to arrange such a summit conversation, but the private office of No. 10 said it was out of the question. 'Don't even ask until after Thursday,' was the Private Secretary's frosty response. Unfortunately, after Thursday would be too late. In British political terms, however, No. 10 were setting the priorities of that particular week correctly, because the Prime Minister was preparing to open an emergency debate on the Maastricht Treaty Bill in the House of Commons. A cliffhanging vote was expected and if it went the wrong way, a no-confidence motion would follow and the survival of the Government would be on the line. John Major could not be faulted for giving the preparation of his Maastricht Bill speech a higher priority than making telephone calls to Kuwait about a defence export contract.

Having reached this impasse, I could see GKN's order going down the plughole. Then I had a brainwave. How about trying to enlist the help of Margaret Thatcher? This was an unorthodox, indeed risky manoeuvre. Because of her increasingly critical views on Maastricht, the former Prime Minister was a long way from being flavour of the month with her successor. When I told my officials that I was thinking of asking Lady Thatcher to make a last-ditch appeal to the Kuwaiti leaders, my idea was greeted with sharp intakes of breath, pursed lips and disapproving murmurs of 'Are you sure that would be wise, Minister?'

I brushed these warnings aside and, with the help of my old friend Julian Seymour, the head of the Thatcher office, I arranged to call on the Iron Lady at her home in Chester Square at 6 p.m. on Tuesday 6 July 1993 – some 13 hours before the vital Kuwaiti Cabinet meeting was due to take place. The action of the next 40 minutes was a marvellous demonstration of Thatcher power at its fiercest, funniest and most effective.

As I recounted the sequence of events in the contract battle so far, my narrative was punctuated by a succession of explosive epithets from Margaret Thatcher: 'Outrageous!' 'Appalling!' 'Disgraceful!' and finally, 'I will not allow this!'

Having roused Queen Boadicea to wrath, my next move was to persuade her to charge at the right target. No such persuasion was required. The lady was for phoning.

'Do you have the Crown Prince of Kuwait's home telephone number?' she demanded. Fortunately I had and dialled it. Amazingly, Sheikh Jabr Al Sabah answered the line himself.

'Your Highness, I am in Margaret Thatcher's house. She is right beside me and would like to speak to you about an urgent matter,' I began.

'Jonathan, you must be joking,' chuckled the bemused heir apparent.

Before I could explain that jokes were not on the evening's agenda, Margaret Thatcher seized the receiver. In tones of rising passion she reminded the Crown Prince of the part Britain had played in the liberation of Kuwait and of his pledge that Britain would get its fair share of the armed forces re-equipment programme. She also reminded him that debts of honour were debts of honour, and that only a month or so ago he had personally assured her that Britain had won the armoured vehicle competition.

'Now what I want to know is: do Kuwaitis keep their promises?' The answer was apparently less than satisfactory.

'Your Highness, I do not like what I am hearing. Let me ask you again. Do Kuwaitis keep their promises? Are you going to keep your word or break your word?'

'I'm beginning to feel a bit sorry for this chappie,' observed Sir Denis *sotto voce* as he sipped his gin and tonic. His sympathy was evidently not shared by his spouse. Her decibels rose as she enlarged on her strong feelings to the Crown Prince.

'So what exactly are you going to do at your Cabinet meeting tomorrow?' she crescendoed. 'You are not going to run away from your responsibilities, are you?'

I was beginning to wonder whether my bright idea would provoke a major diplomatic incident in Anglo-Kuwaiti relations when sweetness and light broke out.

'Thank you so much, Your Highness. I knew you would be a man of your word,' I heard Margaret Thatcher coo in dulcet tones.

'He was wobbly, but he'll be all right,' she declared as she put down the receiver. 'Now I must sort out the Americans. Let's get Al Gore on the line.' I confessed that my skills as an impromptu switchboard operator did not include carrying around the telephone number of the Vice President of the United States.

'Well then, get Robin Renwick. He'll know it.' The number of the British Ambassador in Washington was not at my fingertips either.

Margaret Thatcher was in no mood to be thwarted by these pettifogging obstructions. 'Then I must speak to Ray Seitz at once. He must be made to order the Clinton Administration to stop their dirty tricks immediately.'

With some difficulty I tracked down the Ambassador of the United States to the Court of St James, only to be told by the butler at the official US Embassy Residence in Regent's Park that His Excellency was unavailable to come to the telephone because he was having a shower.

For the second time Margaret Thatcher seized the receiver from me. 'This is Margaret Thatcher. Please tell Ambassador Seitz that I will hold on until he comes out of the shower.'

The butler did not argue with these orders and apparently delivered them to the Ambassador's bathroom, for a couple of minutes later a presumably wet and dripping Raymond Seitz came to the telephone to receive a broadside, from which he escaped only by promising to pass on a 'back off' message to Washington immediately.

Justifiably pleased though she was by her evening's work, Margaret Thatcher had not quite finished. 'Now, our last task tonight is to tell the Prime Minister exactly what's been happening. I'd like him to know that I can still bat for Britain.'

I said I would tell John Major about all the boundaries his predecessor had scored in the morning. That was not good enough. 'A Prime Minister likes to know these things at once. Do it now!' was the command.

With some trepidation, I rang No. 10 and was relieved to be told that the Prime Minister could not be disturbed. 'And perhaps it might be wiser not to disturb him at all on this one,' murmured the well-trained Private Secretary. 'Let's take stock in the morning.' I agreed with alacrity to this proposition.[5]

By the time we got round to taking stock the following morning in Whitehall, the Cabinet in Kuwait had approved the final details of the armoured vehicle contract and had authorized the Defence Minister to sign it in the British Embassy. So GKN got its £1 billion order and the Warrior subsequently performed superbly both in the snows of Bosnia and in the sands of Kuwait. Britain had achieved a great export success – but we would never have done it without Margaret Thatcher.

During my first two years as a Defence Minister, Britain's annual defence export sales more than doubled from £3.5 billion to £7.2 billion. As the responsible minister I took both praise and blame for this spectacular growth, which its admirers thought was due to good salesmanship and its detractors believed was a corrupt arms race. In reality, however, the improvement was largely attributable to impersonal factors such as the increased competitiveness of British industry, the booming economies of Asia and the Middle East, and the re-equipment programmes of the Gulf States. If there were individual sales heroes they were to be found within the export departments of the companies concerned and in the MOD's Defence Export Services Organization which, under the leadership of Sir Alan Thomas, was a remarkably effective government promoter of British interests in this field.

Occasionally, however, a Defence Minister plays a pivotal role in helping to win an overseas export contract because the personal or political touch can make a vital difference. I often tried to play these cards with my opposite numbers in governments as far afield as Australia, the USA, the UAE, the Netherlands, Malaysia and Oman, sometimes with success and sometimes without. But there was one government and one defence contract where my personal role did make the difference between triumph and disaster. This was the 1993 Al Yamamah extension agreement between the Governments of Britain and Saudi Arabia.

The defence relationship between Britain and Saudi Arabia is of the highest strategic, military and commercial importance to both countries. As was demonstrated in the Gulf War, Saudi Arabia is the fulcrum of security in the region. It is the West's most dependable Arab ally. Its British-trained Air Force is one of the finest in the Middle East, second only to Israel's in firepower and pilot skills. Its bases, military infrastructure and computer systems in fields such as AWACS (Airborne Warning and Control Systems) and secure communications are lynchpins in the security arrangements that safeguard the peace of the Gulf. This military interdependence is matched by considerable commercial benefits to the Western military powers who support the Saudis. In the last decade, the US, Britain, France and Germany have won well over $100 billion worth of export orders from Saudi Arabia in the defence and security field. Calling this 'an arms race' is a superficial oversimplification, because without it there would have been an arms disaster. One only has to envisage the Gulf and its oil reserves dominated by Saddam Hussein to realize that even if the price of vigilance is costly in both manpower and machinery, it is well worth paying if it secures peace and stability.

All this was the background to the British–Saudi negotiations for an extension of the Al Yamamah agreement which arrived on my desk at the MOD towards the end of 1992. Al Yamamah, 'The Dove', had been a government-to-government defence concordat operating successfully for the previous seven years. It was now coming up for renewal. There was great confidence on the British side that the Royal Saudi Air Force continued to need the facilities, the training and the equipment which we had provided with such good results before and during the Gulf War. The only difficulties were with the contractual details of prices, but these were thought to have eased because of recent changes in the exchange rate to the Saudi advantage.

According to the briefings I received from our Foreign Office and MOD experts in December 1992, Al Yamamah Two (as the extension was called) was all over bar the signing. I was advised that my role as minister would be more ceremonial than substantive. The latest round of negotiations between British Aerospace (the prime contractor on Al Yamamah) and the Royal Saudi Air Force had gone so well that all I had to do was to fly into Riyadh on ministerial autopilot, make a formal presentation of the final offer to Prince Sultan bin Abdulaziz, the Saudi Defence Minister, and then take out a gold pen for the signature of the contract.

From my past experience of doing business in Saudi Arabia, I had some instinctive forebodings that the optimistic expectations of Whitehall might not turn out to be quite such plain sailing as the Al Yamamah specialists were predicting. I therefore insisted on being given a total immersion briefing on the contract and its complex ramifications. Nothing, however, could have prepared me or anyone else for the shock that was to come.

On 8 January 1993 I took a large entourage of British Embassy, British Aerospace and British military personnel to see Prince Sultan. I described in detail Britain's offer for an extension of the Al Yamamah contract which included 48 new Tornado ADV aircraft, 24 Hawk trainers and extensive additional programmes for training and maintenance. I then fell silent, confidently expecting a positive response from my host.

To the consternation of the British team, Prince Sultan answered me with a totally negative reply which he read out in a formal monotone from a prepared script. His message was that the Council of Ministers had carefully considered the British offer but had regretfully concluded that the Kingdom of Saudi Arabia could not proceed with it. Citing budgetary pressures and hinting that other, more cost-effective proposals for re-equipping the RSAF had been received, Prince Sultan firmly closed the door on the deal that had been under negotiation for over a year. So definite and decisive was the rejection of our offer that the entire meeting lasted less than 30 minutes. There were no discussions on points of detail, since it had been made crystal clear to us that Al Yamamah was not to be extended as a matter of principle.

To say that Prince Sultan's announcement was seen as a severe blow to Britain's national interests would be a massive understatement. 'Total disaster' was how one of my senior officials described it, and he summed up the feeling of our entire delegation as we returned to the British Embassy in a mood of cataclysmic gloom.

In the post-mortem discussion that followed, it was said that up to 100,000 British defence industry jobs could be lost in this debacle – many of them in Lancashire, where the BAe factory at Wharton desperately needed to keep its Tornado production line open for at least another three years before the EFA project started to create new employment opportunities for its own workforce and those of its supplier companies. Fears were also expressed that an announcement of the end of Al Yamamah could undermine our credibility as a defence-exporting nation, blow a hole in our balance of payments figures, and even affect the value of sterling.

As we stared into these disturbing abysses, the only slender lifeline of hope to emerge from our discussions was the idea of an urgent appeal to King Fahd. The thought was that, if we could get an audience with the Saudi monarch, perhaps he might be persuaded to reconsider the Council of Ministers' decision on strategic grounds. Unfortunately, this plan was scotched when a telephone call from our Ambassador, Sir Alan Munro, to the Head of Royal Protocol elicited the information that King Fahd had just gone away on a camping trip in the desert and would not be accepting any official engagements or appointments for the next few days.

Our gloom was deteriorating into doom when Sir Alan Thomas, the MOD's tenacious Head of Defence Sales, took me aside and urged me to try an initiative through my personal contacts. 'Surely, Jonathan, you could ask Prince Mohammed bin Fahd to get you helicoptered out to the desert to see his father?' said Alan. 'I know it's a long shot, but you've always said that Prince Mohammed is a real friend of yours and a genuine Anglophile. Couldn't he do a big favour for you on a personal basis?'

Although this seemed the longest of shots and the biggest of favours, it was our only straw to clutch at, so I gave it a try. I tracked down Prince Mohammed at his Governor's Residence in the Eastern Province and explained the gravity of the crisis as seen through British eyes. In this conversation, and in a subsequent meeting, I implored the Prince to get me an emergency appointment to see his father.

Prince Mohammed delivered. He persuaded his father to break off his desert holiday in the interests of British–Saudi relations. Four days later, at the late, but in Arabian terms not unusual hour of 1 a.m., the British Ambassador and I entered the marble halls of the Al Hasqua Palace in Riyadh and were duly ushered into the King's presence for what was to become the most important appointment of my ministerial career.

It was a negotiator's chance of a lifetime. In this moment of high tension I knew I would only get one shot at my target, which was to change the declared policy of the Saudi Government and to reopen negotiations on the Al Yamamah extension.

I knew enough about Arabia to make haste slowly, well understanding that a head-on attempt to put direct pressure on as formidable a figure as King Fahd would fail. So I began with prolonged pleasantries, making the King laugh with reminiscences of our previous encounters in family settings and with gossipy anecdotes of my more recent ministerial travels around the region. Changing the tone, I moved for more than an hour into an analysis of the threats to security in the Gulf, covering topics such as Iran's rearmament programme, Saddam Hussein's chemical and biological warfare capabilities, disputes over islands such as Abu Musa and Hawar, and Qatar's border skirmishes over the Jubal al Udayd peninsular. Gradually we worked round from these subjects to Britain's role in preserving stability in the area, to the importance of the British–Saudi relationship in war and peace, and to the political importance of Al Yamamah, strategically, economically and symbolically.

King Fahd on his best form (as he certainly was that night) is a highly perceptive regional and geopolitical strategist. However, his clear vision can be obscured from the uninitiated by his use of what might be called a Delphic style of expressing his thoughts. As I was among the uninitiated, I probably missed some of the regal nuances in the early part of our dialogue. But as we talked long into the early hours of the morning of 12 January, I began to decode the almost telepathic signals in the King's sentences, whose complexity brought into my mind Henry Kissinger's description of another contemporary statesman's negotiating methods: 'One came to realise that his words were like billiard strokes. What mattered was not the initial impact but the carom.'[6]

As this comparable game of intellectual and political snooker played out towards dawn in the Royal Palace in Riyadh, I sensed that the King was slowly turning Britain's way. In reaching this understanding I was immeasurably assisted by the brilliant simultaneous interpreting of Prince Bandar bin Sultan, the only other person in the room besides the King, the British Ambassador and myself. Prince Bandar, the Saudi Ambassador to Washington, has long been an outstanding builder of bridges between the heartlands of Islam and the capitals of the Western Alliance. The briefing he gave me shortly before my audience proved to be the ideal curtain-raiser to the King's concerns on security issues. So when I eventually steered the conversation to Al Yamamah and the devastating impact its loss could have on Britain, King Fahd was already receptive to the thought that this might not be the right time to weaken any aspect of the British–Saudi defence relationship.

Two hours and 55 minutes after our audience had begun, King Fahd said he would reconsider the negative decision on Al Yamamah communicated by Prince Sultan four days earlier. Indeed, the King went on, he would personally try to find a formula which would allow the purchase of the 48 Tornado aircraft to go ahead. He believed that a solution could be reached. He would ask Prince Bandar and Prince Sultan to work closely with me in the coming days to see if a mutually satisfactory result could be achieved.

With the calls to dawn prayer wailing across the deserted streets from the mosques and minarets of Riyadh, Ambassador Munro and I drove back to the British Embassy and debriefed our Al Yamamah team, who had been standing by on all-night vigil. Their jubilation was great but, on reflection, qualified. 'The Minister played his hand well, but we have not yet won the rubber,' was how one bridge-playing diplomat summed up the situation.

After a few hours' sleep, my own thoughts on 'winning the rubber' began to focus on the importance of engineering an early summit meeting between King Fahd and John Major. I went to have lunch with Prince Bandar, who agreed with this strategy and said he thought he could get it implemented on his side fairly quickly. I said I would do the same, although my words were a great deal less confident than they sounded.

Rearranging a Prime Minister's travel schedule is no easy task. I was already unpopular with the logistics team at No. 10 for having persuaded John Major to reroute his homeward journey from the Far East and India to include a stopover in Oman. Now I was doing it again, asking the prime-ministerial aircraft to make a further detour to Riyadh.

'I have a hunch it will come out all right on the night,' I told the Duty Clerk at No. 10.

'Hunch? All right on the night? Do you want me to pass it on like that?' was the sceptical response.

Fortunately I was able to speak to Rod Lyne, the Prime Minister's more sympathetic Foreign Affairs Private Secretary in India, and he worked the necessary rescheduling miracle for a day towards the end of January. It was a case of flying on a wing and a prayer, but it worked.

King Fahd was genuinely delighted to see John Major, one of whose many undervalued qualities is an ability to establish excellent personal relationships with foreign heads of state on a one-to-one basis. It was the first time the two leaders had seen each other since the Gulf War, so a spectacular state banquet of welcome was laid on, followed by private talks between King and Prime Minister with their respective Defence Ministers in attendance.

Unfortunately, the Prime Minister arrived in Riyadh in a tense and fractious mood. This was partly due to tiredness, since he was already into the twenty-first hour and third time zone of a hectic working day which had begun with a businessman's breakfast in Bombay. The factor that was causing him most angst, however, was a mendacious burst of media poison back in London, where the *New Statesman* and *Scallywag* magazine had splashed a story claiming that the Prime Minister and a catering lady who cooked occasional dinner parties at No. 10 were having an affair. This was malicious fiction but, as the rest of the British media were also now running with the story, John Major decided to sue the *New Statesman* for libel and had spent most of his previous night in India talking to lawyers and issuing writs.

The British contingent waiting to welcome the Prime Minister at Riyadh airport were unaware of these journalistic shenanigans. So we were mystified by the febrile questioning from some members of the accompanying press party who tumbled off the aircraft like barking puppies, evidently believing that serious affairs of state in Saudi Arabia were far less newsworthy than imaginary affairs of the heart in the Downing Street kitchen.

To his credit, John Major brushed aside the rat pack's prurient interest in his private life and gave his full concentration to the complex briefing I had prepared for him. However, the romantic allegations about the cook were never far from his mind all evening. 'Do you think I should mention the *New Statesman*'s story to King Fahd?' the Prime Minister murmured nervously into my ear as we were about to set off for the state banquet. 'He may be wondering about it.'

Touched by this display of personal vulnerability, I did my best to reassure John Major that the *New Statesman* was unlikely to be required reading in Saudi Arabia and need not be mentioned in the summit discussions. This was to no avail. Sitting on the King's left at dinner, I was startled to overhear the conversation on the King's right turn at full volume to the fanciful tales of upstairs-downstairs dalliance at No. 10.

'I'm afraid some sections of our media will invent anything,' said the Prime Minister.

'I know they will,' replied the King with a merry laugh. 'The British press said I was in love with Margaret Thatcher!'

Further explanations about the non-love story in the kitchen continued as the Saudi monarch and the British Prime Minister talked on. The interpreter seemed to become confused. King Fahd evidently got the wrong end of the stick for, turning to me, he whispered conspiratorially, '*Hadha tabakh – haliya bint jamila?*' (This cook, is she a pretty girl?)

I said I had no idea, and that the story was nonsense anyway.

'Well, your boss is a good looking and strong young man,' observed the King with a twinkle in his eye.[7]

John Major needed to be a strong young man that night in Riyadh, for the Saudi–British summit lasted for nearly seven hours of intensive talks. I was proud of the Prime Minister, who conquered his travel fatigue, performing with statesmanlike perspicacity on the strategic *tour d'horizon* part of the talks and with commercial tenacity on the difficult details of the Al Yamamah negotiations. However, it emerged that King Fahd was uneasy about finalizing the deal on the spot. He proposed that the actual agreements and announcements should be delayed and be subject to further negotiations between the Defence Ministers of the two countries during the following few days. As the discussions began to stall, with both King and Prime Minister visibly tiring, John Major passed me a note: 'KF has now said three times that he wants you and PS [Prince Sultan] to handle it from now on. Shall I back off and agree?'

I scribbled back, 'No! Keep fighting! We are almost there. We must get a public announcement tonight.' Like a battle-weary knight returning to the charge, John Major responded to my exhortation by rallying his negotiating skills and making one final, impassioned plea to his host in which he emphasized the importance to both Kingdoms of releasing a decisive public announcement that evening. King Fahd listened and gracefully agreed. Prince Sultan and I, with useful input from Sir Alan Thomas and the Saudi Information Minister, Sheikh Ali Al Sha'er, quickly hammered out the wording of a five-line press statement for immediate release. It announced simply that the Governments of Britain and Saudi Arabia had agreed to an extension of Al Yamamah which would include the purchase of 48 Tornado ADV aircraft.

As we landed seven hours later at Heathrow airport, the morning's national news bulletins were all leading with the overnight story of the Prime Minister's record-breaking £4 billion Saudi arms-deal triumph securing 100,000 British jobs. 'I think one could say that you earned your pay today, Minister,' purred my Private Secretary over the car telephone as I headed off to Thanet and the down-to-earth realities of my weekly constituency surgery. It had been an Arabian night to remember.

CHAPTER ELEVEN

First Clash with the Guardian

THE FRENETIC NATURE OF 'Yes Minister' life at the MOD, together with the importance of some of the decisions which had to be taken there, ensured that my Arabian adventures on Al Yamamah soon faded into the background. Within months of those regal negotiations in Riyadh, my focus had switched to domestic issues such as the future of the Royal Dockyards, the contract for a new helicopter carrier and, most absorbing of all, my chairmanship of an across-the-board defence costs review entitled 'Front Line First'.

Away from the deskwork of Whitehall, it was sometimes easy for a Defence Minister to confuse movement with action. Such confusion was understandable when the movement was provided by one's own RAF aircraft and the action consisted of *Boys' Own Paper* exploits such as days on patrol with the SAS in the jungles of South America or nights test-firing torpedoes from a Trident submarine in the waters of the North Atlantic.

In the midst of these exciting duties, the Al Yamamah extension did manage to rear its head on rare occasions, eventually in a form that triggered the *Guardian*'s implacable hostility towards me.

The background to this episode was that the contractual details for Al Yamamah Two took far longer than expected to finalize. Although the Saudi King and the British Prime Minister had announced their agreement to the deal in January 1993, the lawyers for both Governments were still nit-picking at the small print of it in June. Occasionally the nit-pickers became so intransigent with each other that the whole contract looked in jeopardy. However, the ubiquitous Prince Bandar kept the show on the road, flying in and out of London to exercise his supervisory role over Al Yamamah as King Fahd's personal envoy.

Prince Bandar, a Cranwell-trained fighter pilot, had a considerable affection for Britain. His Anglophilia ran deep and I gained some interesting insights into the roots of it when one evening in the early summer of 1993 he telephoned me to say, 'How would you like to come to a pub with me on Saturday night?'

Prince Bandar's idea of going to a pub was to take one over for a weekend. He had invited his entire class at Cranwell for a reunion at the Fox and Anchor at Rotherhithe. Twenty years on from their days as novice fast jet pilots, the Gingers, Pongos and Busters of 214 Squadron had lost none of their irreverence for top brass, nor their enthusiasm for high jinks. His Royal Highness Prince Bandar was immediately demoted to 'Woggie', his 1970s' nickname in the officer cadets' mess. I was christened 'Hacker' after the inept minister in the television series *Yes Minister*. Both of us were teased good humouredly all evening by the erstwhile fighter aces of Cranwell '72 as they drank pints of beer standing on their heads, sang songs such as 'One wing on my Chipmunk / I'm just rolling along', and told ripping yarns of their prangs, pile-ups, shunts and snafus. Former Flight Lieutenant Bandar joined in these activities with unfeigned enthusiasm. Just as he was being asked to perform the role of starter for a tobogganing race down the pub staircase on tea trays, I extracted from him a promise to sort out the last remaining details on the Al Yamamah contract, made my excuses and left him and the other true Brits to get on with the fun.

Prince Bandar's sense of humour became rather strained a week or two later, when he was named as the central figure in a sensational story which appeared on the front page of the *Guardian* on 22 June 1993 under the headline 'TORIES FACE SAUDI CASH CLAIM'.

Carefully timed to coincide with an Opposition debate in the

House of Commons on the ethics of party-political fundraising, the article by Paul Brown alleged that £7 million in cash had been handed over to a British Cabinet minister[1] by Prince Bandar in the London home of his father, the Saudi Defence Minister Prince Sultan bin Abdulaziz, as a donation to the Conservative Party just before the 1992 General Election.

As soon as I read this explosive *Guardian* accusation, which was immediately recycled as the lead story on all the day's news bulletins, I knew it was nonsense but feared it might be dynamite.

My certainty that the *Guardian*'s allegations were a malicious invention stemmed from my knowledge of the leading personalities named in the story. Just as any sane Whitehall observer would instantly have known that a story in a Middle Eastern newspaper stating that the British Ambassador in Washington had, with the connivance of the Secretary of State for Defence, delivered £7 million in cash to the Hizbollah Party of Iran was a ludicrous fantasy, so any competent Saudi-watcher in Britain could have made the immediate and accurate judgement that the *Guardian*'s story about the Saudi Ambassador in Washington giving £7 million in cash to the Conservative Party of Britain was equally preposterous pie in the sky. It was the sort of black propaganda fabrication which might have appeared in a particularly deranged edition of *Private Eye*, but on the assumption that lunatics had not suddenly taken over the asylum at the *Guardian*, the question arose as to how on earth such a story could have appeared as the front-page lead in a newspaper which in those days still had the reputation of being a fair and reliable broadsheet.

My bewilderment at the *Guardian*'s transformation into a paper of fiction was nothing compared to my trepidation about the damage this journalistic calumny might do to Britain's national interests in Saudi Arabia. The Saudis are prone to over-reaction at hostile Western media coverage. They have a track record of cancelling, freezing or switching big orders and contracts away from countries whose newspapers or television programmes have caused them displeasure. My fear was that the *Guardian* story would put the Al Yamamah extension deal in jeopardy and that many thousands of aerospace jobs would be lost as a consequence.

These forebodings were initially shared by the Al Yamamah specialists within the MOD and British industry. By chance I was able to pass them on to Peter Preston, the Editor of the *Guardian*, who coincidentally came into the MOD to have lunch with Malcolm Rifkind on the day the accusation against Prince Bandar was published. I probably spoilt Preston's lunch by giving him my forthright views on the incredibility of his paper's story. From the shiftiness of his body language and the evasiveness of his answers to my questions, I could see that the Editor was already extremely nervous about the quality of his reporter's sources.

More bad news was in the pipeline for Preston, because the Saudis decided on what for them was the novel step of seeking redress through the courts. Prince Bandar, whose outrage at the *Guardian* was increased by the fact that their reporters had neither approached him for a comment nor attempted to check the story with his office in Washington, issued a writ for libel.

Two days later I was due to fulfil a long-standing speaking engagement to the annual conference of the Commonwealth Press Association. This goodwill organization, which maintains the old connections between newspapers in Canada, Australia, New Zealand, Malaysia and other parts of the Commonwealth, may have been expecting a light-hearted lunchtime address from me with anecdotes about Lord Beaverbrook, Sir Frank Packer, Roy Thomson and other newspaper proprietors who had ruled the roost in my 1960s' days as a journalist. But I was so steamed up by the *Guardian*'s irresponsible report that I cut down on the humour and instead tackled the serious theme of declining standards in contemporary journalism.

My thesis was that while most newspapers strove to achieve high editorial standards, and while the provincial press in the United Kingdom and the leading big-city newspapers of the Commonwealth had on the whole a good record of fair and accurate reporting, nevertheless a disease had been creeping into British journalism which might be called 'hatchet-job reporting', whose weapons were dubious sources, dodgy rumours and sometimes palpable fictions. In this genre of journalism, the old-fashioned editor's blue pencil was taking a poor second place to the headline writer's urge to rush into print with a negative and all too often untruthful story. The old Fleet Street editor's rubric 'If you can't check it, don't print it' was being changed into 'Don't look too closely at an exciting rumour' by some journalists, particularly in the marketplace of the tabloids.

At this point in my speech I turned my fire on the *Guardian*, whose founder C. P. Scott had coined the maxim, 'Comment is free but facts are sacred.' I said that C. P. Scott would be turning in his grave if he could read his old paper's front-page lead story of the previous Tuesday morning, for its sins were as bad as any of the worst tabloid fictions. Warming to my theme, I said that any thorough or fair-minded editor would have insisted that this sensational story was checked out carefully with the prominent individuals who were named in it as wrongdoers. So why had the *Guardian* not made a telephone call to the office of Prince Bandar at the Saudi Arabian Embassy in Washington? This fact-checking failure would, I said, most likely cost the *Guardian* dear in terms of both money and reputation, since Prince Bandar had now issued instructions to his solicitors to commence proceedings for libel.

Seen with the wisdom of hindsight, I probably went too far in the sharpness of my attack on the *Guardian*, accurate though it was. For, unknown to me at the time, the Chairman of the *Guardian* had taken a large table at the Commonwealth Press Association lunch. He and his assembled company of guests and editorial executives were not only humiliated by my strictures, they were shocked to hear for the first time that they were about to receive a writ for libel from Prince

Bandar – a revelation which was confirmed to them when they returned to their offices. Although my speech had been applauded by the rest of the audience, therefore, it had stirred up a hornets' nest in the *Guardian* which was to seethe and sting for many months to come.

A few days after my speech to the Commonwealth Press Association, Peter Preston and Mohamed al Fayed had a meeting in London and made the first moves towards cementing the alliance that was to bring about my downfall. There must have been a *frisson* of embarrassment in the air when these unlikely bedfellows began their mating game, because Preston's previous comments on Mr al Fayed's sterling qualities of character and veracity had been scathing. 'FAYED LIED OVER HARRODS', 'LIES, LIES, AND MORE LIES: THE MOUNTAIN THAT CAME FROM MOHAMED', and 'DECEIT ON A MASSIVE SCALE' were just three of the *Guardian*'s headlines on 8 March 1990. On that day Peter Preston devoted three pages of his paper and its main editorial to condemning Mohamed al Fayed for his mendacity over the takeover of Harrods as exposed in the DTI report.

But what are a few old lies between new friends? Preston now badly needed Fayed's help, to solve what could have been a horrendously expensive problem for the *Guardian* over Prince Bandar's libel action, so this was the main topic of conversation between the two new allies when they met for the first of their many assignations in June 1993.[2] At the end of the evening, the owner of Harrods promised his full co-operation to the Editor of the *Guardian*, and during the coming weeks Fayed worked hard to fulfil his side of the bargain.

In early August 1993, Fayed telephoned Prince Bandar's long-standing friend Mr Wafic Said at his home in Marbella. Presenting himself as 'a close friend' of Peter Preston and his paper, Fayed offered to arrange favourable coverage of Prince Bandar by the *Guardian*. He said that the *Guardian* would send a top journalist to

Washington to interview Prince Bandar and that the paper would adopt a 'positive attitude' towards him, provided he could be persuaded to withdraw his libel action.

Wafic Said replied that, while he could not speak for Prince Bandar, he did not believe His Royal Highness had any need to be interviewed by the *Guardian*. What was required was for the *Guardian* to accept that the story it had published on 22 June was untrue and to issue a proper apology. 'The *Guardian* does not like to apologize,' responded Mohamed al Fayed, and on that unsatisfactory note the conversation ended.[3] In due course, however, an apology was given in court.[4]

Mohamed al Fayed's curious activities as the *Guardian*'s go-between on this libel case had at least one more spasm of subterranean activity. On 3 September 1993 Prince Mohammed bin Fahd checked into the Ritz Hotel in Paris. He was shown into his suite by the hotel's owner, Mohamed al Fayed. To the considerable surprise of the Prince, Fayed suddenly began talking about the *Guardian*, claiming to be representing the newspaper. According to the eyewitnesses present, Fayed gave a number of reasons why the libel action would be extremely damaging to Prince Bandar and urged that it should be settled. He (Fayed) had been asked by the *Guardian* to arrange a settlement. Would Prince Mohammed help in this endeavour?[5]

Prince Mohammed was visibly offended by Fayed's approach. Because of it, he checked out of the hotel three days later, leaving word to Fayed that if he wished to contact Prince Bandar he should do so via the Saudi Embassy in Washington. Fayed was later said to have felt affronted by this rebuff.

I was unaware of these Fayed–*Guardian* initiatives and of the rejections they had received. Indeed, I was oblivious to the Fayed–*Guardian* alliance, which by this time had also moved into other areas of collaboration connected to the cash-for-questions allegation Fayed was making against Neil Hamilton MP. So when I checked into the Ritz Hotel myself on 17 September 1993, I had no idea that all my movements and telephone calls would be monitored by the hotel's owner on behalf of his friends at the *Guardian*. The trap had been set and I fell well and truly into it.

CHAPTER TWELVE

What Really Happened at the Ritz

'WHEN I DIE YOU will find the words *Ritz Hotel* engraved upon my heart.' The thought is paraphrased from Mary Tudor's epitaph on the loss of Calais in 1558. Writing nearly four and a half centuries later, I have some fellow feeling for the English monarch's misery, because in its own, if much smaller, way my personal catastrophe on French soil was a comparable heartbreak.

Some disasters are important more for their symbolism than for their significance. My nonpayment of a £900 Ritz Hotel bill fell into this category because it set a match to a bonfire of 1990s' discontents, including the unpopularity of John Major's Government, the venality of Tory sleaze, the mendacity of politicians under pressure, the victimization of Mohamed al Fayed over his citizenship application, and the deceitful tendencies of some investigative journalists. How many of these perceptions were fair, others must judge, but true or false they boiled up into a cauldron of conspiracy theories, spiced by other exotic ingredients such as allegations of British arms deals, MI6 espionage, Arab bribery, al Fayed eavesdropping, Mossad traps, ministerial corruption and *Guardian* forgery. The saga offered a field day for score-settlers and fiction-writers. Beat this one:

...the gigantic Al Yamamah Tornado contract lies at the heart of the Ritz mystery. King Fahd of Saudi Arabia was reluctant to distribute £600 million in commission to the middlemen who had brokered the Tornado contract. The plan, elaborated at the Ritz, was to persuade King Fahd to approve these vast bribes. In exchange for an even larger chunk of commission, Prince Mohammed would lean on his father to approve the vast payments. Meanwhile, Jonathan Aitken MP ... as usual, would be rewarded for his efforts.[1]

The above paragraph was the *Guardian* reporting team's first verdict on the Ritz Hotel affair on the final page of their book about the libel case, published in December 1997. The team had a second bite at this cherry in March 1999 when they published a three-page article claiming they had discovered the 'true story behind the Ritz'. This revolved around a claim that Said Ayas had formed an offshore company called Marks One in 1993 to receive commissions from two British defence companies with whom Marks One had consultancy agreements. 'If there is a more serious act of corruption in post-war British politics we would be interested to know of it,' thundered the *Guardian*, although confusingly, some 25 lines earlier in this same editorial the paper stated, 'We cannot know if Mr Aitken himself would have benefited.'[2]

The *Guardian* was not alone in jumping to dramatic – and wrong – conclusions about my visit to the Ritz Hotel. The *Independent* suggested that I was there trying to arrange nuclear arms exports to Iraq via Saudi Arabia,[3] while the foreign press invented a multiplicity of sensational scenarios which ranged from an Aitken sex scandal to a trap set by Mossad.

After such exotic journalistic theories, what I have to offer is mundane in comparison. However, for those who are interested in a factual account of what really happened at the Ritz, here it is.

My visit to the Ritz Hotel in September 1993 had its origins in the 20-year-old friendship between Prince Mohammed bin Fahd and myself. I had last seen him in Saudi Arabia nine months earlier in January 1993, when he had been the key figure in arranging my appointment with his father, King Fahd, for a meeting which had rescued the Al Yamamah contract from cancellation.[4] The extension of that contract, known as Al Yamamah Two, secured 100,000 British jobs and was worth over £4 billion in export orders to British factories. Prince Mohammed, who is the Governor of Saudi Arabia's Eastern Province, had no commercial involvement in the contract and earned no commission or reward from it. Nor did Said Ayas.

My visit to the Ritz Hotel had nothing to do with Al Yamamah and nothing to do with rewards for me. The visit took place because Said Ayas, Prince Mohammed's closest aide at that time, had telephoned me a week or so earlier to say that the Prince would like to see me during his summer holiday in Europe. I was pleased by the invitation, partly because I was glad to have the chance to keep my friendship with Prince Mohammed in good repair and partly because I wanted, through talking to him, to try to read the mind of his father, King Fahd, on one or two defence and security issues which were on my agenda as a Defence Minister. The most significant of these issues was the threat to the stability of the Gulf posed by Iran.

Nobody who knew me or Prince Mohammed should have been at all surprised that we wanted to meet and talk with each other, both as old friends and as ministerial players within our respective Governments. For my part, with the wisdom of hindsight, I think that the temptation of pride was an additional factor in my motivation for the meeting. For I *was* proud of my friendship with the son of the Saudi King. I was proud of being well regarded in Whitehall as a minister with specialist Middle East expertise. I was proud of my track record of batting for Britain as the minister responsible for promoting defence exports. I was proud of the successes I had enjoyed in my first 18 months as a Defence Minister and, as an ambitious politician, I wanted to go on succeeding in my responsibilities. So perhaps I was too ambitious and too proud for my own good, which was one reason why I ran into the trap of the Ritz Hotel too eagerly and too recklessly.

The arrangements for my meeting with Prince Mohammed had been a constantly moveable feast. I had chosen the date of Friday 17 September because the Prince was scheduled to be in Geneva and I was intending to be there on that date also, accompanied by my wife and daughter Victoria, who was going to a new school, Aiglon College, in the nearby Swiss town of Villars. Then Prince Mohammed's plans changed and he had to be in Paris. Then my plans changed too, because I was unexpectedly required to visit Poland on ministerial duty with the Duke of Edinburgh for the funeral obsequies of General Sikorski.

This ceremonial reinterment of Poland's de Gaulle was a moving occasion but also a prolonged one. It included a service of committal in Kracow Cathedral, a three-mile walk behind the gun carriage bearing the General's remains to the Castle of Kings, an open-air High Mass with a 45-minute sermon by Cardinal Glemp, the reburial ceremony in the royal vaults, a post-burial drink followed by a private meeting with President Lech Walesa, and a two-and-a-half-hour flight back to Balmoral. 'We seem to have done a lot of flying and a lot of praying,' observed the Duke of Edinburgh genially as we stepped off the HS 146 aircraft of the Royal Flight.

I had even more flying ahead of me, and still further delays at Northolt and Heathrow airports. The end of this colourful if protracted day in the life of a Defence Minister was that I turned up at the Ritz Hotel in Paris, not at 6.00 p.m. as expected, but shortly after 11.30 p.m. Prince Mohammed had, not unreasonably, given up waiting for me, so I arrived alone and unmet. At reception I was relieved to find that a room had been booked for me by Said Ayas. I checked in with the usual French routines of form-filling and was glad to get my head down and sleep. Nothing was said to me about the payment of my bill.

The next morning, Saturday 18 September, Said Ayas said that Prince Mohammed would have supper with me that evening. I dawdled away most of the day, shopping, reading, correcting the proofs of the new US edition of my Nixon biography, and jogging in the Jardin de Tuileries. I had no meetings with anyone other than Said Ayas. The cast of characters I was later to be accused of seeing for business purposes by the *Guardian* and/or Mohamed al Fayed (i.e. Messrs Wafic Said, Fahad Somait, Sheikh Essam Darwish, Peter Custer and Mark Thatcher) were conspicuous by their absence. My Saturday was uneventful to the point of being tedious.

I used words rather sharper than 'tedious' when, at around 7 p.m., I learned from an apologetic Said Ayas that my supper with Prince Mohammed had been cancelled. Apparently, family pressures in the form of a summons from one of his uncles, who was also visiting Paris, had intervened. As an old Saudi hand, I was neither unfamiliar with these social *forces majeures* inside the royal family nor unused to Prince Mohammed's oblivion to other people's schedules. I did feel some irritation at the cancellation, but was placated by a telephone call from the Prince who rearranged to see me the following evening, not in Paris but in Geneva, to which we were both travelling separately for our own reasons.

After this conversation I stayed in my hotel room, alone, for the rest of the evening. I made one or two telephone calls to Lolicia in Villars, who told me that Victoria had settled in well to her new school; had a light supper from room service; and read until well after midnight. The following morning was spent church-going, jogging and having coffee with Said Ayas who, in passing, said, 'I'll take care of your bill.'

'Thanks,' I said, unaware that I was crossing the Rubicon to future trouble and strife. Over the past 20 years Said Ayas had taken care of many of my hotel bills in foreign cities almost as a reflex action of automatic Arabian hospitality to a guest and fellow company director. I should not have let him do it on this occasion now that I had resigned all my directorships to become a Minister of the Crown, and therein lay the seed of my self-destruction.

Half an hour later, I left the Ritz and caught the TGV train to Geneva. I met Lolicia in the Hilton Hotel and had dinner with her there. After dinner I met Said Ayas and Prince Mohammed for the appointment that should have taken place in Paris two days previously.

My conversation with Prince Mohammed ranged far and wide, covering British politics, intelligence matters, defence issues and old friends' gossip. However, there was really only one topic of importance on my agenda. I wanted to know how King Fahd was reacting to the latest American intelligence on Iran and, in particular, to the activities of Iran's new Kilo-class submarines, which had recently been purchased from the Russians and were now operating on patrols in the Gulf from the naval bases of Bandar Abbas and Char Bahar. I particularly wanted to know how King Fahd viewed the discussion that had been in progress between senior officers of the British Royal Navy (RN) and the Royal Saudi Navy (RSN) about a proposal to lease the RSN four second-hand Upholder submarines. These were surplus to the RN's military requirements, but with the appropriate MOD training package they could give the Saudis a future submarine capability to counterbalance Iran's Kilos.

Prince Mohammed said he had been away from Saudi Arabia for some weeks, so did not know his father's latest thoughts on these matters. 'I will see His Majesty on my return and will give you an answer,' was how he ended the conversation. Said Ayas and I made arrangements for channelling such future communications, and that was that.

The next day, Monday 20 September, I flew back to London on the 7.30 a.m. flight out of Geneva and was met on schedule by Pat Kelly, my MOD driver. I reported the gist of my inconclusive conversation with Prince Mohammed on the Upholders to Sir Alan Thomas, the head of the Defence Export Services Organization (DESO), and then resumed my normal MOD duties with a four-day tour of Scottish military installations. Travelling round firing ranges such as St Kilda, Benbecula and Ardnacarry, my memories of the previous weekend soon faded away like evanescent Highland mist. Moreover, within a couple of months of these events, my responsibilities within the MOD dramatically changed when Malcolm Rifkind put me in charge of the important costs review known as 'Front Line First'. This huge overhaul of the MOD's £23 billion budget absorbed so much of my energies that I had virtually no time to devote to promoting Britain's defence exports. Even huge projects like Al Yamamah seemed unimportant in comparison to getting Front Line First right.

Looking back on the weekend of the Paris Ritz with these simple facts in mind, I have often asked myself: What did I do that was so terribly wrong? It was, seen retrospectively, incorrect of me to allow my hotel bills for this weekend – both at the Ritz in Paris and at the Hilton in Geneva – to be paid for directly or indirectly by Prince Mohammed. But the sums of money were small (in total about £1,200) and the rules of guidance relating to the acceptance of hospitality in such circumstances from a fellow minister in a friendly foreign government were blurred. Those rules, known as Questions of Procedure for Ministers, do not forbid the acceptance of hospitality. They merely advise ministers not to accept hospitality in conditions which might put them under an obligation to their hosts.

Was my acceptance of hospitality from Prince Mohammed or Said Ayas in this category? I did not think very much about it at the time. It was a debatable question, given my long-standing friendship with my hosts and the reciprocal hospitality I had in the past given them in my own home, but I now recognize that I was in the wrong. Where else I went wrong, I do not know. I engaged in no improper behaviour and held no improper conversations. My discussion with Prince Mohammed was entirely above board, appropriate and in furtherance of British interests. I had no commercial or business conversations either with him or with Said Ayas.

Turning to Said Ayas and his offshore company Marks One, this is a *Guardian* red herring rather than the red meat of a ministerial corruption scandal. I had never heard of this company and its 3 per cent consultancy arrangements with shipbuilders VSEL and GEC until the matter was raised with me by the *Sunday Times* in July 1998. At that time I said to the paper's reporters:

I know nothing about Marks One or any such arrangement ... I was always extremely careful as a Defence Minister to act on civil service advice from the Defence Export Services Organization to make myself scrupulously apart from – and without knowledge of – all commission arrangements between Saudi Arabia and British companies.[5]

The *Sunday Times* printed this statement and, after doing its own checking, accepted its veracity. It also pointed out that none of the potential export sales concerning Marks One and British companies was ever achieved, so no consultancy fees were ever paid.

By the time the *Guardian* had followed up the *Sunday Times* story and turned the same basic facts into an attack on me for 'corruption' in March 1999, I had been able to discover from Said Ayas that he had indeed set up the Marks One consultancy agreements on behalf of his Saudi colleagues in 1993. However, as a result of the involvement of MOD officials in the DESO – which had known and approved of these consultancy arrangements – neither Said Ayas nor the officials concerned had disclosed any such details to me. This was because of a long-standing 'Chinese wall' rule that ministers are never given this sort of commercial, in-confidence information about arrangements between defence exporters and their agents or consultants. Against that background, it is difficult to see how the *Guardian*'s 'corruption' charges stand up, since I had no knowledge of any Marks One agreements and, of course, no commercial involvement or partnership with Said Ayas or his company.

Even if I had known the details of Said Ayas' consultancy activities – which were perfectly legitimate for a Saudi Arabian businessman – I do not believe that I would have said anything significantly different in my conversations with him and Prince Mohammed during our meetings in Paris and Geneva in September 1993. At that time, as the minister responsible for Britain's defence exports, one of my prime concerns was the disposal of the Royal Navy's Upholder submarines. They were on offer to Canada, Pakistan and Saudi Arabia. What I was trying to establish was the extent of the Saudi Government's interest in the Upholder package, which incidentally was a government-to-government deal which would not have involved commissions to third parties. So that was the extent of my 'arms-deal' discussions with my interlocutors. The answer eventually came back that there was no Saudi interest in leasing or buying the Upholders. End of story and surely, in the eyes of most reasonable observers, end of 'corruption scandal'.

For these and other reasons, my conclusion on the saga of the Ritz Hotel weekend is that it turned into a disaster not because of any wrongdoing by me at the time, but because of the wrongdoing I got into some weeks afterwards when I started to cover it up.

It is painful for me now to set out, even in an abbreviated form, the lies I told to the *Guardian* about my visit to the Ritz and my non-payment of the bill. As the cover-up story unfolds, the question that now troubles me most is simply this: Why did I do it? The answer to that is two words: fear and arrogance. The fear came from not wanting to be embarrassed about a possible breach of Questions of Procedure for Ministers at a time when I was in the frame for promotion to the Cabinet. In the climate of rising hysteria about 'Tory sleaze', I was nervous that my comparatively minor transgression over the hotel bill could be ramped up into a career-damaging story by a hostile newspaper. So instead of sorting the matter out with a little penitence (which at worst would have meant some short-term media embarrassment), I toughed it out with a lot of arrogance. I thought I was smarter than an anti-Government newspaper and stronger in my defences than its reporters and editors could be in their attack. How wrong I was!

The cat-and-mouse game that was played out between Mohamed al Fayed, the *Guardian*'s Editor Peter Preston and myself was a ruthless one which does not reflect much credit on any of the protagonists, but at the end of the day my hubris was greater than anyone else's, so the nemesis for my deceit was far worse.

The first sign of trouble with the Ritz came in a telephone call, promptly followed by a letter, from the *Guardian*'s reporter David Pallister almost exactly a month after I had stayed in the hotel. He wanted to know if he could come and discuss 'the meeting you had over the weekend of September 18 in Paris with Mr Ayas and Dr Somait of Al Bilad (UK) and Mr Wafic Said'.[6]

It did not seem difficult to swat this journalistic fly away, for I had held no such meeting. Indeed, when I received Pallister's letter, I had no idea whether Dr Somait or Wafic Said (neither of whom I had seen for months) had even been in Paris at the same time as myself. Later inquiries revealed that Dr Somait had not but that Wafic Said had. In any case, the only member of the *Guardian*'s trio I had seen was Said Ayas, so I replied coldly, 'I had no meeting with Mr Ayas, Dr Somait and Mr Wafic Said in Paris over the weekend of 18 September or at any other place or time.'[7] I also suggested that the *Guardian* should, in future, communicate with me in the normal way via the MOD Press Office.

The next move was by Peter Preston, the Editor of the *Guardian*, who took the unusual step of writing personally to me. His letter of 22 October was bewildering. It started with a rambling paragraph about my 24 June speech to the Commonwealth Press Association, chiding me for being 'strenuously critical of the *Guardian*'s reporting of the Saudi money for Conservative funds story' and complaining that I had appeared to know about Prince Bandar's legal proceedings before the newspaper itself had received notification of them. This inside knowledge, he implied, had led to the *Guardian* keeping a watch on me through their reporters' sources.

Turning to the Ritz, Preston continued, 'By chance, one of the sources many weeks later happened to be in the Hotel in Paris on entirely unconnected business over the weekend of September 18. He saw you at the Ritz. He also observed Wafic Said and a third gentleman who he found to be Mr Ayas. With holidays intervening, he reported that back...'[8]

As the *Guardian* later admitted, this source, who just happened to be in the Ritz Hotel on entirely unconnected business, was in fact the owner of the Ritz Hotel, Mohamed al Fayed. He was by this time a close collaborator with the *Guardian* for complex reasons of his own, linked to the Home Office's recent refusal to grant him British citizenship and an earlier DTI report which had severely criticized him for telling lies at the time of his takeover of Harrods. 'The Government have shat on me,' Fayed raged to Preston,[9] evidently volunteering to reciprocate this activity on the Government through the pages of the *Guardian*. At a meeting in Harrods with Preston on 16 October 1993, Fayed's first movement in this process was to assert that he had seen Said Ayas, Wafic Said and myself sitting at a table together at the Espadon Restaurant of the Ritz Hotel during the weekend of 17–19 September.

'Just imagine if you see the Attorney-General sitting with Al Capone, it will be exactly the same,' he expostulated.[10] Preston faithfully passed on this allegation of the sighting of the three conspirators in the Espadon Restaurant to me in another letter, dated 27 October. It was not difficult to swat this fly away either, because the allegation was untrue, as Preston later conceded, saying that 'the informant who said he had seen Mr Aitken, Wafic Said and Mr Ayas dining together proved frail'[11] – the word 'frail' being a *Guardian*speak euphemism for 'untruthful'.

I had no idea who Preston's informant was at this stage, nor did I know he was becoming a most dedicated conspirator with the *Guardian*, for it was around this time, in November 1993, that Fayed, Preston and Pallister hatched the plot that became known as 'the Ritz–*Guardian* forgery'.

What happened was that Fayed told Preston that he had seen my bill at the Ritz for 8,010 francs and knew that it had been clearly stamped 'Débiteur A/C Mr Ayas 626/7'. Preston asked for a copy. Fayed at first declined, on the grounds that the reputation of the Ritz would be damaged. Then Preston came up with the idea of the forgery. He proposed that the *Guardian* should mock up a letter on my House of Commons notepaper addressed to the accounts department of the Ritz Hotel. The letter, purporting to come from me and signed on my behalf with the forged signature of my MOD private secretary, would ask the Ritz to fax a copy of my bill to a fax number at the top of the letter which was, in fact, the *Guardian*'s office. Fayed agreed to this plan and on Preston's instructions it was executed by his reporter David Pallister, who falsified the notepaper, typed the letter and forged the signature. The forgery read as follows:

From: JONATHAN AITKEN, MP
HOUSE OF COMMONS
LONDON SW1A 0AA

Fax: 071 239 9997
Telephone: 071 278 0586

24 November 1993

PERSONAL & CONFIDENTIAL

The Accounts Department
Hôtel Ritz
15 Place Vendôme
75041 Paris

Dear Sir

I wonder if you could kindly assist me with a small administrative matter. I was staying at the Ritz for two nights on 17 and 18 September in room 526. As your records will show, my bill was debited to the account of my friend, Mr Ayas, who was, I believe, in room 626/7.

Regrettably I seem to have mislaid my copy which I require for personal accounting reasons. Could you please confirm that billing arrangement and send me a copy of my account at the above fax number. Thank you for your co-operation.

Yours faithfully

pp Jeremy Wright, private secretary
Jonathan Aitken

This ruse worked. Whether or not Fayed was an active participant in the plot at the Paris as well as the London end of these machinations is unclear but, whatever the process may have been, the *Guardian* were duly sent my bill. By early January 1994 they were ready to attack.

During the late autumn of 1993, after the Preston–Aitken correspondence seemed to have fizzled out into silence, the channel of communication which Prince Mohammed, Said Ayas and I had set up in Geneva on 19 September became active and, in one or two instances, dramatically so. I must tread carefully at this point in my narrative because it concerns matters which may still be pertinent to the national security interests of Britain and Saudi Arabia. Nonetheless, because of earlier press speculation in this area, I can lift the veil a little and say that it suited both Governments to conduct certain sensitive communications through the Prince Mohammed–Ayas–Aitken channel.

At first the traffic passing through the channel was low-level material, most of it linked to defence matters such as the naval issues that had been discussed between Prince Mohammed and myself in Geneva. In December 1993, however, the channel was used at a far higher level of importance and classification when, at the request of the SIS, I flew to Jeddah carrying with me a top-secret report for the King's eyes only.

My appointment to see King Fahd was arranged by Prince Mohammed after messages through our channel had been passed by our intermediary, Said Ayas. Not even the British Ambassador, one of the five people who attended the meeting, knew what it was going to be about. I presented the King with an Arabic version of the SIS report which was, in effect, the transcript of a tape recording, and took him through its more important passages. To say that King Fahd was startled would be an understatement. As one rather overexcitable Saudi official put it, 'This was the equivalent of a Minister in our Government flying in to London to see your Queen and presenting her with the IRA battle plans for the next six months.'[12]

Explaining and interpreting the British intelligence coup to the King was a challenging task but, by the small hours of the morning, I had accomplished it. The next day, the King's principal security adviser, Sheikh Ibrahim Al Angari, came to see me for a further discussion on the report's implications and to express the Saudi Government's gratitude. He told me that King Fahd had been concerned to hear that I was intending to fly home on a commercial flight. He would like to put his personal 747 at my disposal. With some difficulty, I extracted myself from this offer of regal hospitality (the cost of the aviation fuel alone would have been worth at least a hundred times more than my Ritz Hotel bill) and instead travelled home with my private secretary on British Airways, stopping off in Dharan, at the King's request, to brief Prince Mohammed on the security implications of the SIS transcript for the Eastern Province. Various changes in security arrangements for the area were put in place. Soon after I came home, the SIS gave a dinner in my honour at their headquarters, expressing many warm words of thanks for a job well done.

The Prince Mohammed channel was also active again in early January 1994, this time concerning problems of high sensitivity relating to Qatar. I had to fly to Doha for two days of talks with the Qatari Crown Prince, and later to Riyadh for a three-hour meeting with the Kingdom's Defence Minister Prince Sultan. These matters, which were of interest to Foreign Office specialists in Britain, had a far higher importance rating to the national security concerns of Saudi Arabia.

I have given a circumspect account of these silent missions because they were to make a considerable impact on the Saudi reactions to the next moves in the Ritz saga. These began on 11 January 1994 when Peter Preston wrote to me once again.

Dear Jonathan

I'm sorry to resume our fitful correspondence on that Paris weekend in September, but one further matter has arisen which I think I should put to you. A combination of circumstances and inquiries surrounding my chaps' original inquiries meant that one or two loose ends were left in the hands of others, and it has naturally taken some time for them to fall in place. But one, in particular, causes obvious bafflement.

It is now clear to me that Mr Ayas didn't merely join you for a family dinner but himself paid for your two nights at the Ritz – a bill of around £1,000. That may have been an act of extraordinary generosity between old friends; though to some it may reinforce the impression of some kind of business meeting. In any case, my team are naturally concerned to know how it fits in with section 126 of the Questions of Procedure for Ministers. That seems to me a legitimate, even urgent question in current circumstances: and, in the context of our previous exchanges, I thought I should put it to you directly.

Yours sincerely

Peter Preston

When I received this letter, my pulse raced. Until this point in the saga, I had not really worried about the *Guardian*'s inquiries – which, so far as I could see, consisted largely of barking up wrong trees about Prince Bandar's libel action and donations which had not been made to the Conservative Party. I had not focused at all on the payment of my Ritz bill and my vulnerability to criticism over it. Now that it was clear that the *Guardian* were in possession of some embarrassing information on this score, I had to think carefully about how to respond to Preston, for the cat-and-mouse game we had been playing in our correspondence so far had become dangerous, at least for the mouse.

My first thought was that while the *Guardian*'s evidence that Said Ayas had paid my bill was unassailable, there was at least one explanation for it which was likely to prove acceptable. For Said Ayas was not an 'Al Capone'. He was a genuine friend of over 20 years' standing who had introduced me to my wife at a party in London in 1977, who had been a dutiful godfather to our daughter Victoria, and who had received frequent hospitality in our home with his family. Could I not legitimately argue that his picking up of the tab at the Ritz was part of a wider picture of long-standing friendship and reciprocal hospitality? With this thought in mind, I telephoned Said Ayas to get his view on how best to respond to Preston's letter.

I tracked Said Ayas down on his boat in the Caribbean. Stirred into action by my anxiety, he made many telephone calls to Saudi Arabia and came back from them with a solution which looked better than the reciprocal hospitality explanation. According to Said Ayas, my bill at the Ritz had been paid at the last minute in cash by a French book-keeper employed by Prince Mohammed. This French book-keeper was a woman who had been brought up to Paris from the Prince's office in the South of France, was unknown to the Ritz, and looked rather like Lolicia. 'If you said Lolicia paid your bill in cash, how the hell can a cashier at the Ritz contradict you six months later?' asked Said Ayas with a rhetorical flourish. 'I can get you the receipt proving it was paid in cash. That will be that – *halas* [finished]!'

Until this moment I had not heard of the French book-keeper, nor that my bill had been paid by her in cash. All I wanted was the quickest possible escape from the clutches of the *Guardian*, with the minimum of embarrassment. To my everlasting shame and regret, I took the line of mendacious expediency and made the idiotic decision to go along with the new suggestion. Another Rubicon on my journey to disaster had been crossed.

In fairness to Said Ayas, it should be explained that he was under pressure from a different direction to come up with a solution to my problem which did not involve a damaging linkage to myself or to anyone else from Saudi Arabia. As he explained in a later witness statement:

The time when the *Guardian* and Mohamed al Fayed jointly began to try and expose Mr Aitken's connections with the Saudi Royal Family and to make a scandal out of the payment of Mr Aitken's hotel bill at the Hotel Ritz by Prince Mohammed occurred in the period November 1993–January 1994. This was also the period when the Jonathan Aitken–Prince Mohammed–King Fahd secret channel of communication was most active and successful in the security interests of both governments. Prince Mohammed instructed me to cover up the Ritz Hotel episode and to conceal all material that might lead journalists to publish material which would enable those who were hostile to the security interests of Saudi Arabia and Britain to know about the existence of the secret channel. So I followed Prince Mohammed's instructions which I am sure were given to me as a matter of state.[13]

Whether or not matters of state were relevant to the Saudi end of the cover-up, I do not know. At my end, I was merely grateful to have been given a cover story. In an act of consummate folly, I adopted it and recycled it to Peter Preston in a letter dated 13 January 1994.

Dear Peter

Thank you for your letter of 11th January. You have again been misinformed. Mr Ayas did not pay my hotel bill. There had been no 'act of extraordinary generosity between old friends'. There was not 'some kind of business meeting'. There has been no breach of any section of Questions of Procedure for Ministers.

The facts of this matter are that the hotel bill was paid by my wife, with money given to her by me for this purpose, some hours after I had left Paris.

Since receiving your letter the only possible connection I have been able to discover between your wrong information and the correct facts, is that in my absence Mr Ayas (whom you will recall from our earlier correspondence is an old family friend) did help my wife with some minor administrative and transportation arrangements at the time of her departure. However, these arrangements did not include any financial help with the hotel bill which, I repeat, was paid for with our own money.

I hope this makes the position clear.

Yours sincerely

Jonathan

Almost every line in this reprehensible letter was untrue. For Lolicia had never paid my hotel bill and had never been in Paris at all on the weekend in question. The whole story was a lie.[14] But since we were dealing (as I then believed) with a bill which had been paid in cash by an unidentifiable woman to the anonymous cashier of an hotel which, in its own advertising, praised itself for being discreet about its clients, there did not seem any reason for believing the lie could be detected. I had unfortunately reckoned without the hotel's less than discreet owner, Mohamed al Fayed.

When Said Ayas returned from the Caribbean to tidy up the loose ends on the cover-up, he found that the story he had given to me was beginning to unravel. The first difficulty was that the Ritz management were surprisingly unco-operative with him. The second and more serious blow was the discovery that the Aitken bill had *not* been fully paid in cash by the French book-keeper. When her accounts were inspected, it emerged that, in the course of a classic Arabian entourage departure muddle, she actually paid only 4,257 francs of my 8,010-franc bill, leaving the remaining 3,753 francs debited to Said Ayas' account.

This revelation made the cover story look highly improbable. I was furious about the new mess I had now been dropped into by these revelations about the French book-keeper's accounts. However, having nailed my colours so firmly to the mast of the lie that my wife had paid the bill, I could not haul them down again without abject humiliation. Sinking deeper into the quagmire, I stuck to the line that yes, my wife had paid the bill; that she had paid the only sum asked of her; and that she had only now been informed that, as a result of other people's mistakes at the check-out, there had been a shortfall in her payment of 3,753 francs.

Although this unlikely story convinced no one, it was not so wholly unconvincing as to be incredible to everyone. Indeed, to those who have endured the chaos of simultaneous hotel check-outs by members of large groups, the possibility of financial error over multiple bill payments is an all too familiar reality. Hanging tough on the line that a muddle had taken place in my absence between my wife, the Ritz cashier and assorted Arabs checking out alongside her was therefore not a wholly unbelievable explanation.

The first figures of authority to listen to this explanation were the Prime Minister's Private Secretary Alex Allan and the Cabinet Secretary Sir Robin Butler. They had been copied into the entire

Preston–Aitken correspondence from the beginning and had enjoyed the initial exchanges, which one of them described as 'game and set to Aitken'. But not match. Once the Preston–al Fayed collaboration had produced the bill documentation, Aitken was in sufficiently serious trouble to be summoned to the Cabinet Office to see these two important civil servants.

What I remember most about this appointment on 17 February 1994 was the feverish clicking of Alex Allan's calculator as he endeavoured to work out what had really happened at the Ritz in financial terms. 'I'll just tot these figures up. I enjoy this sort of puzzle,' he confidently declared as he began adding up the various bills of Said Ayas, May Ayas, Danielle Ayas, Hodder Abdul Rahman, Hadi Abdul Rahman, Izzedin Abdul Jawad, Moheddine Ayas, Jonathan Aitken, Old Uncle Sheikh Cobbleigh and all who, at various times, had their bills debited to the account of room 626/7 and then credited by various cheque and cash payments from another cast of characters in the Prince Mohammed entourage. Later in the saga, I described this bill-paying activity as a 'Carry on Arabia' scenario[15] and it was too much for the 'Carry on Calculating' activity of the Prime Minister's private secretary. 'I'll never stay in the Ritz if this is the way they present their bills,' said Alex Allan despairingly. 'None of these figures add up.'

Having established, with the help of the No. 10 Downing Street calculator, that some sort of accounting muddle appeared to have taken place at the cashier's desk, the conversation turned to my conduct at the Ritz. Sir Robin Butler neither investigated this nor cleared me from the *Guardian*'s allegations. He simply accepted my explanation at face value and advised me that on that basis there had been no breach of the guidelines in Questions of Procedure for Ministers. He also advised me to repay the shortfall in the bill of 3,753 francs to Said Ayas, which I duly did – although, at the Saudi's request, the repayment was actually made to his nephew, Abdul Rahman.

The light watchdog touch in Whitehall was almost matched at first bite by the *Guardian*. When Peter Preston finally published his musings on the affair, which he headlined as 'THE MINISTER, THE MANDARIN, THE PREMIER, THE EDITOR', they were so opaque as to be only semi-comprehensible. In an act of what appeared to be gross editorial self-indulgence, Preston spread himself over three pages of turgid prose in the magazine section of the *Guardian*, boring for England as he laid out various al Fayed theories in painstaking detail and ending in his final paragraph with this less than resounding conclusion:

Hospitality, like paid-for holidays, is a very muddied area, maybe because some senior ministers are invited away by friends and can't draw the line easily when that friend is a person of wealth or influence.

But no one we talked to in Whitehall seemed very clear. Civil servants knew where they stood. Ministers, and ex-ministers, were deeply uncertain. And who, on this small case, can wonder at that?[16]

No one, it appeared, was inclined to wonder at all about the *Guardian*'s small-case revelations. This dampest of journalistic damp squibs provoked no criticism of me at the time and no parliamentary or media interest either. The sole follow-up report in the rest of the press consisted of an acerbic comment in the diary of the *Independent*: 'Now we know what the *Guardian*'s Magazine Section Two is about. It is for publishing stories which aren't good enough to stand up in the main body of the newspaper.'[17]

I thought I could breathe easily. Indeed, my complacency turned to contempt when, the day after the publication of Preston's article, I received a remarkable letter from the Manager of the Ritz Hotel:

Dear Mr Aitken

A copy of today's *Guardian* has been brought to my attention. I have already sent it to our lawyers asking them to initiate proceedings against the

Guardian in France for invasion of the hotel's privacy and the privacy of its guests and to examine the possibilities of a successful action against the newspaper for fraud and malicious misrepresentation. It goes without saying that the hotel is appalled by this article and regrets any embarrassment which it may have caused to you and the other guests named.

In the hours since I have seen the article, I have caused further investigations to be made in the hotel archives because of the *Guardian*'s reproduction of what appears to be your bill for last September. This search has revealed a letter which until today I was unaware of. It was received by fax here on November 24, 1993. It follows for your inspection. Unbeknown to me this fax was answered by the guest accounts department. A copy of the reply also follows. The person in charge of this department has since left the Ritz and therefore I have not yet been able to interview her about the circumstances of her decision to reply in the way she did. It is not unknown for us to receive such correspondence from guests and to answer as required. I note that the fax number does not correspond to yours (the one I have always used in the past). I fear that some fraud has been perpetrated upon the hotel but I will leave that question to you for further investigation.

I remain at your disposal.

Yours sincerely

Frank J. Klein
President[18]

The letter which followed for my inspection was the first revelation of the *Guardian*'s forgery described earlier in this chapter. To this day I do not know whether Frank Klein's indignation about it was synthetic or sincere. Initially I presumed the latter, but in view of the co-operation Klein subsequently gave the *Guardian* in areas such as providing them with monitored records of my telephone calls from the hotel, I am now by no means certain.

The likeliest explanation for the appalled tone of Klein's letter is that the management of the Ritz were terrified that the collaboration between their owner and the Editor of the *Guardian* might leak out and damage the hotel's self-proclaimed reputation for discretion. In glossy magazines all over Europe and the USA throughout 1994 the Ritz was running a series of advertisements under the headline 'NOW YOU WILL UNDERSTAND WHY WE'RE DISCREET'.

The text of these advertisements boasted about the large numbers of heads of state, princes, dukes, senators, rock stars, government ministers, supermodels, Nobel Prize winners and other celebrities who had stayed in the hotel in the past year. It then continued, 'If today our hotel is renowned throughout the world, it is because our notion of service implies an unspoken agreement of trust between us and our clients. And that trust has never been broken.'[19]

This solemn declaration that an hotel owned by Mohamed al Fayed never breaks its trust deserves to be set to music as the theme song of an Egyptian comic opera. I could at least see the funny side of it but, back in Whitehall, the evidence of the Ritz–*Guardian* forgery was causing real anger, although no real action.

Sir Christopher France, the Permanent Secretary at the Ministry of Defence, expressed much sound and fury at the counterfeiting of a civil servant's signature, but after consulting various oracles within the Home Office, the Department of Heritage and the Press Council, he decided to do nothing. Sir Robin Butler penned a stinging rebuke to Peter Preston for transgressing 'the margins of criminality'.[20] The Prime Minister seethed privately that the forgery was 'utterly disgraceful and contemptible'.[21] I shared his view, but like Brer Rabbit, I decided the best policy was to lie low and do nothing.

So that was the way the first round of the Ritz battle ended, not with a bang but a whimper. It would probably have faded away altogether had it not been for two subsequent developments. The first was my promotion to the Cabinet as Chief Secretary to the Treasury in July 1994, which made me a much bigger and more exciting target for the *Guardian* to attack. The second was an explosion of Mohamed al Fayed's insatiable hatred for the Conservative Government and all its ministers which erupted in the wake of the decision, ratified in September 1994 by the European Court of Human Rights, not to grant him British citizenship. This hatred, which spilled out into ever closer collaboration between Fayed and the *Guardian*, was the force that moved the Ritz affair back onto the centre stage of British politics and the media.

CHAPTER THIRTEEN

More Pleadings and Prayers

MOHAMED AL FAYED WAS to me what Banquo's ghost was to Macbeth – a weird and wraithlike figure whose haunting presence kept reappearing at various times in the story with alarming and destabilizing effect.

Macbeth may have deserved his Banquo, having arranged his murder according to the Shakespearean plot, but I had never met Mohamed al Fayed, let alone crossed swords with him. It was a mystery why Fayed should have decided to make me the principal target in his plot, feeding editors, reporters, television producers, politicians and even the Prime Minister with anti-Aitken rumours which, with the exception of my nonpayment of the Ritz Hotel bill, were all false. Perhaps the most convincing explanation for the furies driving Fayed is the one given by the *Guardian* in its account of why it returned to the attack on me six months after Preston's original article on 10 March.¹

...in September 1994, the saga took a fresh twist. Mohamed Al Fayed heard that he had lost his case in the European Court of Human Rights, which might have had the damning DTI report into his Harrods take-over declared in breach of the Convention. Fayed went ape. At his penthouse suite in Harrods the air hummed with expletives as Fayed stomped and chafed.

On the evening of 19 September 1994 Preston went to Harrods and saw the Egyptian multi-millionaire alone. Mohamed looked a little dishevelled, shirt undone, jacket discarded, grim and upset. They drank whisky. There was, as he saw it, no justice. He had decided to go public with his allegations...[2]

I hope the two collaborators enjoyed each other's scintillating company and conversation on this evening *à deux*, but all that aping, stomping and chafing should have come as no surprise to the Editor of the *Guardian* because Fayed had been going private with his allegations for some weeks. His most extraordinary move had been to send an emissary to see the Prime Minister on 31 August 1994 in order to allege that I was the owner of two brothels in London and Paris; that I regularly arranged whores for Arabs; and that while I had been at the Ritz Hotel on 19 September 1993 I had split £1 billion in cash with my partners Mark Thatcher and Wafic Said as our divided spoils from an arms deal.[3]

It did not take the head of the British Government long to establish that these claims were false. Unfortunately, other listeners to Mohamed al Fayed were more gullible. As the Harrods whisky continued to flow, so did its owner's obscenities as he asserted that the Chief Secretary to the Treasury had a secret life as a multimillionaire pimp and arms dealer. Although most recipients of these confidences soon decided that their source and his stories were unworthy of belief, a handful of journalists accepted the allegations with such devotion that they came to adopt Mohamed al Fayed's obsessions and hatreds almost as if they were their own.

Interesting politicians must expect to become hate objects at certain stages in their careers. I was never afraid of unpopularity or isolation, but I was taken aback by the virulence of the hostility which swirled in my direction during my year in the Cabinet and throughout my subsequent libel battles with the *Guardian*.

Not being a hater of opponents, I found it hard to understand why I provoked so much journalistic enmity. Was it the temper of the anti-Tory times? Resentment of my Eton and Oxford background? Settlement of old scores and ancient rivalries? Animosity towards my

Guardian-created image as a plutocratic pimp and arms dealer? Social or sexual jealousy? An envious desire to cut down a tall poppy? Or was it these journalists' belief that I was an evil and verminous political animal who needed to be torn to pieces that set the hounds baying for my blood? All these theories have been floated at various times by columnists and commentators, but none are convincing. Yet it cannot be denied that the hatred was in circulation. I knew it and gradually became alarmed by it.

'They're out to get you,' was a frequent refrain of my friends in 1995–6, particularly after they had seen the fruits of the *World in Action–Guardian*–al Fayed collaborations. With the wisdom of hindsight, I should have said, 'So what?' and ignored my opponents' campaigns. Unfortunately, I had too much pride to take such an emollient course of action and too much combative spirit to restrain myself from going into battle against my tormentors.

In the months after the writs were issued in 1995, the libel battle became rough, dirty and expensive. From the earliest exchanges of the pleadings, it was clear that my adversaries were long on assertion but short on evidence. To cover this up, they embarked on a war of attrition. The pleadings expanded from the original 40 or so pages to over 500 and the pre-trial court appearances from an anticipated one to 14. Libel practitioners had never seen anything like it. In the legalese jargon of litigation, as defences and replies were followed by amended defences and amended replies; followed by court orders for further and better particulars; followed by rejoinders and amended rejoinders; followed by more court orders for further and better particulars of rejoinders; followed by yet more court orders for consolidation, discovery and direction; followed by appeals from Masters to Judges and from Judges to the Court of Appeal, the war of attrition was assuming epic proportions. So were the costs.

By the end of 1996, still six months away from getting into court, I had spent over £350,000 on mere legal paperwork. This is a fleabite to big media groups but a heavy burden for an individual. My solicitor's original estimates had suggested that the case would cost me around £150,000 in pre-trial expenses and another £250,000 or so if we fought to the bitter end in court. This price had now more than doubled. I had to arrange heavy borrowings to meet the bills.

These financial pressures were worrying. Yet with Lolicia's support I battled on, telling my family and my friends, 'I just can't let my opponents get away with their assertions that I was a pimp, an illegal arms dealer, and a corrupt minister. These falsehoods have to be laid to rest.' This may have been an excessively prideful stance, but in terms of the legal battles it was not a foolish one. For the results from the pleadings suggested that I was gradually winning the war in nearly every area of the case.

The purpose of pleadings and the pre-trial activity that accompanies them is to flush out the foundations of the cases being presented by the parties. Mere assertion is not, or should not be, enough. For example, the *Guardian* had pleaded that 'the extent of the plaintiff's dependence on Prince Mohammed was such as to impact upon his ability to act and speak wholly independently as a Member of Parliament and as a senior Minister of the Crown',[4] and that this 'dependency on a foreign power compromised his ability to act independently in the interests of his constituents and the electorate generally'.[5]

However, could the *Guardian*, when asked for further and better particulars, provide any examples of this dependency, any examples of my failure to speak independently as an MP and minister, or any examples of how I had let down my constituents in the way suggested? The answer was no, they could not. The most they could do was to claim that I had been 'richly rewarded'[6] by Prince Mohammed but that 'the defendants can give no further particulars pending discovery'.[7] The intrusive discovery process yielded up basketfuls of my bank statements, tax returns, property deeds and other financial documentation, but nothing that remotely substantiated either the claim of financial dependency or the connected dereliction of parliamentary duty.

The best the *Guardian* could do in these areas was to suggest in the pleadings a rags-to-riches fairy story based on my houses:

At that time [1976] he was not wealthy and lived and worked in his mother's house. When that lease expired in or about 1977, the plaintiff could not afford to renew it ... in consequence of the plaintiff's lucrative association with Prince Mohammed by the early 1980s the plaintiff was in a position to buy the freehold of 8 Lord North Street.[8]

This was baloney. The lease of my mother's house, in which I owned a self-contained flat, had 17 years to run in 1979. It was extended for a further 70 years at a price of £74,000 and was profitably sold a year or two later for approximately £500,000. My wife and I bought our first matrimonial home, 39 Connaught Square, for £183,000 in 1980 with money given to us by my father-in-law, whose bank transfers were meticulously recorded by our solicitors. In 1982 we sold Connaught Square for £202,000 and with these proceeds (following the repayment of a temporary bridging loan) and a £40,000 mortgage from Coutts Bank, we bought 8 Lord North Street for £225,000. The financial documentation on these transactions completely destroyed the assertions made on screen by *World in Action* and implied in the pleadings by the *Guardian* that Prince Mohammed had been instrumental in buying our house for us.

The sloppiness of the journalistic research which backed up the defendants' pleadings became more and more apparent as the paperwork rolled backwards and forwards, encompassing the procedure known as the exchange of witness statements.

Could the *Guardian* produce a single Parliamentarian or constituent to back up their damaging claim that 'the plaintiff arranged his Parliamentary and constituency commitments so as to enable him to spend time attending to Prince Mohammed's requirements which in case of conflict took precedence over any constituency business'?[9] No, they could not, whereas I was able to obtain witness statements from many constituents and Parliamentarians (including two ex-Speakers and two Labour MPs) who were willing to testify to the contrary.

Could the *Guardian* support their assertion in the pleadings that Prince Mohammed had subsidized the *East Kent Critic*, 'a constituency magazine which provided publicity for the plaintiff'?[10] No, they could not, whereas the outraged editor and sole proprietor of the magazine, a Labour county councillor called Derek Molock, came forward with evidence that his journal's shoestring budget had never seen a penny of these fictional princely subsidies.

As for TV-am, could the *Guardian* back up their sweeping assertion that during my years on the board, 'the plaintiff would as director invariably serve Saudi interests whenever they were involved'?[11] No, they could not, later deleting the allegation at a pre-trial hearing.

Finally, on arms deals, could the combined resources of Granada and the *Guardian* come up with any evidence to suggest that BMARC or any other part of Gerald James' Astra group of companies (with whom I had been accused of fuelling 'the bloodiest war of the decade') had ever won any contracts to export arms to Iraq, Iran or Saudi Arabia? No, they could not even do this, let alone substantiate their claims that I had been instrumental in winning such contracts or enriching myself from them. Even an allegation emerging from an internal Gerald James memorandum in 1989 suggesting that BMARC was theoretically intending to pay enough commission to 'look after Jonathan Aitken's interests' was demolished when the BMARC executive David Trigger, who was supposed to have made this remark in a telephone conversation, totally denied it.[12]

These tactical successes in the pre-trial skirmishes were encouraging. So was the political community's attitude to the case. On the domestic scene, my local constituency party stayed rock solid in their backing, intermittently passing unanimous motions of confidence and issuing press notices rebutting hostile media stories. In the House of Commons the number of parliamentary colleagues from all parties who voiced expressions of support grew steadily month by month. This sympathy was reflected at the highest levels. Tony Blair, then Leader of the Opposition, had the kindness to murmur encouragingly to me during an encounter in the division lobbies, while John Major showed his loyalty by inviting me to No. 10 and Chequers with touching frequency. A week's holiday on Malcolm Pearson's[13] Perthshire estate with Margaret and Denis Thatcher in August 1996 left me in no doubt where their sympathies lay, while on the international stage I was equally well supported.

In the USA, Henry Kissinger invited me to be his guest at the Bohemian Grove Club – an annual assembly of America's great and good in the redwoods of Sonoma County, California. Camping al fresco with the likes of George Bush, Steve Bechtel Jnr, James Baker, Walter Cronkite, Gerald R. Ford, Herbert Hoover III, Ed Meese, George Schultz and many other such luminaries, it was flattering to be introduced on foreign policy discussion platforms as 'a man who will soon be restored to a position of the highest leadership in Britain'.

Rather similar accolades were part of the introductions when I went to give speeches in Bonn, Washington, New York and Chicago, while in the Middle East I was greeted with exceptionally warm demonstrations of friendship when I travelled to countries such as Jordan and Oman bearing letters to their heads of state from the Prime Minister. As for Saudi Arabia, Prince Mohammed asked me to come and see him and his uncles within days of the arrest of two British nurses in Dharan on charges of murder. Thereafter I played a discreet, behind-the-scenes role on this case by persuading the Saudis to treat the accused with compassionate favour (by Sharia law standards) in terms of early access to defence lawyers, transfers to the hospital wing of the prison where they were being held on remand, and regular visits from their families and British Embassy officials. None of this was easy, given the ignorant noises about the nurses' case both in the British media and in the Saudi religious establishment, but – not for the first time – Prince Mohammed showed himself to be a wise and fair Governor when dealing with a difficult controversy.

Although it was agreeable to be well occupied and well supported both at home and abroad in the difficult 18 months or so after my resignation from the Cabinet, I was under no illusions about the difficult battles that lay ahead of me in the libel case, particularly as my opponents seemed to be moving into the murky waters of sexual muck-raking.

Sex reared its head because the defendants introduced into the case three ladies of doubtful reputation.[14] The first of these demimonde figures was Paula Strudwick, with whom I had had a brief relationship 15 years earlier. Another was Lindy St Clair, a notorious madam and self-publicist who came forward to claim that she had plied her trade at Inglewood. The third was a New Zealand air hostess who had been a member of the aircrew on Prince Mohammed's aircraft for a few months in 1979 before being dismissed for drugtaking, and who now alleged that she had been seduced by various prominent Saudis.

All three ladies were, at best, peripheral to the real issues of the libel case and I suspected they had only been recruited to the defendants' cause as 'frighteners' to scare me off. Paula Strudwick could no doubt rake up more of the kiss'n'tell anecdotes she had already sold to the *Sunday Mirror* for over £100,000 about our fling in 1980, but her tales were hardly germane to my libel claims against the *Guardian* on totally unrelated matters in 1995. The defendants' lawyers disagreed, saying that they wanted to place Paula Strudwick's lurid reminiscences before the jury. 'It went to the heart of his [Aitken's] credibility,' said the *Guardian*'s solicitor Geraldine Proudler. 'He was always painting himself as a family man and a religious man. We wanted to show the jury that was a sham.'[15]

After much pre-trial manoeuvring on both sides, Paula Strudwick was removed from the case. A similar fate befell the defendants' two other heroines. Lindy St Clair was dropped as a witness against me after it became clear that I had never met her and that, far from plying her trade at Inglewood, she had actually been prevented from doing so by the hydro's management, who had asked her to leave as soon as they had discovered her identity. As for the New Zealand air hostess – who had been recruited by a Saudi company, rather than by me, as a successor to one of the original 1977 cabin crew – her revelations about her romantic trysts with sheikhs and princes were somewhat devalued by her refusal to give a witness statement about them. Instead, a Granada employee, Mr Quentin McDermott, solemnly presented to the court his account of what the air hostess had told him in New Zealand about her bedroom romps in Riyadh 17 years earlier. As Mr McDermott's tape recorder was switched off when his interviewee's most exciting kiss'n'tell stories were being divulged, it did not take the pre-trial judges long to decide that such dubious evidence was inadmissible as well as wholly irrelevant to the case against me.

These tawdry attempts at scare and smear tactics by the defendants all failed. But making them fail involved legal battles of considerable length and expense, linked to profound personal anxieties on the home front. When the *Guardian* decided to exhume the skeleton of Paula Strudwick from my cupboard of past sins in order to demonstrate, as their solicitor Geraldine Proudler put it, that my family life was a 'sham', they must have calculated that this cynical manoeuvre would take its toll in terms of family nervous strain. It did. Lolicia and I decided we could not and should not let this sort of muckraking explode in a courtroom to the embarrassment of our teenage children. If the fight was going to get as dirty as our opponents were trying to make it, with the Paula Strudwicks of this world coming to court as the *Guardian*'s witnesses, I felt inclined to throw in the towel on the libel case and retire from public life.

Although in this particular case the *Guardian*'s ploy with Paula Strudwick had been removed from the legal arena, the whole tenor of the defendants' strategy began to stir me into a mood of introspection and soul-searching. What had started out as a relatively straightforward libel action was gradually turning into a quite different scenario in which I seemed to have become the defendant, being put on trial for all my past sins, misjudgements or mistakes, whether in business, in private life, or in any of my associations with Arabs. I may be over-dramatizing here, yet it did feel oppressive to be compelled to disprove the flow of onslaughts in the pleadings to the effect that just about every move in my life, in Parliament, in my constituency, and in my merchant-banking career, had been affected by my alleged role as a corrupt Saudi placeman. Although I knew these attacks were unfair, I began to ask myself much deeper questions: Have large parts of my whole life been wrong? Have I been obsessed with the rat races for power and money? Have I been a bad husband and father? Did I do anything improper with my Saudi clients and colleagues? What is the great evil in my life which provokes such extraordinary hostility from the *Guardian*?

This self-interrogation brought me back to my spiritual journey, which had been gathering momentum long before the attacks from the *Guardian* had commenced. Some of Lolicia's penetrating questions about my relationship with God, first made some five years earlier, started to wake me up in the night during the 1996–7 period. Was there a disconnection between my life and my lips when it came to practising my faith? Was there a contradiction between my self-interested head and my God-interested heart? If so, why did my self-interested head keep winning, encouraging me to exercise a convenient selectivity of choice between those of God's commandments I chose to obey or disobey?

As I wrestled with these contradictions, a screen of darkness separated me from the transcendence of God's reality. Perhaps my greatest fault at this time was that I hived off my libel case journey on one side of this screen and kept it away from my inner or spiritual journey. Indeed, I spoke quite irrationally to myself with words to the effect of: 'Once I've won the libel case, then I will really be able to move deeper into my spiritual life.' The absurdity of this contradiction did not become apparent to me until after the libel case was over.

Yet confused though my soul-searching must have been at this time, one truth did dawn on me because, contrary to all outward appearance, I had at least managed to identify my worst and greatest sin – pride.

I remember well how this realization about my pride came to me. While I had been staying at the Bohemian Grove with Henry Kissinger, we had a long conversation about some of the leading alumni of the Nixon Administration. One of the names mentioned was that of Charles W. Colson who, as Special Assistant to the President, had earned himself the accolade of being described by historian Theodore H. White as 'the shrewdest political mind, after Richard Nixon's, in the White House'.[16] Colson, however, had also earned a number of less complimentary labels, such as 'The Administration's chief dirty tricks artist' and 'Nixon's hatchet man'.[17] In the fallout from Watergate Colson had eventually been scalped by other hatchets, for in 1974 he pleaded guilty to charges of obstruction of justice and served a seven-month prison sentence.

In our California conversations, Henry Kissinger had been somewhat negative about Charles Colson, whereas I had been far more positive. I had got to know him fairly well while writing my biography of President Nixon, and had been impressed by the sincerity of his post-Watergate Christian writings and by his outstanding work as a prison reformer.

A week or two later, when browsing in an airport bookstall, I picked up a paperback edition of Colson's best-selling autobiography *Born Again* and began to re-read it. About a third of the way through the book, I came across the passage in which Colson is introduced to the writings of C. S. Lewis by a friend, Tom Phillips, who reads aloud to him these words:

There is one vice of which no man in the world is free; which everyone in the world loathes when he sees it in someone else; and of which hardly any people, except Christians, ever imagine that they are guilty themselves ...

The vice I am talking of is Pride ... Pride leads to every other vice: it is the complete anti-God state of mind ... For pride is a spiritual cancer: it eats up the very possibility of love, or contentment, or even common sense.[18]

When I reflected on these words, my reactions were very similar to Colson's, who wrote that when he first heard this passage he had felt 'naked and unclean, my bravado defences gone. I was exposed, unprotected, for Lewis's words were describing me.'[19] And me too. I had often been described as 'conceited' and occasionally as 'arrogant' by my critics, from my schooldays through to my Cabinet minister days. 'Jonathan Aitken thinks he walks on water,' was a taunt I recall from some Oxford debating society encounter, and there had been echoes of it many times since. Some of this criticism may have been due to height, a woodenness of body language and a shyness of manner which could make me seem brusque. But even after making all such allowances and excuses, the fact remained that I had been an excessively proud person all my life. At least I was now starting to recognize this fault line in my character.

Interestingly, in view of the subsequent correspondence we were to exchange between 1997 and 1999, I thought about trying to see Chuck Colson during the summer of 1996 to seek his advice on the subject of conquering pride. But this good intention never turned into action, so the opportunity was missed and I set about working out my own cure for the affliction. The medicine I chose was a good strong dose of what sounded like the perfect antidote for pride – spiritual poverty.

Spiritual poverty is an ideal to which many pay lip service when they read the first beatitude of the Sermon on the Mount, 'Blessed are the poor in spirit' (Matthew 5:3), but which few understand. I wanted to understand it and to do so I turned for guidance to the priest who became my spiritual tutor for the third and last of my Parliamentary Retreats, Father Gerard Hughes SJ.

'Spiritual poverty means a mind and heart which so trusts in God as its rock, refuge and strength that nothing in creation can deflect it from God,' said Gerry. 'Would you like to seek the path to such a heart and mind?'

'I'd like to try,' I said nervously, conscious of my hopeless inadequacy for the task.

'Then let's work on the meditation of the Two Standards,' he responded.

So it was that, throughout Lent of 1997, I found myself being patiently led by my sensitive Jesuit mentor through what is perhaps the deepest and most challenging of the spiritual exercises devised by St Ignatius Loyola – the Meditation of the Two Standards.

Simplified to its bare essentials, the meditation consists of picturing two rival armies hoisting their standards for battle. The first army is commanded by Satan, who sits 'on a great throne of fire and smoke inspiring horror and terror'.[20] From it, he dispatches his devils into every individual heart with orders to tempt people with riches, with worldly honours, and finally with pride.

After Satan the meditation turns to Christ, who is standing on the plain near Jerusalem, 'his appearance beautiful and attractive'.[21] Instead of devils, he dispatches apostles and disciples from his army with orders to help people by attracting them 'to perfect spiritual poverty'[22] which he warns may well be accompanied by actual poverty. From this, the meditator is asked to accept three steps: poverty as opposed to riches; insults and contempt from the world as opposed to its honours; and ultimately true humility.

After going deeply into this meditation throughout most of Lent, I leaned towards postponing the uncomfortable choices it posed, but the combination of God and Gerry Hughes did not seem inclined to let me get away with such procrastination.

'Are you willing to accept the challenge of the Standard of Christ?' asked Gerry at our final tutorial in Easter week.

'Yes, I think so,' I replied, with considerable uncertainty, for the programme of poverty, contempt from the world and enforced humility was far removed from my agenda.

'You may not quite be ready for it,' said Gerry perceptively, 'so you should pray for the grace to accept the challenge.'

'I will,' I said, and so I duly prayed, because somehow I had instinctively come to know that the lessons of this third Parliamentary Retreat were even more important than those of the first two, which had moved me so deeply in the Lents of 1995 and 1996.

Nobody's spiritual journey moves forward smoothly and easily like a well-oiled machine. There are unexpected pauses, silences, hesitations, reverses, jerks of pain and leaps of joy. Moreover, a soul does not move towards God by a logical process of conversion from the head, but from mysterious and incomprehensible changes within the heart. Perhaps what matters most in times of doubt and difficulty is to keep on striving, which usually means to keep on praying.

My spiritual posture at this crossroads in my life was ludicrous, if not contemptible, for what I really wanted was to have it both ways. So I prayed in one direction with my lips and went in another direction with my life. Thus, while asking to be shown the route to spiritual poverty, I continued to charge ahead at full throttle of pride into the furnace of the libel battle, fuelled by an arrogant determination to defeat my unlovable neighbours at the *Guardian*. It was inevitably a wrenching experience – the spiritual equivalent of doing the splits. The conflict between prayerfulness and pridefulness created within me an acute sense of tension, restlessness and, at times, misery. Beginning to recognize the problem, I also prayed for the conflict to be resolved – which in the end it was.

CHAPTER FOURTEEN

Countdown to Catastrophe

DESPITE THE INTERNAL TENSIONS that were troubling me, I put on an external mask of confidence as I prepared for the legal and political battles that lay ahead in the make-or-break year of 1997. In the libel case my prospects received an unexpected boost at the last of the pre-trial skirmishes when my lawyers won a significant victory or, to describe it more accurately, when the *Guardian* scored a damaging own goal.

The war of attrition on documents eventually rebounded on the defendants. They had overplayed their hand so heavily with oppressive demands made under court orders for discovery that their paper chase became a paper mountain. As ancient files were brought up by the barrow load from the vaults of Aitken Hume, Al Bilad (UK), Astra, BMARC, Companies House, the Independent Broadcasting Authority, Inglewood, the Inland Revenue, the MOD, six banks and numerous other sources, it became apparent that the discovery process was spiralling out of control. In addition, after spending at least £100,000 on subpoenas for such papers, the defendants reaped a huge harvest of chaff with virtually no wheat at all, because their central allegations of pimping, arms dealing and dependency remained conspicuously uncorroborated. The only certain effect of all this paper-farming was that it would extend the length of the case from weeks into months, because jurors would be asked to grapple with haystacks of trial bundles in search of whatever straws were being clutched at by the defence lawyers.

'I think we've got a good chance of hoisting the *Guardian* on their own petard,' said my QC Charles Gray, telling me of his plan to make an application for court that the interests of justice would be best served if the case was heard by a Judge sitting without a jury. The basis of his argument was that the documentation had become impossibly complicated. The trial Judge, Mr Justice Popplewell, agreed. He decreed that, under a rare but established procedure, *Aitken v Guardian* would be tried as a Judge-alone case. The defendants, in considerable disarray, appealed against this ruling but were turned down by the Court of Appeal. A despondent George Carman QC told his clients that losing the jury was a 'mortal blow'.[1]

The *Guardian's* barristers had already given their clients some earlier intimations of mortality. 'This is a classic case to settle,' they advised at a case conference held in mid-April 1997.[2] The paper's Editor, Alan Rusbridger, agreed to heed the advice. The first I knew of the *Guardian's* moves towards a settlement was on a showery morning of electioneering on the Kent coast when I received a message: 'Ring Lord Saatchi.' As Maurice Saatchi was the advertising and public relations overlord for the Conservative Party's General Election campaign, I assumed as I rang back that the call must have something to do with the electoral battle now in progress. Not so.

'Can you come and have lunch today with me and Alan Rusbridger at Wiltons?' asked Saatchi, apparently under the illusion that my South Thanet constituency was somewhere just around the corner from Jermyn Street. I explained that I was committed to a midday meeting with voters which I simply could not drop at two hours' notice, for I was an election candidate first and a libel defendant second. Nevertheless, even in my absence, I was mightily intrigued at the prospect of settlement negotiations and knew that Maurice Saatchi was the right conduit for them. Eighteen months earlier he had brokered a private meeting between Rusbridger (Peter Preston's replacement) and myself over a cup of coffee at Wiltons. 'There's no personal ill will from me to you,' I had told the new Editor of the

Guardian, 'but you can't expect to call a member of the Cabinet a corrupt minister, a pimp and an arms dealer and get away with it.' Later in the conversation I added, 'When you accept what I'm saying, I'll be glad to talk about a settlement. You will find me reasonable on damages but I'll need a proper apology.'[3]

We had parted amicably enough on that occasion, agreeing to keep our contacts secret and to channel future communications through Maurice Saatchi. After a year and a half of silence, the channel was now being reactivated at the *Guardian's* request. What was Rusbridger offering?

Nothing much, it transpired. The *Guardian's* proposal, as relayed by Maurice Saatchi, was that they were willing to walk away from the case without giving an apology, without paying any damages and without making any contribution to my costs. Their only concession was that they would not challenge any announcement I might care to make unilaterally. Rusbridger advised that I should delay such an announcement until the day of the General Election. He also suggested that I should make it coincide with the news that I would accept the £30,000 which the *Independent* had already paid into court in response to my libel action against them for their articles and editorials in March 1995 accusing me of being knowingly involved in illegal arms deals to Iran.[4]

I was underwhelmed by this proposition on the grounds that an announcement by me unaccompanied by any sort of apology from the *Guardian* would be the hollowest of victories. However, I did not reject it out of hand. I sent word back via Maurice Saatchi that if the defendants were serious about settling the case, they should initiate a discussion between George Carman QC and Charles Gray QC. That discussion did subsequently take place, but it was a desultory and half-hearted affair. Charles Gray said that damages were not likely to be a problem for his client, but he must have an apology. George Carman, after checking back, said that his clients were not prepared to give any sort of apology. On the basis of those instructions, there was no deal. Charles Gray formed the general impression that the defendants, unlike their lawyers, were not seriously interested in trying to reach a settlement of the case.

My sister, Maria Aitken, came to a similar conclusion after she had launched a settlement initiative of her own through a channel involving a well-known theatrical producer and a senior editorial figure at the *Guardian*. At the end of these clandestine discussions Maria reported, 'They aren't interested in coming to terms with you. They've got something up their sleeve.' I had no idea what this 'something' might be.

While these abortive manoeuvres were taking place, I was in the thick of the May 1997 General Election battle. The seat which I had represented in the House of Commons for the past 23 years was widely regarded as 'safe', since it needed a 12 per cent swing to Labour for me to lose it. But this was exactly what I feared was likely to happen. During the previous few months I had been regarded by my closest colleagues in Parliament as an archpessimist, whose Election predictions were so apocalyptic as to border on the unhinged. My view was that the nation had made up its mind to give the Conservative Government the order of the boot with great vigour and to elect Labour by a landslide that would rival Attlee's massive victory over Churchill in 1945. I kept telling anyone who would listen that there would be a Labour majority of over 150 seats and that South Thanet would fall in the process. I even made this my forecast for a pre-filmed Channel 4 television documentary which was to be broadcast after polling day.

When the Election campaign started, I hoped that my Cassandra-like warnings would be negated by the usual narrowing of the gap between the parties in the run-up to polling day. To my dismay I soon discovered evidence from the doorsteps that the gap was widening. I shall never forget one particular evening's canvassing in Worth, near Sandwich. This was a Tory stronghold, ye olde Kentish village with only 400 voters on the electoral roll, many of them living in gentrified cottages picturesquely scattered around a seventeenth-century church, two eighteenth-century pubs and a war memorial duck pond. I personally knocked on the doors of nearly 100 electors in Worth, virtually all of whom had voted for me in the 1992 election. Over a dozen of them said they were switching to Labour.

The last house I canvassed was a Georgian six-bedroomed mansion whose owner I found watering the roses in his large garden. I knew him fairly well, having solved a problem for him when he had come to one of my weekly surgeries a year or so earlier. 'You've been a good MP but I'm afraid I'm definitely voting for Tony Blair,' he said. 'I'm just totally fed up with the Tories and so is my wife.' Like many other constituents at this time, he was impervious to argument, even though he admitted to prospering in business on the back of the Government's economic policies.

Later that evening, over a beer with my fellow canvassers, I said to my Chairman and agent, John Thomas, 'There's a real sea change in the political mood out there. On tonight's figures it's running at the rate of a 15 per cent swing to Labour.'

I fought hard to avert a disaster of this magnitude. The biggest problem was how to win back the disaffected Conservative supporters and to prevent them from being 'won't vote' stayaways. My last-minute weapon in this damage limitation exercise was Margaret Thatcher. She disbelieved my pessimistic assessment that South Thanet was about to go Labour, yet she was sufficiently disturbed by it to do me the great favour of coming down from London to be the star of a special Saturday Election rally in Ramsgate. On the hustings that afternoon, she was Margaret the Magnificent, rolling the audience in the aisles with a fiery speech which ended with a peroration so militantly Eurosceptic that it came close to a declaration of war on Brussels. Thatcher oratory of this potency came as a much needed boost to the beleaguered spirits of our party workers, but it also inflamed the passions of my opponents, who turned out in force for a sizeable anti-Thatcher demonstration on the streets of Ramsgate.

Despite such excitements, the tide continued to roll Labour's way. Six days later, within hours of the polls opening, I knew I was doomed when I saw an unprecedentedly high Labour turnout from the council estates, matched by an unprecedentedly low turnout from the traditional Conservative districts. On the afternoon of 1 May, I took an hour off from touring committee rooms to attend evensong at Canterbury Cathedral. With Lolicia and our 16-year-old daughter Alexandra (a sixth-former at Kings, Canterbury) beside me in the pew, I prayed to be able to show dignity in defeat and to be given the opportunity for other forms of service in the life after politics.

At 2.30 a.m. on 2 May in the Winter Gardens ballroom at Margate, the South Thanet result was declared. My likeable Labour opponent, Stephen Ladyman, had won the seat by a majority of 2,878 votes on a swing of 14.9 per cent. I made a loser's speech which was regarded as gracious in its tone. The hardest part of its delivery was seeing many of my friends and supporters at the count, including my dedicated secretary Lynn Fox, breaking down in tears as I spoke. My own stiff upper lip trembled too, but having expected to be defeated I felt no sense of shock or devastation. After a long round of poignant farewells, I walked out of the hall with the ever-supportive Lolicia on one arm and Alexandra, whispering 'I love you Daddy', on the other. Then it was home, to what I thought would soon be a life of obscurity, if not oblivion.

In the aftermath of the Election result, I suffered several twinges of sadness, but had none of the feelings of depression which affected some of my defeated colleagues. 'It's time for the caravan to move on,' I told my family. 'I hope I can soon find some other outlet for public service.' In making such a pronouncement I was not ruling out a return to the political arena, for the scale of the Conservative catastrophe had been so massive that it was impossible to take my loss as any sort of personal humiliation. There had been no evidence to suggest that the media brickbats thrown at me before the Election had affected the result, for the swing to Labour in South Thanet had been almost identical to the swing in most other constituencies across the region.

During the three weeks of the campaign, just about the only references to my troubles with the *Guardian* had come from voters – including Labour voters – saying things like, 'Don't worry about all that crap in the newspapers about you. No one believes it.' As a prevailing sentiment in the constituency, this was probably true. When you have been a local MP for almost a quarter of a century, your constituents have had plenty of opportunity to make up their own minds about their Member's character, irrespective of what the national media are saying. The electors of Thanet may have had all sorts of views about me, but I do not think they included many subscribers to the *Guardian*'s accusations that I was a procurer of prostitutes for Arabs, an illegal arms dealer, and so on.

To their credit, neither my Liberal nor my Labour opponent used these or any other 'sleaze' arguments against me in the campaign, which was a fair and decent one on all sides. One other indication of local feeling was displayed immediately after the result. In a characteristically British mood swing of sympathy towards the vanquished, I found myself becoming much more popular in my constituency in the days immediately after the Election than I had been throughout the last five years of Conservative government. When I went round the towns and villages of South Thanet to say my goodbyes and thank-yous, I was overwhelmed by the genuine emotional warmth with which I was greeted, not only by my supporters but also by large numbers of people who a few days earlier had cast their vote in favour of dismissing me as their parliamentary representative. This was puzzling, but, as my great uncle Lord Beaverbrook used to say, 'Politics is the best of lives and the worst of lives.' South Thanet had, at different times, encompassed both extremes in my life, but I departed from it with a gratitude and an affection which seemed, to some extent, to be reciprocal.

Returning to London, I had some emotional pangs of nostalgia on the first few occasions when I walked past the Houses of

Parliament. What had I achieved during my 23 years in that palace of varieties? On balance, quite a lot. Few MPs contribute more than a thread or two to the tapestry of history, but I like to think that mine had been strong, positive and colourful strands of good public service. I could reasonably claim that I had represented my constituency well; changed a few lives for the better; championed the causes in which I believed without fear or favour; altered the perception of one or two key political issues; and exerted a modest measure of both power and influence for the greater good. It would be tedious to list these achievements in specific form, but looking back on my parliamentary life in the round, I felt much more fulfilment than disappointment. That is not a bad epitaph on any career in any walk of life.

One way and another, therefore, I took my electoral defeat philosophically and peacefully. This acceptance had something to do with the growing importance of the spiritual dimension in my life, although my impulses to do God's will were still confused, contradictory and sometimes downright contrary. Nowhere was this muddle more apparent (although to me only in retrospect) than in the preparations for my impending courtroom battle with the *Guardian*.

In the five weeks between the ending of my parliamentary career and the beginning of the libel case, my life was a combination of being furiously busy and busily furious. The first of these states of activity came from the long hours of homework I had to do in order to prepare to be examined and cross-examined in the High Court. I was told that I should expect to be in the witness box for at least a week – a far tougher assignment than even the most demanding of Parliamentary Question sessions. So I worked hard at mastering my brief, carefully assessing all the strengths and weaknesses of my case and preparing diligently for the predictable lines of attack I would face in the cross-examination by George Carman, the defendants' QC. This preparation exercise was an onerous but not particularly difficult task, except in one area of the case – the Ritz.

Defending a false story in the witness box was always going to be a dangerous task, but there was one good reason why the danger seemed limited. As far as anyone could tell, no proof existed that my story was untrue. 'Lolicia paid the bill in cash' remained an improbable proposition, especially since the revised version, 'Lolicia paid only 4,257 francs of the 8,010-franc bill in cash owing to a muddle', needed a lot of explaining. Yet who or what could contradict it? There was a cashier from the Ritz who claimed on the basis of photographs that Lolicia had not paid the bill. However, he had mysteriously disappeared from Mr al Fayed's employment without signing his witness statement. His unsigned testimony was hardly a strong card, particularly as he had already contradicted part of his identification evidence in an interview with the *Sunday Times*, but it appeared to be the *Guardian*'s only card in this part of the game. After more than two years of sending their journalists and solicitors all over Europe in search of Ritz evidence, after close collaboration with Mohamed al Fayed and his staff at the hotel, and after the massive discovery of documents exercise, there was neither an available witness nor any piece of paper before the court that could destroy the 'Lolicia paid the bill' story.

A libel case is decided on the basis of facts, not assertions. By the time we reached the eve of the trial, the *Guardian* were in serious and obvious difficulties on many fronts in the case because of the number of factual errors in their articles and pleadings. With a track record of so many false assertions, why should their true assertion about the Ritz win the day with the court if it could not be substantiated by factual evidence? Using this reasoning I stuck to my 'hang tough' strategy, explaining to my suppressed, if not inaudible, voice of conscience that it was necessary to defend the Ritz bill part of the case with my lie in order to nail the far more important (as I saw them) falsehoods published by the *Guardian* about my alleged pimping, arms dealing and corrupt business activities. It was a ruthless strategy based on the notoriously immoral principle that the end justifies the means.

In the aftermath of the collapse of the libel case, I was often asked the question, 'Didn't you realize that the *Guardian* might produce some evidence that would destroy your case?' The answer was that I had worried about this possibility but had discounted it for two reasons. The first was that, if such evidence existed and was in the possession of the defendants, under the rules of the High Court they were required to produce it *before* the case began. Exceptions to those rules are permissible if new evidence comes to light while a trial is in progress. It seemed incredible, in view of the lengths the *Guardian* had gone to during the last two years in order to seek a mass of irrelevant documents to their case, that they could have failed to seek any key documents that were potentially relevant to the Ritz episode.

The second reason for my misplaced confidence about any 'smoking gun' evidence that might emerge – such as Lolicia's air tickets – was that three weeks before the libel trial began I had talked to a friend who is a senior director at British Airways and, without telling him why, had asked the question: 'If my opponents wanted to trace old air tickets or passenger lists on a BA flight nearly four years ago, can they do so?'

'No,' he replied, 'we destroy all such records after two years. There is one secure computer which might keep older passenger lists, but you'd have to be from Interpol or the security services to get access to it.'

The fact that I had this conversation with my friend from British Airways in the month before the libel trial shows how thoroughly I was preparing to defend my deceit. Were there any chinks in the armour I had built around the false story of the Ritz bill? There were none that I could discover and none that the defendants seemed to have discovered either. That appeared to be the position on the day the trial opened.

There was, however, one other potential weakness in the Ritz bill deceit, which was that my false story might crack open under the ferocious cross-examination which would be launched by George

Jonathan Aitken leaves a Cabinet meeting at No. 10 Downing Street, March 1995.

A family portrait in the drawing room at Lord North Street, 1995

Sister Mary Finbar, the nun who nursed the young Jonathan at Cappagh Hospital in Dublin when he had tuberculosis in the 1940s.

Prince Mohammed bin Fahd, the son of the King of Saudi Arabia, Aitken's friend and colleague.

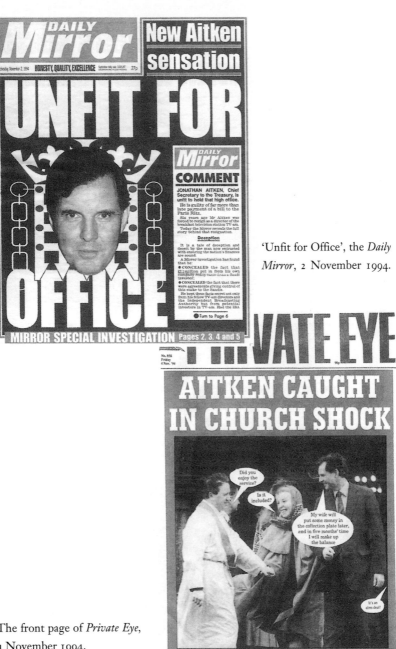

'Unfit for Office', the *Daily Mirror*, 2 November 1994.

The front page of *Private Eye*,
4 November 1994.

Lolicia, Jonathan and Victoria leaving Conservative Central Office on 10 April 1995, the day of the 'sword of truth' speech. This was also the day on which he launched the libel action against the *Guardian* and Granada.

Jonathan with his mother, Lady Aitken, and Lolicia outside the High Court during the libel trial, 10 June 1997.

The front page of the *Guardian* on the day after Aitken's withdrawal from the libel case was announced.

'The battle of College Green', in which Aitken was the focus of media attention after his return to London from America, 17 July 1999.

Victoria with her aunt, Maria Aitken, near her London home on the day of her arrest, 16 March 1998.

Aitken arriving at Bow Street magistrates' court, where he was committed to stand trial for perjury and perverting the course of justice, 8 December 1998.

Aitken at the Old Bailey with the homeless Bill Ledlaw, 8 December 1998.

A cartoon in the *Spectator*, 30 January 1999.

Aitken at the Old Bailey with his mother, Lady Aitken, 19 January 1999.

Victoria, Alexandra and Petrina Khashoggi arrive at the Old Bailey to hear Aitken sentenced, 8 June 1999.

Jonathan Aitken with Charles Colson. Colson wrote many letters of encouragement to Aitken in the post-libel period, and arrived in London to support him on the day of sentencing.

Carman. He would have two bites at the cherry – one at me and one at Lolicia. Would either of us get chewed to pieces?

I was reasonably confident that I could fight my duel with Carman without suffering any mortal wounds, but Lolicia would be an unknown quantity in the witness box. She had always disapproved of my strategy on the Ritz. When she eventually found out about it, she told me I had been 'arrogant and stupid' – an entirely justified comment. For many months she supported me only by her silence. It was far from certain whether she would give evidence at all. Her attitude to the drama varied from day to day. On the big picture of the case as a whole she was usually steadfast in saying that the evil forces, as she saw them, who had told such terrible lies about us had to be fought and defeated. Yet on the discrete issue of the Ritz bill she was equivocal as to what she would or would not say if she ever got as far as the witness box.

I was not the only participant in the drama who could not work out what Lolicia might do as a witness. It became a cliché amongst certain journalists that she was the 'weak link' in the case. This much repeated observation could be right or it could turn out to be 180° wrong. I knew that Lolicia had the capacity to make or break the case because she was and remains a lady of surprises.

About 10 days before the trial began, Lolicia was herself the target of some disagreeable surprises. These arrived in a steady stream of envelopes and packages addressed to Paula Strudwick, 8 Lord North Street, London SW1. Sometimes they were additionally addressed to Paula Strudwick c/o Lolicia Aitken, and sometimes they came in outer envelopes addressed only to Lolicia, but with the Strudwick name inside. The contents of these missives were bizarre. Sometimes they contained pornography or suggestive photographs. Sometimes they were pointless junk mail offering cut-price package holidays or discount air travel. Sometimes they contained little statuettes or wax figures of soldiers, dancers and the like.

Usually I opened the Paula Strudwick mail offerings myself and put them straight into the wastepaper basket. When I told my solicitor,

Richard Sykes, about them he agreed with my view that these childish games should be ignored. Since Paula Strudwick's evidence of my affair with her in 1980 had been struck out of the case in the pre-trial rulings, she was no danger to me and so I initially had no feelings of alarm about whoever was sending us this rubbish. Unfortunately, Lolicia felt differently.

'I know this is a campaign to get me down,' she declared. If this was its purpose, the campaign backfired on the day when Lolicia opened a package to find one of the statuettes and saw that it had been impaled with pins. 'Witchcraft!' she screamed, forbidding me to touch or see the offending package. Within hours a Russian Orthodox priest specializing in exorcism had been summoned to the house to preside over a complicated ritual for the destruction and immolation of the bewitched object. Not for the first time in this saga, I felt as though I had entered the scene of a play as I watched the flames consuming the latest of the unsolicited parcels. What did it all mean? Nothing very much was my conclusion, except perhaps that someone with a considerable knowledge of the case had an extremely warped and weird personality. This was hardly a revelation to me, but it did cause great distress to Lolicia. When I saw how upset she had become, I was furious on her behalf. I need not have worried. Far from getting Lolicia down, the effect of the 'witchcraft' campaign was to put Lolicia up, transforming her from the reluctant supporter into the avenging angel. If she had met the purveyor of the Paula Strudwick packages, I dread to think what celestial forces she would have summoned into the attack!

The episode was an unpleasant irrelevancy, but it did reveal a glimpse of the pressures that were being applied to my family. I was so self-centred at this time, however, that I cared little about anyone else's feelings under pressure. All that mattered to me now was winning the war. I had become so desperate to achieve this objective that I let go all the anchors of the spiritual teachings that had been important to me in recent years, and I ignored all the potential risk factors, even to my nearest and dearest. It was this dimension to my pride and selfishness which would later cause the greatest torment of all.

CHAPTER FIFTEEN

The Courtroom Battle

A BIG LIBEL TRIAL has few rivals as a human drama, especially when it is supercharged with scandalous allegations, surprise twists and a sensational climax. As the final curtain fell on *Aitken v Guardian*, the defendants' counsel, George Carman QC, was quoted as saying that in all his 44 years at the Bar he had never seen a case with a more dramatic ending. This was one Carman judgement with which I could not disagree, for I too was overwhelmed by the intensity of the battle and came close to being destroyed, as well as defeated, by its denouement.

From the moment I walked into Court No. 10 of the Royal Courts of Justice on the morning of Wednesday 4 June 1997, I had the feeling of being on centre stage of a great theatrical as well as a great legal production. It was not just the huge crush of cameras outside the court, nor the high-voltage atmosphere of expectancy inside it which created that impression. Somehow there was an awareness of deeper personal and political passions underlying the case which made everyone concerned with it realize that this was going to be a fight to remember.

'Mr Aitken sues the *Guardian* over an article entitled "Aitken tried to arrange girls for Saudis",' were the opening words spoken by my counsel, Charles Gray QC, who spent the next five hours taking the Judge, Mr Justice Popplewell, through the *Guardian*'s articles and Granada's videotapes of the two *World in Action* programmes. In painstaking detail, Gray highlighted the most serious libels against me.

'It is no exaggeration to say they have butchered Mr Aitken's personal, political and professional reputation,' he declared,[1] as he ran through the all too familiar litany of charges by the defendants about my alleged activities in the areas of arms dealing, pimping and financial dependency on royal Arab paymasters. On this last charge Gray was scathing as he pointed out the gravity of the allegation that I had 'lost the independence essential to the proper discharge of the responsibilities of an MP and Minister of the Crown',[2] and the paucity of the defendants' evidence in support of it.

He drew the Judge's attention to the fact that the defendants could produce no evidence at all in support of their imputation that I had handled, distributed and benefited enormously from the proceeds of Saudi bribes; no evidence that I had been involved in some 'dubious, if not downright corrupt arrangements'[3] for the nonexistent GEC–Philips bid for a contract for the street lighting of Riyadh; no evidence that Prince Mohammed had helped me to buy my house in Lord North Street; and no evidence that Prince Mohammed had been in any way financially involved in Inglewood, the *East Kent Critic*, or Investment Intelligence Ltd (a small unit trust company in which I had been a partner in the early 1970s). All these claims had been wrongly made in support of the dependency allegation in the *Guardian*'s original pleadings.

'The defendants have nevertheless pursued their case against Mr Aitken on the basis of particulars which are nothing more than bald assertion and flannel,' said Charles Gray. 'This total dearth of evidence has not prevented the defendants from pursuing Mr Aitken remorselessly and oppressively for documents relating to his private financial affairs in the hope of being able to make out the case of dependency. This they have manifestly failed to do.'[4]

Gray then turned from the evidence that did not exist to the evidence that had been withdrawn by the defendants' lawyers 48 hours before the trial opened. The alleged presence of prostitutes at Inglewood in 1990, prostitutes in Prince Mohammed's house in the

1970s, and my alleged recruitment of air hostesses as prostitutes in 1977 had been suddenly cut out of the *Guardian*'s case, presumably because last-minute doubts had arisen over the reliability of the evidence on which these assertions were based.

'Mohamed al Fayed, Valerie Scott and Gerald James are the fertile sources from whom the defendants have drawn much of the ammunition used against Mr Aitken,' said Gray, using some high-velocity ammunition of his own to fire at these targets and striking particularly hard at Gerald James as the foundation of the arms-dealing allegations, saying of him, 'It would be hard to conceive of a foundation more shaky and more prone to subsidence.'[5]

To judge by the body language and later the reported actual language of the *Guardian*'s representatives who sat in court listening to my counsel's opening speech, they were worried. 'The first few days of a libel trial are always the worst. You sit there and have buckets of wet brown stuff tipped all over you,' Alan Rusbridger murmured to a colleague.[6] In fact, Charles Gray's delivery methods were rather more subtle, consisting mainly of quiet understatement, forensic precision and occasional but lethal thrusts of the soundbite stiletto. There was no doubt which of these caught the imagination of the headline writers, for the evening news bulletins and the next day's papers all led with variations on 'AITKEN'S REPUTATION BUTCHERED'.

The following morning I took the witness stand and remained there for the next eight days. The first two days were taken up with my evidence-in-chief, which is when a witness is asked questions by the counsel for his side of the case. One of the more time-consuming aspects of my evidence-in-chief was dealing with the large number of unsubstantiated allegations made in the defendants' publications and pleadings which, for one reason or another, they had simply got wrong. Most of these were of secondary importance compared to the principal libels, but I had to be taken through them because they were so indicative of the damaging effect of accumulated inaccuracy. There were around 20 of these lesser journalistic misrepresentations which had to be corrected as subplots around the main themes in the case. On these I was asked broad, general questions by Charles Gray, first about my reactions to the *Guardian*'s publications.

Gray: Was a single one of the allegations which were published in the issue of the *Guardian* for 10th April put to you in any way orally or in writing by the *Guardian* prior to publication?

Aitken: Absolutely not. The *Guardian* gave me no notice of when they were going to publish; no warning of what they were going to publish; and no opportunity to respond to the very serious allegations which they were going to make...

Gray: Can you describe for His Lordship in your own words your reaction when you saw the headline ['Aitken "tried to arrange girls" for Saudi friends'] and the text of that story.

Aitken: My reaction was to be horrified. I felt poleaxed by this headline and the ensuing story. It was almost the equivalent of having a heart attack in terms of the shock and the pain I felt on reading it ... it was so astonishing to read on the front page of a serious newspaper an allegation of this serious-ness which I knew in my own heart and soul was completely untrue, and then to feel such pain because it is just such a sordid story and I remember just sort of burying my head in my hands and saying really to no one in par-ticular 'The *Guardian* have now said on their front page that I'm a pimp' and I just remember my small son politely enquiring 'What is a pimp Daddy?'[7]

These last words were grist to the media's mill on Day Two of the trial, although they were rivalled in the reporting of my answer to a question about my reactions after watching the broadcast of the *World in Action* programme 'Jonathan of Arabia'. 'Clearly this was a hatchet job,' I replied. 'This was character assassination television not current affairs television. There was no attempt at balance or fairness or objectivity. It was "Destroy Aitken Time".'[8]

It was no doubt hoped by the defendants that the latest instalment of 'Destroy Aitken Time' would arrive when George Carman QC launched his cross-examination of me. He did his best by unveiling, after a few general questions, a prophetic trailer for the attack he would later be making on my evidence on the Ritz Hotel episode.

Carman: If in this courtroom, in the course of these proceedings, My Lord has eventually to make the melancholy decision that you have lied to the Cabinet Secretary whilst a Cabinet Minister; that you have lied to your own Prime Minister as a Cabinet Minister; and that you have lied to the House of Commons as a Cabinet Minister; and lied to this court on all occasions to do with your stay at the Ritz, if that were to be so, you would accept that such a series of lies would prove you totally unfit for public office?

Aitken: I don't accept any of these melodramatic hypothetical allegations you are putting to me ... but if his Lordship were to make those dramatic judgements it would obviously be a shattering blow to me, yes...

Carman: It would butcher your reputation.

Aitken: My reputation has already been butchered.

Carman: It would butcher it again.

Aitken: It would.[9]

Having given the court a taste of the red meat that was to come, George Carman moved slowly and, on the whole, rather ineffectively towards the butcher's shop a.k.a. the Ritz. As a prelude to this part of his cross-examination, he made what seemed to me to be a rather half-hearted stab at the dependency issue. Instead of focusing on Prince Mohammed as a source of dependency, as his clients had so inaccurately done, he parcelled together a number of Arab names who had been clients of or shareholders in Aitken Hume, trying to make them sound as though they were a mysterious network of connected paymasters on the grounds that 'they know each other'.[10]

High on the Carman mystery list came Mr Wafic Said. After a dozen or so questions about this distinguished gentleman's birthplace, antecedents, business activities and links with the Saudi royal family, I turned the tables on my interrogator.

Aitken: Mr Carman I do not want to play-act with you.

Carman: No, no, no.

Aitken: Mr Wafic Said has retained you as his lawyer for many years. You know him very well.

Carman: I do not know him very well. I have advised him once in consultation.

Aitken: And been retained by him for some considerable time.

Carman: Probably retained at the time, but I have never appeared for him in court.

Aitken: We need not play-act about our knowledge of Mr Wafic Said.[11]

Laughter in court, with some of the loudest chuckles coming from the Judge. Aitken's suspicious Arab paymaster had been paying the defendants' leading counsel large retainer fees for many years. Collapse of stout barrister, who looked greatly discomfited. He quickly switched to the buying of Prince Mohammed's BAC 1-11 at the Paris air show in 1977. Carman suggested that I had been 'assisting and promoting' the purchase of the aircraft.[12] I pointed out that my assistance had been limited to making the chance introduction of the Prince to the Chairman of Rolls-Royce and that I had only started to do something concrete after the sale had been agreed, when one of the Prince's colleagues had asked me late on a Saturday evening, 'Where do we find lawyers?'

'Where do we find lawyers?' Carman repeated in a mocking tone.[13] I looked round the first few benches of the courtroom, which were overflowing with some 20-odd leading counsel, junior counsel, senior solicitors, junior solicitors, legal assistants and paralegal notetakers.

'Yes,' I replied. 'It has not been my problem since.'[14] More laughter in court. I was having an easy ride.

The ride inevitably became more difficult in the cross-examination over the Ritz. I told several bad lies about it, of which the worst was to say in direct evidence that Lolicia had met me in my room in the hotel at lunchtime on Sunday 19 September 1993, and that I had arranged with her that she would pay my bill later that afternoon following my departure. However, none of these lies could be nailed with any proof or evidence. Carman huffed and puffed with scornful suspicion, but he did not blow the house down. This was the *Guardian*'s verdict on this part of the trial:

As the defendants poured out of the court, they felt uneasy. Aitken had held up remarkably well in the witness-box. Where he was weak – in his letter to Sir Robin Butler – he resorted to the 'verbal subtleties' … Otherwise, he had given no ground at all.[15]

Once we were over the Ritz (which took two full days) I was on a good wicket, finding myself largely untroubled by Carman's bowling.

As the case progressed, it became obvious that the *Guardian* was in serious difficulty on issues such as Inglewood, Saudi dependency and the Makhzoumi 'impropriety' episode, for their counsel had produced little or nothing in the cross-examination to dent my position. Moreover, on one of the most important issues of all – arms dealing – the defendants were forced to concede defeat. Following a clear but inevitable ruling from the Judge on the meaning of the words used by the defendants when they had attacked me with arms-dealing allegations, George Carman QC withdrew his clients' defence of justification to what was known as the second action.[16]

This concerned the campaigns against me by Granada and the *Guardian* on BMARC, Astra, Project Lisi and other alleged arms deals to Iran, Iraq and Saudi Arabia. This surprise withdrawal on the sixth day of the trial was a huge boost to my morale and case-winning prospects. My opponents had devoted many articles and an entire television documentary to the proposition that I had been knowingly and lucratively involved in arms deals, most of them to illegal destinations. Now they were surrendering without offering any evidence or argument to justify their original publications. By any standards, this was a humiliating climb-down.

When I eventually climbed down from the witness box myself, after some 45 hours of intense questioning, I felt like a boxer who has gone the full distance with a reigning champion and won on points. It had been a great ordeal physically, mentally and morally. In physical terms I had prepared myself like an athlete before a race, going to bed early, eating and drinking sparingly, having regular massages and doing *qigong* relaxation exercises under Lolicia's expert instruction. Mentally my preparations were far tougher. I had to master every detail of each day's expected proceedings in order not to be wrong-footed in the witness box by my formidable cross-examiner. This required almost as much intense study each evening and early morning as had been required of me when I was Chief Secretary to the Treasury, steering the relevant Cabinet committees through round after round of detailed decisions on the nation's public expenditure budget.

The toughest test of all, however, was the moral one. It required a Jekyll-and-Hyde performance. On the one hand I could easily fire myself up with positive moral fervour on those large areas of the case where the defendants had made false allegations against me. On the other hand I made myself tell some highly immoral lies about the Ritz bill in order to defend my own false story against the defendants. The contradictions in such a stance were an appalling strain. Night after night during the trial I wilted under the burden of my secret deception, suffering greatly from sweaty hours of sleeplessness punctuated by stabbing heart-thrusts of anxiety. Yet despite this inner turmoil, I somehow steeled myself to preserve an outer demeanour of calm professionalism. In the witness box adrenaline not only kept me on my mental toes, it also anaesthetized my moral conscience.

The general opinion in and around the courtroom, as my eight-day duel with George Carman ended, was that my evidence had been impressive and that I had probably won the case with it. This view even seemed to prevail among the *Guardian*'s reporting team, whose assessment of my testimony stated:

Aitken's performance in the witness-box over eight days was awesome. His eyes twinkled, he was confident, fluent and charming. A bemused half-smile, almost a smirk, played on his face, lending him an aura of good-humoured stoicism.[17]

'We had always expected him to be a very good witness,' they quoted a prominent barrister as saying. 'He was intelligent, seemed to me very credible, and performed extremely well. I don't think Carman really laid a glove on him.'[18]

This analysis was too flattering. For a start, George Carman did lay his gloves on me quite effectively once or twice, although it would be fair to say that he never came close to delivering any knockout blows. Leaving aside the Ritz (and even there the combined resources of Mohamed al Fayed and the *Guardian* had not produced any hard evidence with which Carman could land killer punches), the fact of the matter was that the defendants' journalists and their sources had produced two anti-Aitken television documentaries and numerous articles, large parts of which were grossly misleading because they were so heavily based on material which was either factually wrong or incapable of standing up to the test of fair comment in law.

These exposed flanks of the defendants took more painful blows from the first shoal of witnesses from my side of the case. First came several Inglewood witnesses, who between them destroyed the defendants' false claims that I had called in the police to investigate the fraud and theft allegations against Kirk and Wilson; that I had fired these individuals to deny them a £15,000 commission; and that Inglewood had been the scene of pimping and prostitution activities during my 11 years as a director.

When we moved on to Saudi dependency and my consequent lack of ability to speak with an independent voice in Parliament, only one witness, Richard Shepherd MP, gave evidence before Carman appeared to throw in the towel on this issue. There is a practice in civil trials by which a witness statement can be 'taken as read' – in other words, accepted as fact without any sort of questions or challenge. To my surprise, this procedure was extended to many of my best witnesses, including the two former Speakers of the House (George Thomas and Jack Weatherill), the Labour MP Stuart Bell, and half a dozen constituents from South Thanet. The latter witnesses all made it clear that I had never rearranged my engagements to give priority to demands from Saudi princes, as the defendants' pleadings had asserted. It looked very much as though the *Guardian*'s lawyers were letting their clients' claims about my dependency, subservience and failure of parliamentary duty go by default because of lack of evidence.

The only constituency witness who did make an appearance in court was my former Constituency Association Chairman, Mrs

Irene Maggs MBE. An elderly and disabled lady in her late eighties, she had been tricked by the producers of *World in Action* into giving them a filmed interview for 'Jonathan of Arabia' after being told that the programme was one of a series of profiles of future contenders for the Conservative leadership. Mrs Maggs had allegedly corroborated for *World in Action* a story told on the programme by Valerie Scott that Prince Mohammed had given me a Jaguar car in 1976 and that I had subsequently ordered her to make sure Mrs Maggs kept quiet about this gift. Mrs Maggs demolished this nonsense, not only in her evidence but also by being taken through the transcript of her original interview with *World in Action*. Far from corroborating the Valerie Scott story about Prince Mohammed's gift of a Jaguar, what Mrs Maggs had actually said to Quentin McDermott of *World in Action* was this:

I can tell you absolutely definitely I have no knowledge of him buying Jonathan a car or even having any conversation with Valerie Scott about a car and I'm sure I would know ... No there's no way that Valerie Scott, certainly never, she never rang and said he had a car. Never ... she romances like mad, yeah, romances like mad does Valerie Scott.[19]

Offstage from the courtroom, Valerie Scott was giving the defendants even more serious worries. She was in theory their key witness, for most of the material in the pleadings and publications on the sleaze and dependency issues came from her. Now that the trial was under way she was having a crisis of conscience. She tried to pull out of the case. This provoked a panic-stricken stream of telephone calls to her from David Leigh of the *Guardian*, pleading with her to stay onside. She was also the recipient of a threat (or was it a bluff?) from the defendants' camp when she was told that if she did not co-operate she would be summoned to the High Court by subpoena and cross-examined as a hostile witness.

These grave problems over Valerie Scott were not the only crisis troubling the defendants at this time. According to later press reports,[20] when my cross-examination ended, Granada's libel insurers took the view that they had lost the case. They called an emergency meeting in George Carman's chambers and urged a settlement. Alan Rusbridger opposed them, which at the time must have looked a foolhardy, if courageous, stance. But he won the day and the case continued, even though one half of the defence team thought they were dead in the water.

Meanwhile, back in the courtroom the next trickle of witnesses were putting nails into various other coffins that were part of the defendants' case, such as their claim of impropriety in relation to my meetings with Fouad Makhzoumi at the MOD and Lord North Street in 1993. Sir Alan Thomas, the former Head of Defence Sales at the MOD, gave particularly effective testimony. He firmly rejected the defendants' assertions that my meetings with Makhzoumi (all of them known to the MOD and often attended by civil servants) had been in any way improper, and he also gave valuable evidence on the contribution to the national interest which the Prince Mohammed–Jonathan Aitken communication channel had made on Al Yamamah and related issues in 1993. The following exchanges referring to my visit to the Ritz Hotel in Paris were particularly helpful.

Gray: You mentioned Prince Mohammed. Can you just explain to His Lordship what discussion you did have with Mr Aitken after his visit to Paris?

Thomas: We had a number of discussions on this particular aspect but the outcome of the discussions we were focusing upon was whether Prince Mohammed had been able to establish, with his father especially, whether it was likely that the Saudis would be interested in buying four Upholders that we had decided to release.

Gray: And we know about the Upholders as submarines that basically you, I suppose, were in charge of selling or trying to sell. Is that right?

Thomas: Indeed.

Gray: Just so that we are clear about it, what point in time did this conversation between yourself and Mr Aitken about what he had said to Prince Mohammed, what time did this conversation take place?

Thomas: I couldn't be sure but we had a pretty constant dialogue and feedback. When Mr Aitken had been able to speak to Prince Mohammed, who is the King's ... son, he is a very, very useful form of communication as far as understanding and thinking in the Saudi Arabian Government.[21]

Even though my cross-examination about Prince Mohammed in the Ritz was over, I remained nervous about it. One reason for this was the body language of the Judge. Mr Justice Popplewell was later to be caricatured by the *Guardian* reporting team in their book on the case as some sort of establishment old fogey who leaned towards my side of the arguments throughout the trial because of class solidarity. I saw it differently. Any Judge in any case has to lean where the evidence is taking him, yet on the Ritz I sensed that Sir Oliver Popplewell was almost as suspicious as George Carman. One symptom of this suspicion was his attitude to an interesting but inconclusive item of evidence which arrived in court some days after the trial had begun.

The *Guardian*'s solicitor, Geraldine Proudler of Olswang, had made a belated request to her clients on 1 June, asking them to investigate whether any hotel records were available at the Hotel Bristol in Villars, where Lolicia had spent the night of 18 September 1993 when taking Victoria to Aiglon College. A *Guardian* reporter was duly dispatched to Switzerland and was able to overcome the usual Swiss attitude to client confidentiality because the Hotel Bristol was in bankruptcy, with its old records stored in the basement under the control of an uncharacteristically helpful insolvency accountant. The reporter extracted Lolicia's bill, which showed that on the night of 18 September 1993 her room had been in single occupancy.

This was not in itself of momentous importance, but it did cast doubt on a segment of my evidence when I had been required by George Carman to explain one particular telephone call I had made from the Ritz. Mohamed al Fayed, still collaborating to the full with the *Guardian*, had supplied his allies with the records of all my calls from his hotel. One of them had been made to the Hotel Bristol in Villars at 10.15 a.m. on the morning of Sunday 19 September. If I had spoken to Lolicia in this call, the whole edifice of my false story of the Ritz bill payment would have come crashing down. It would have been impossible for Lolicia to have been in Villars at 10.15 a.m. and in the Paris Ritz by lunchtime on the same day, because the journey between these two locations took at least four hours.

To paper over the cracks on this problem, I had told another lie in the witness box. My false story was that my mother-in-law (a Swiss resident) had also been staying in the Hotel Bristol, sharing Lolicia's room, and I had spoken to her not to Lolicia at 10.15 a.m. on Sunday 19 September.

This story was shaken, although not shattered, by the production of the Hotel Bristol records. These were confusing, with manuscript amendments, references to rooms with communicating doors and some pages which appeared to contradict each other between double and single occupancy. The most telling point, however, was that for the night of 17 September Lolicia had been billed for a room with double occupancy and on 18 September she had been billed for a room with single occupancy. The Judge frowned as this evidence emerged and asked me a question:

Popplewell: Where does your wife's mother live normally?

Aitken: In a place called Schlieren, which is effectively in Zurich.

Popplewell: She is alive and well?

Aitken: She is alive and not very well.[22]

To those with sharp antennae, the Judge was signalling his scepticism over the telephone call evidence and suggesting that my story needed corroboration from my mother-in-law. I knew that this corroboration might be impossible to obtain. My mother-in-law would probably refuse to condone my false story and, even if she agreed to do so, she was quite genuinely such an ill and forgetful person that she could not be expected to be a reliable source of written or oral evidence.

At this point in the story, I lurched into my worst and most shameful mistake of the entire case. I decided to ask Victoria, our 16-year-old daughter, for help in corroborating my false story about my mother-in-law's presence in the Hotel Bristol in Villars on 19 September. There can be no excuses for this terrible decision by me. The only explanation was that I was desperate to shore up this small hole in my wall of deceit over the Ritz bill episode and was prepared to go to any lengths to prevent it from widening. A short and simple witness statement from Victoria, I thought, would do just that.

Victoria, who was studying for her A levels in Germany at the time, was excited at the prospect of getting a day or two off from school. She flew into London and, soon after arriving at Lord North Street, cheerfully signed the witness statement, already written by me, which was waiting for her. She may not have read it thoroughly and she certainly did not understand its implications fully. Remembering travel arrangements to Villars from one of the many trips she had made to her schools in that town between the ages of 10 and 13, and specifying what had happened on a particular one of her grandmother's visits to her there some four years earlier, was well beyond her power of accurate recall. So Victoria relied on her father and loyally signed a witness statement to help him. This loyalty was later to be the source of her father's greatest shame, disgrace and remorse.

Victoria's witness statement was a fairly anodyne document which was helpful but not essential to the case. After setting out her travel arrangements to Villars via Paris and Geneva (also false but needlessly so), the vital passage in Victoria's statement read as follows:

On the Saturday morning my mother and I went up to the school where I tried on my uniform. At some time during the day we met my grandmother Madame Azucki. My mother and I then went to the school where after saying good-bye she left me. This would be some time in the afternoon and I slept the night at the school. The following morning I felt very unhappy and telephoned the Hotel Bristol. My grandmother was there and I spoke to her...[23]

As I read my own handiwork, I thought it would neatly block off the small weakness about the presence of my mother-in-law in the Hotel Bristol on the morning of Sunday 19 September. 'That will do nicely,' I said to myself, blinkered to all imperatives save that of winning the battle.

Back in the courtroom, the battle was continuing to go nicely. My witnesses were testifying well. Outside the courtroom, however, things were going far from well for, unbeknown to me, the *Guardian's* legal team had been in successful overdrive ever since unearthing Lolicia's Hotel Bristol bill. It remains a mystery why the *Guardian* waited for over two years before commencing the energetic overseas document hunt which they appear to have carried out in two days halfway through the trial. Yet they were now fired up, and with this fire they discovered evidential gold.

On the afternoon of Wednesday 18 June, I became aware of some curious *frissons* of body language among the journalists covering the trial. One of them asked if she could have an exclusive interview with me later that day. What could this mean? My solicitor said perhaps there were rumours that the *Guardian* were about to settle the case – an improbable, but by no means unlikely development since the defendants had been losing ground daily.

Meanwhile, the latest of the witnesses, David Trigger, a former Astra executive, took the oath and exploded yet another myth about arms-deals commissions. This one was about a conversation he was supposed to have had in Saudi Arabia to the effect that I would be financially 'looked after' by BMARC's local agent. 'Absolute rubbish,' said Trigger robustly,[24] also making the point that BMARC never won any business in Saudi Arabia.

All of a sudden George Carman became unusually robust. In a voice which rang with barely suppressed excitement, he rose to his feet and said, 'My Lord, before any further evidence is called by my learned friend, I am in a position to provide the plaintiff's solicitors, Mr Gray and your Lordship with a signed witness statement of a lady called Wendy Dawn Harris who is employed by British Airways. I think, My Lord, if I may respectfully say so, it might be very important for Mr Gray and your Lordship to read it immediately.'

A few seconds later I too was reading this statement from Wendy Dawn Harris. As I scanned its pages, my heart sank. My head pounded. My confidence exploded into tiny pieces like flying shrapnel. I knew at once that I had lost the libel case and that with it I had lost my whole world.

CHAPTER SIXTEEN

Disaster Strikes

THE STATEMENT FROM WENDY Harris of British Airways was dynamite, for it blew a huge hole in my carefully constructed story about the Ritz bill payment. The full text consisted of six pages of technical explanations about airline records and ticketing procedures but, boiled down to the essentials, it contained conclusive proof that my Ritz story was false.

The first falsehood to be exposed was my statement that Victoria and Lolicia had passed through Paris on their way to Geneva on 17 September 1993. The air ticket microfiche records showed that they had travelled directly from Heathrow to Geneva. More importantly, Lolicia's return air ticket showed that she had flown back to London from Geneva, rather than from Paris, on the night of Monday 20 September. This evidence effectively proved, when linked to some Swiss car hire documents, that Lolicia had never been in Paris at all on the weekend when she had supposedly been paying my bill at the Ritz.

As soon as I read the British Airways statement, I knew it was all over. I had been caught red-handed. I immediately recognized that the libel action would have to be withdrawn, despite the appalling consequences, and that my life would never be the same again. It was the moment of truth and the moment of disaster.

On the surface, there were few signs in the courtroom that an earthquake had struck me. According to the *Guardian* reporters who were watching me closely as I read the Harris statement, 'a look of bemusement and then of stone' came over my face.¹ It must have been a tombstone, for at the time I felt totally dead and buried. Such a fate, if I had been able to exercise any choice in the matter, might well have seemed preferable to the media torture I was going to have to endure in the coming weeks. However, for the next half hour or so in court, I somehow found it possible to maintain a veneer of impassivity as Judge, barristers and witnesses droned on as though nothing out of the ordinary had occurred.

To the uninitiated, almost the only clue to the explosion that was about to break came just before the court retired at the usual time of 4.30 p.m., when Mr Justice Popplewell rather grimly observed, 'No doubt Mr Gray you will want to consider the position overnight. I shall be ready to see counsel in chambers tomorrow morning.'

As I sat waiting for the suddenly meaningless proceedings to draw to a close that afternoon, my frozen feelings of shock gradually thawed into warmer emotions of release. This was extraordinary but true. My mind quickly clutched at one or two straws of gratitude as I braced myself for the coming storm. Firstly, I was grateful that the thunderbolt had fallen at a time when I alone (as I then thought) could take the rap. Lolicia had been due to give evidence the following day. At least she would emerge legally unscathed from the nuclear fallout that would soon be descending on my head. So I quietly gave thanks – wrongly and prematurely, as things turned out – for that mercy.

Secondly, I was suffused by a sense of relief that the nightmare was over. Of course, I had expected that, when the bad dream ended, I would wake up to the trumpets of victory. Instead, I was now hearing the dirge of defeat and the drumbeat of disaster. But the immediate drama and the high tension of keeping up my own courage and other people's morale had suddenly dissolved. *La commedia è finita*. Even if my curtain call was not going to be the one I had planned, the thought of leaving the libel stage in *any* new direction did not seem the worst of options at this particular moment.

It was, however, an unreal moment. Immediately after the court closed, I went round to Charles Gray's chambers for an emergency conference. As we sat down my first words were, 'I'm afraid this is a mortal blow. We will have to surrender.' In an atmosphere of funereal gloom Charles and his junior counsel – Mark Warby and Justin Rushbrooke – agreed. My solicitor, the eternally optimistic Richard Sykes, had an alternative point of view, which was that I should fight on in order to get judgement on the other issues in the case, especially on the second action relating to the arms-dealing libels which the defendants had already conceded. I thought that such a separation of the issues, even if it was legally feasible, would be impossible in its practical implications for me on the wider political and media stage. Richard said he thought the other side would be expecting me to fight to the bitter end because I was bound to win on so many issues. After a while the discussion started to go round and round in circles. I was not making much sense in my contributions to it. Charles Gray tactfully said that we should all sleep on it and reconvene at 9.00 a.m. the following morning.

The first move I made after leaving the conference with my legal team was to go and break the news to Lolicia. In order to escape from the remorseless patrols of the paparazzi around Lord North Street, she was temporarily encamped in a studio flat near Sloane Square owned by my close friend Richard Shepherd MP. She was chatting with Alexandra and Victoria. All three of them had attended earlier sessions of the court hearing and were optimistic, as so many others were, about my rising prospects for victory.

'Terrible news, I'm afraid,' I said as I walked in. 'We've lost the case. There's been a mega-disaster.'

After I had explained the events of the afternoon there was a moment's stunned silence, followed by an impulsive display of love and solidarity by the Aitken women.

'We love you, Daddy,' said Alexandra, coming over and kissing me, immediately followed by Victoria and Lolicia. We hugged each other with impassioned feeling.

'God's will has been done,' announced Lolicia. 'So many people were praying for us that the light broke out of the darkness and illuminated the real truth.' I nodded, sinking into new levels of misery as it began to dawn on me that I had let down not just my family but also a huge army of friends, supporters, lawyers, constituents, well-wishers and prayer-givers.

Victoria, full of courageous sparkle, said, 'Let's be practical and look at the future.' She began running through an agenda of questions. Could we afford the legal bills? Where would we live if we had to sell our house? Could we keep on paying the school fees? Could I get a job and make some money? To all such questions I gave sanguine answers, not because of false optimism, but because at that moment I genuinely believed in brighter prospects for my future than eventually materialized.

The conversation then turned to William. 'We can fight our way through the media war that's coming, Daddy, but William's far too young for it – he's only 14,' said Alexandra with the assured self-confidence of a 17-year-old sister (the girls' birthday had been just a few days before). 'He'll be shattered – you must take him away.'

'We'd better all go away,' said Lolicia. 'The reptiles will be after our blood. Life won't be liveable here for some time.'[2]

Quickly we worked out an exit strategy. Within the next 48 hours Victoria would go back to her school near Munich, taking Alexandra with her as a 'guest pupil' for the last two weeks of term. Lolicia would seek refuge as a patient under an assumed name in a nearby German health clinic, while I would fly incognito to America for a holiday with William. These travel plans and the elaborate secrecy precautions that accompanied them might have seemed melodramatic to a fly on the wall. But we were a battle-scarred family who had learned how to survive many earlier paparazzi sieges. As things turned out, we were correct in our calculation that life would be made impossible for us by the media during the ensuing days. However, we seriously underestimated the frenzy of the various hunts in which the tabloid press would soon be pursuing us around the world.

After we had made our dispositions, breaking the news to William was the next priority. I drove down to Eton and had one of the worst hours of my life alone with him in his housemaster's study. I explained how I had lost the case, giving him a no-holds-barred description of my feelings of shame at having been caught lying. I added that it was not impossible that I could be prosecuted for perjury and be sent to prison. The thought had occurred to me for the first time while driving down to Eton.

William was then in that most fragile of masculine phases midway between boyhood and manhood. As I unveiled the horror story he crumpled, childlike, into my arms as we sat together on the sofa. 'Can I just ask one question?' he sobbed. 'Why did you go ahead with the case if there was a real chance you would lose it?'

Now it was my turn to break down. 'I'm afraid the answer is pride, foolish pride,' I answered. 'I've made the greatest mistake of my life because I've been proud, arrogant, blind and dishonest – now I'm going to pay a heavy price for those sins.'[3] We hugged and shed more tears. When we recovered we had a practical discussion about our immediate plans. I told William he could choose to come away with me from school that night and fly with me into exile the next day – which would mean missing the last week of the summer term. Alternatively, he could finish his school term – which would probably mean a miserable few days for him with the media firestorm crashing around his head, tabloids on his trail, and perhaps some teasing by unsympathetic contemporaries. He could then join me in the USA for a father-and-son holiday a week or so later.

'I'll stay here and take the heat,' was William's reply. This was an unexpected decision in view of his well-known lack of enthusiasm for end-of-term exams, not to mention the emotional pressures, but it was a good one. As his housemaster Charles Milne pointed out, Eton was a school that knew how to cope with media intrusions and parental disasters. 'We'll look after Will,' he assured me. It was no empty promise. During the next few days the school was put through all sorts of difficult tests in protecting and supporting Aitken Jnr, but both boys and masters gave him so much sympathetic understanding that William was kept afloat and well stabilized even at the height of the storm.

Before I left Eton that night, I gave William every ounce of fatherly comfort I could squeeze out of my own cracking heart. 'If this cloud has a silver lining,' I told him, 'it is that the breaking of me could be the making of you. If you will learn the lessons from this mess – and by far the most important one is always tell the truth – you will grow up to be a much bigger and better man than your father.'[4]

In a silence too deep for tears, we walked to my car holding hands and parted after a rib-crushing hug worthy of two grizzly bears. 'Whatever happens, Daddy, I'll always love you,' were William's parting words to me.[5] I thought about them continuously on the drive back to London.

I had a sleepless night before attending the 9.00 a.m. conference in Charles Gray's chambers. The lawyers looked as though they too might have had sleeping problems, for a bedraggled air of exhausted disappointment pervaded the room. We had become close as a team during the 26 months between the issuing of the original writ and the moment of defeat. My lawyers had believed in me and in my story. They were far too polite to be reproachful to their client, but I could see the pain on their faces, especially that of Richard Sykes. All of them had been badly betrayed by my deceit.

As we talked, the option of fighting on was quickly discarded. We were not even engaged in a salvage job. The task in hand was damage limitation. The best we could hope for was a bad deal on costs and a quiet surrender in court – which would inevitably be followed by a loud media explosion. After an exploratory discussion on the possibilities for an agreed costs order, I raised the question which had been on my mind all night: 'Am I vulnerable to a perjury charge?'

'Good question, and one to which we have been turning our minds,' said Charles Gray crisply, picking up a marked copy of the court transcripts. As we ran through one or two highlighted passages, the consensus was that I would be extremely unlucky to be prosecuted, particularly as the evidence against me, for technical and legal reasons, did not look to a lawyer as clear-cut as it might to a layman.

'I think you'll find that this would be a difficult perjury charge to make stick,' said one voice. Another added that perjury convictions in civil cases were rare and in libel cases unknown. The point was also made that I appeared to have given little in the way of direct eyewitness evidence that was untrue, for the false parts of my story about the payment of the Ritz bill, as well as the account of Lolicia's and Victoria's travel arrangements, were indirect or hearsay testimony. We spent a few minutes clutching inconclusively at such straws. 'A great deal will hang on what the Judge says,' observed Charles Gray. 'If he thinks the matter is serious enough, it's for him to announce that he will refer the papers to the DPP [Director of Public Prosecutions].'[6]

On that disturbing note, the lawyers set off without me for the court. Their brief was to ask for an adjournment, to hear what the Judge had to say in his chambers, and then to start negotiations with the other side on costs. As all this was likely to take at least a couple of hours, I went home and began the doleful task of breaking the bad news of the imminent collapse of my case to various close friends and relatives, starting with my mother.

My 87-year-old mother had been one of the silent heroines of the drama. She had seen many tragedies in her life, including the loss in childhood of three siblings, my father's RAF air crash, his premature death, and many brushes with disaster in her own health. In the last few weeks she had demonstrated a physical and emotional commitment to my cause which would have been impressive for someone 20 years her junior. She had attended almost every session of the trial, cooked meals for her grandchildren at all hours of the day and night, and sustained me with encouragement at many points during my marathon evidence-giving in the witness box. My mother's life had been so dedicated to her children that I knew she would be sent reeling by the shock of my catastrophe. Breaking the news to her was hard, therefore, yet she took it with amazing resilience. 'Don't worry about me, darling, take care of yourself. The first thing you need is a large cognac with your coffee,' she said. 'Then you must have a proper breakfast and a proper sleep.'

I felt as though I was 14 years old rather than 54, but I took her maternal advice, for the morning was slipping by in a haze of deepening gloom and crushing tiredness. The late editions of the *Guardian* had transmitted a clear signal that my case might be in trouble with a story headlined 'SURPRISE TWIST TO AITKEN CASE AS DOCUMENTS SURFACE'.[7] This was enough to start a new media siege outside our front door, and a new surge of friends called up to discover what was happening. I did not have the energy or the inclination to explain the surprise twist to them in any detail. 'It's a disaster. I've been caught lying about the Ritz,' was just about all I could manage. 'There'll be an announcement later today and it'll be very bad news.'

In fact, there was no announcement on Thursday 19 June because the private discussions in front of Mr Justice Popplewell and the negotiations between the two sides on costs took far longer than expected. The Judge was formally told in open court that an adjournment was required, ostensibly for further investigations into the new evidence, but in reality for surrender terms to be negotiated. In the course of the talks in chambers between the barristers and the Judge, someone had raised the issue of whether I had committed perjury. 'It was mentioned in passing rather than as a burning question,' I was told. 'The Judge did not seem to react one way or the other.' Richard Sykes read these runes as an encouraging sign that Mr Justice Popplewell would not be minded to refer the papers to the DPP.

This was the only note of encouragement I received all day, for my opponents were hanging extremely tough on the question of costs. The way my legal team saw it, we had already won the second action (on arms dealing) so were entitled to our costs from the defendants for that part of the battle, while they were entitled to costs from me for the first action which I was about to withdraw. The logic of this equitable position did not appeal to the *Guardian* and Granada, who wanted all their costs paid in full. 'Why should we back off when we have our foot on his windpipe?' said Alan Rusbridger.[8]

This militancy prevailed for most of the day, with demands from the *Guardian* for 100 per cent of 'indemnity costs' – a term which meant that their lawyers were in an advantageous position when it came to having the costs assessed by a taxing master. 'That's like writing a blank cheque. They're out for your blood,' observed Richard Sykes. He estimated that when taxed (assessed), the defendants' costs would come out at below £1 million.[9]

All estimates were pointless at this stage, however, because we had reached a complete impasse. It was eventually broken by George Carman, who proved far more reasonable than his clients. He offered to recommend a deal whereby I would have to pay 80 per cent of the defendants' taxed costs. If Richard Sykes was right in his forecast, that would mean I would have to pay my opponents about £800,000 on top of my own costs, which were then estimated to be around £700,000. A total bill of £1.5 million would be crippling, but just about payable without total devastation or bankruptcy, particularly if we sold Lord North Street well and moved to a smaller house.

It was a day of hard choices, but this one was more or less inevitable. 'Let's take it,' I said, accepting George Carman's offer at around 8 p.m. on the Thursday evening.

The only other choice I had to make was whether to be in court the following day when the surrender was announced. Charles Gray strongly advised against my presence, since the only words that would be spoken by either side in the courtroom would be his sentence, 'I am instructed by my client to ask for the action to be withdrawn on the terms which subject to your Lordship have been agreed on costs.'

After some hesitation, I agreed that there was no sense in my being around to present myself to what would be a near lynch mob of reporters and cameramen outside the court. So I made new plans for an early departure and went off to spend the evening with Lolicia, Alexandra and Victoria.

When I tracked Lolicia down to her temporary refuge in Richard Shepherd's flat, I found her in a decisive mood. 'I want a separation and I want to announce it tonight,' she said. 'It's not that I don't still love you, it's because I want time and space away from you and away from all this media torture. I simply must have a clean break so I can decide what is the right thing to do.'

I was in no position to argue with my wife, who had been pushed past breaking point that very afternoon by the behaviour of the paparazzi in Lord North Street. I too was close to breaking point, but the last thing I wanted was a matrimonial argument. Rather like a boxer who has just been knocked out, I had no stomach for starting an immediate new fight. Punch-drunk with pain, I caved in to this latest blow without objection. 'I'll announce anything you want,' I said, there and then dictating off a two-line separation news release.

After that surrender, with illogicalities piling up by the minute, we opened a bottle of champagne and drank a toast with our daughters, 'To the future'. Reckless bravado, perhaps, for I was under no illusions about the pain I would feel on the morrow once the anaesthetic of alcohol wore off and the media torments commenced. Nevertheless, we parted with the dignity of defeated warriors, scattering to our different destinations, yet bonded by the invisible energies of love. It was in that spirit that I set my alarm for 4.30 a.m. and slept fitfully until dawn.

CHAPTER SEVENTEEN

Flight into Fear

WEARING A WASHINGTON REDSKINS baseball cap belonging to my son and a pair of Armani dark glasses borrowed from my wife, I slipped out of London soon after dawn on the morning of Friday 20 June 1997, catching the 5.08 Eurostar from Waterloo to Paris. My amateurish efforts at disguise gave me the appearance of a ham actor performing the role of an international drug smuggler in a charade, so I abandoned my paparazzi-dodging props on arriving at the Gard du Nord. This was a mistake, for 10 minutes later I was spotted by a passing British tourist.

'Hey! You must be Jonathan Aitken!' bellowed my compatriot, as we both queued to buy a Metro ticket to Charles de Gaulle airport. 'Have you seen this morning's *Daily Mirror*?' No, I had not, so my interlocutor filled this gap in my knowledge by reading out its contents in a booming estuary voice that almost carried back to Essex, particularly when he delivered a fortissimo rendering of the headline 'AITKEN SPLITS FROM WIFE'.[1]

By the time this latest instalment of my misfortunes had been broadcast to the assembled travellers lined up at the Metro guichet, I had all the anonymity of an escaping elephant. My equilibrium was not restored until I was safely on board the first Air France flight of the morning to New York.

I dozed miserably for much of the eight-hour journey to JFK, intermittently wondering what was happening in and around Court

No. 10 of the Royal Courts of Justice. I could picture the press benches erupting as Charles Gray withdrew the action; the media scrum on the pavements in the Strand as the *Guardian* team gave triumphalist interviews glorying in their victory; the hostile headlines in the evening papers. All of these visualizations were accurate, although, as I was soon to discover, they underestimated both the sensationalism and the *schadenfreude* of the media's coverage of my fall.

Soon after arriving in New York, I moved into a friend's apartment on East 56th Street and telephoned my family. 'You won't believe this, Daddy, but you're not just news, you're the only news,' reported Victoria. 'The whole of the TV bulletins are about you and the whole of tonight's newspaper is about you – almost every page of it.'

I assumed this was filial exaggeration, but when I was faxed a copy of the *Evening Standard* I saw that Victoria's description was not far wide of the mark. 'THE RUIN OF AITKEN' was the banner headline, in a magnified typesize usually reserved for national crises, while lower down the page a contents box labelled 'DOWNFALL OF A FORMER CABINET MINISTER' announced how much of the paper's contents were focused on my travails:

Aitken: The Marriage	Page 3
Aitken: The Trial	Page 4
Aitken: The Lies	Page 5
Aitken: The Man	Pages 12 & 13
Leader Comment	Page 9[2]

'Are they gonna name this paper after you, Bud?' said the bemused apartment-house fax operator as Aitken headline after Aitken headline rolled through his machine. Alas, the *Evening Standard*'s coverage was only the hors d'oeuvres, for the next day's papers made an even bigger meal out of my disaster.

Predictably, the *Guardian* led the pack, devoting every single column inch in the first five pages of its 21 June edition to Aitken stories before the real news about Clinton, Blair, Saddam Hussein et al. started to get a look-in after page six. There was one disturbing new angle to the *Guardian*'s coverage: 'DPP URGED TO PROSECUTE AITKEN FOR PERJURY...' was the headline at the top of the paper's front page,[3] followed by a report making it clear that it was Alan Rusbridger who was doing the urging and that he had launched a personal campaign to achieve this objective.

Such initiatives are normally the preserve of the legal authorities. However, Mr Justice Popplewell had made no suggestion on the last day of the trial that the papers should be referred to the DPP, so it was a case of the *Guardian* rushing in where the judiciary had hesitated to tread. Apparently dissatisfied at merely being the civil law victor in the libel case, Alan Rusbridger became the self-appointed promoter of its extension into the criminal law, writing on 20 June to Dame Barbara Mills, the Director of Public Prosecutions, and to Sir Paul Condon, the Commissioner of the Metropolitan Police, in these terms:

Dear Dame Barbara

You will be aware that Jonathan Aitken today discontinued his libel action against the *Guardian* and against Granada TV in the High Court.

He did so because incontrovertible evidence from British Airways, obtained on subpoena, showed that Mr Aitken had perjured himself on oath.

Witness statements from his wife, 17-year-old daughter and from a close family friend – all of whom Mr Aitken had been intending to call to give evidence – were also directly dishonest. There is, therefore, the clearest evidence of a well-laid and carefully co-ordinated conspiracy to pervert the course of justice.

Our solicitor, Geraldine Proudler, of Olswang, has all the documents to support this charge and would be happy to assist you in any enquiries.

I am also writing to the Commissioner of Metropolitan Police, drawing this matter to his attention.[4]

This request set off a new round of headlines, of which the most sensational was 'JAIL HIM', blazoned across the front page of the *Daily Mirror*, which described me as 'a serial liar, coward and cheat', the last charge apparently being based on a creative new claim by Paula Strudwick: 'He promised to marry me.'[5]

There was plenty more in this vein, and not only on the front pages of the tabloids. Some of the serious broadsheets lost their balance too, a prime example being the *Independent*, whose lead story suggested that I had visited the Paris Ritz to arrange nuclear arms deals for the Iraqis via Saudi Arabia ('shurely shome mishtake here', as *Private Eye* might have put it) and whose inside-page profile of me concluded with this paragraph: 'Since we no longer use words like bounder, rogue and cad, other words are needed to describe him. In the language of our time, Jonathan Aitken is a total shit.'[6] Such restrained editorial comments brought to mind the passage from Lord Macaulay's essay on Lord Byron which begins, 'We know of no spectacle so ridiculous as the British public in one of its periodical fits of morality.'[7]

The fits of morality that swept over some journalists in the last few days of June 1997 looked ridiculous too, as they forgot their own forgeries and other transgressions; republished stories they knew had already been proved untrue; and rushed with chequebooks to the housemaids, cooks, bottlewashers, or any other sources who could come up with a good 'kick Aitken when he's down' story. The fictions that were published about me in this period could have filled a large novel, so I tried not to fret about such froth and bubble and to concentrate instead on the essentials.

The first essential decision I had to make concerned Alan Rusbridger's perjury charge initiative, which was being fuelled by hysterical media speculation that I was 'doing a Lord Lucan', 'never coming back to Britain', and 'becoming a fugitive from justice'.[8] As it happened, one or two of my American friends seriously urged me to start thinking along these lines. 'It's obviously a barbaric atmosphere over there. You'll never get a fair trial, let alone a fair shake from the British press. So stay here for the next year or two until it fades away,' advised one New York lawyer. His views were echoed by other friends who offered to arrange jobs, green-card work permits and financial backing for me in the US.

Not for one second did I listen to these siren voices with any seriousness. 'England is my country,' I explained to them. 'Even if I get the roughest of rough rides there, and the *Guardian* succeeds in getting me jailed, I'm going back, and not only because of my family. I love England, warts and all, and I can't think of anything worse than to live in exile.'

Expressing such a view in New York was no answer to the continuing media squawks in London to the effect that I was being 'hunted' by Scotland Yard detectives who wished to arrest, or at least question, me in connection with the *Guardian*'s perjury charge campaign. So I decided to go back and face the music immediately. But who were the musicians and were they really dancing to the *Guardian*'s tune? I asked my secretary, Lynn Fox, to telephone the Metropolitan Police and let them know that I would return by appointment as soon as they wanted to see me, although preferably after the end of my holiday with William. 'Tell them I may be hiding from the press but I am certainly not hiding from the police,' I said.

Lynn relayed this message to a pleasant Detective Superintendent at Scotland Yard, who responded by saying that I could have all the holiday I liked. 'And by the way, tell him not to worry too much,' were the final words of this officer's conversation.[9] It was the first of many clues that the police had markedly less enthusiasm for the perjury investigation than the journalists who were promoting it.

My next essential decision concerned the Privy Council. According to the *Guardian* and other papers, various anonymous voices from the elder statesman establishment were calling for my resignation from this institution, to which one is appointed for life. It did not take long for me to come round to the same view. Without any soul-searching, I recognized that I was so badly at fault for having told lies on oath in court that I could not, in all conscience, retain my title of 'Right Honourable' or my membership of the body which, in the mists of Britain's unwritten constitution, still remains the most eminent group of state advisers to the monarch.

Having resolved these thoughts in my mind, on Monday 23 June I telephoned Nigel Nicholls, the Clerk of the Privy Council, and told him of my wish to resign. I knew Nigel fairly well, for in his previous incarnation he had been a senior civil servant at the MOD, working with me on aviation matters in my days as Minister of State for Defence. To my surprise, Nigel seemed to be urging caution. 'I must emphasize that there is no pressure from anyone here for you to take this step,' he told me after checking back with the mysterious upper echelons of the Privy Council.

'Thank you, but I've made my decision – how do I implement it?' I replied, extracting from him the appropriate form of words. The following day I sent him this fax:

From: Jonathan Aitken

To: N. H. Nicholls CBE, Clerk of the Privy Council

24th June 1997

Dear Mr Nicholls

I am writing, with deep personal sadness, to resign from the Privy Council. I would be grateful if the Queen would consent to the removal of my name from the list of Privy Councillors.

May I also take this opportunity to express my profound regrets and apologies for having created the circumstances in which I believe it is right for me to resign.

Yours sincerely

Jonathan Aitken[10]

On 26 June my resignation was formally accepted at a meeting of the Privy Council presided over, in the Queen's absence in Canada, by the Prince of Wales and the Duke of York. The announcement in the *London Gazette* was greeted with glee by the *Guardian*: 'EX-MP EXITS INTO THE RANKS OF THE PROCURERS AND FRAUDS' was their headline,[11] accompanied by a story pointing out that I was only the third member of the Privy Council to resign in the twentieth century, the other two being John Profumo and John Stonehouse.

Having completed these formalities, I knew that I had left public life for ever. It was a heartbreaking move. I said as much to various friends on the telephone, several of whom kept urging me, 'Don't give up ... don't quit ... don't let go of your fighting spirit ... this witch-hunt will soon blow over...' I now know that these almost hourly exhortations were being delivered in a co-ordinated effort to prevent me from lurching in a downward spiral of depression towards suicide. 'Don't do anything silly, will you?' was how many of these calls ended.

'Of course not,' was my autopilot response, delivered calmly through my lips, but felt uncertainly in my heart. For the truth was that the savagery of the media onslaught had torn and lacerated every fibre of my being. I was in shock and in pain. Inevitably I had sleepless nights, tossings and turnings of agony, long hours of bitter self-recrimination, and the blackest descent into misery I had ever known.

In the depths of such suffering, the chances of my 'doing something silly' were dangerously high. There were mad moments, such as a 4 a.m. walk around the reservoir in Central Park, when I fleetingly considered throwing myself into its dark waters, or when I stared with tearful and transfixed eyes at my bottle of Temazepan sleeping pills, wondering if I should swig them all down with a bottle of Scotch and so put a merciful end to my merciless torment.

Yet terrible though these lonely days after the libel case were, the edge of the precipice was always a few feet away. I was physically disorientated by sleeplessness, extended jet lag, weird walks through the streets of Manhattan at strange hours, missed meals, and several near collapses into total exhaustion, yet I never completely lost my mental or spiritual bearings. What helped me to hang on, and gradually to start recovering, was a personal prescription which I subsequently labelled the 'three Fs' – faith, family and friends.

The first of these three Fs might initially just as well have been called 'failure', for at the beginning of my post-trial ordeal my faith seemed to be letting me down badly. The problem was that I wanted to pray but found I simply could not do so. My emotions were too shocked, my thoughts were too confused and my concentration was too wandering for any meaningful dialogue with the Almighty to take place. Nevertheless, I kept on trying, at least to the extent of going to one New York church after another, kneeling down, telling God I was sorry, asking for his help and then waiting for something to happen – which it did not.

On one of these slightly unhinged ecclesiastical visits, a priest came over to me and asked if he could be of any assistance. At first I resisted this offer of help. But as the American pastor sat silently in prayer beside me, I backed off from my boorish behaviour and gave him a three-minute trailer of my troubles, adding that right now just about the worst of them was that I simply could not find the words with which to pray.

'Don't worry about the words,' said this kindly counsellor, 'you will have to be patient and wait for God to speak to you. But, in the meantime, if you need to fill the space of your impatience with words, try reading some Psalms to yourself. They contain the finest prayers in the world and they'll show you that there is nothing new in your sins, and nothing in them that a loving God will not forgive. You might like to start with Psalm 51.'

A few minutes after this recommendation, I went into a nearby bookstore and bought a copy of the Psalter. However, before I had time to read the first, let alone the fifty-first, Psalm I found myself engulfed in a media-created family crisis. This one started because a social acquaintance of my mother's from Ibiza, Danae Brook, had dropped in to offer her sympathy. My mother had talked emotionally about her thoughts on the disaster to her friend, not understanding that Ms Brook was a freelance journalist who was to publish her comments as an 'interview' on the front page of the *Mail on Sunday*.

The pain that was caused by the publication of what my mother thought were her private musings – many of them unfairly critical of Lolicia – about our marriage was devastating. I had to spend most of the next two days on the telephone, calming down a justifiably incandescent Lolicia, engaging in a damage limitation exercise with my mother, and reassuring our children that the family was not on the verge of civil war. I would come off the telephone from these conversations dripping in sweat and sometimes in tears. Yet whatever could be said about the conduct of others in this subplot of the drama, the heart of the matter was that I was the one who was ultimately to blame for the entire mess, both inside and outside the family.

Despite these and other moments of turbulence, all my nearest and dearest relatives – including Lolicia and my mother – were towers of strength to me in the darkest hours of the crisis, none more so than our three teenage children. It is a seminal moment in the life of a family when a father needs to lean for support and comfort on his children rather than the other way round. The libel case result had so devastatingly reversed this natural order that suddenly I was the weakest and most vulnerable member of our brood. I did not fully understand this, but our children did and they rallied to my battered corner with a loyalty which was wonderful in the circumstances, since they had themselves become targets and quarries in the latest phase of the Aitken media hunt.

Soon after Alan Rusbridger's letter to the DPP had been published, formally lodging the accusation that Victoria had been a criminal conspirator with me in what he called 'a well-laid and carefully co-ordinated conspiracy to pervert the course of justice',[12] other newspapers started to chase her for interviews and photographs. It did not take the tabloid press long to track Victoria down to her German boarding school, Schule Schloss Stein, near Munich, and to set up a stakeout at the gates of this hitherto tranquil establishment. 'Daddy, we're really under siege here,' was Victoria's refrain in the two or three telephone calls she and Alexandra made to me in New York every day. Most of the girls' conversations were devoted to the proposition that their father needed cheering up, an activity which they made successful by the infectious laughter and excitement with which they described their 'secret escape plan'.

After several days of media surveillance outside Schule Schloss Stein had produced no pictures and no interviews, the intrepid guardians of the public interest attempted one break-in (foiled) and many bribes (refused). 'Helge and some of the other girls have been offered 5000 Deutschmarks[13] for stories about us, but they're all snubbing the reporters. Everyone's on our side,' enthused Alexandra.

With mounting excitement, the siege continued for a week, until it was foiled through a joint decoy exercise by pupils, teachers and parents at the school. The gist of the plan, which was exercised with Teutonic military efficiency, was that the British journalists were distracted by the German schoolchildren, while the Aitken daughters escaped out of a back entrance and were guided through a hidden path in the woods to a waiting getaway car driven by a Bavarian countess. It sounded like one of those ripping wartime escape-from-Colditz yarns but, on this occasion, with the Germans as the resistance heroes and the British reporters in the role of the bamboozled SS guards. Anyway, it worked and the girls were successfully spirited away to the hospitable homes of other European friends, where they were eventually reunited with Lolicia.

Meanwhile, back at Eton, a school well trained in protecting another William's privacy, our William was having an easier time of it – until the last day of term, when the tabloid vultures swooped on his house. However, the House Captain Ed Haughey, son of Ireland's Senator Edward Haughey, had devised an Etonian escape plot which, in the planning stages, involved a dawn exit, a helicopter ride to Belfast and then an Aer Lingus flight from Dublin to New York ticketed under the misspelt name of W. Aiken. With variations involving other friends and parents, this plan worked too, leaving the reporters empty handed save for one headline, 'AITKEN'S SON FLEES ABROAD',[14] which gave no further or better particulars of where 'abroad' was.

My reunion with William in New York was an emotional event for both of us, but one which led on to much greater intimacy and mutual understanding. My immediate problem was this: What on earth do you say to a 14-year-old son injured in a train wreck if you have been the train driver? I rehearsed all sorts of lines, but in the end I just ran to him the moment I saw him on the Park Avenue sidewalk, hugged him and said, 'I love you … I'm so sorry for everything…' To which he replied, 'I love you too, Daddy,' words which were balm to the soul of the Prodigal Father.

William and I had a delightful week together in New York, talking the nights away, television-watching, sightseeing, cinema-going and dining out with friends in restaurants. Our principal Good Samaritan in this period was Larry Strenger, a Manhattan corporate lawyer who had been a family friend from the day we first met as protagonists in an Oxford University versus Columbia University student debating competition in September 1964. Almost 33 years later, it was Larry who devoted most of his time to binding up my wounds, pouring oil on my troubles and wine down my thirsty throat, and paying money to many an innkeeper for the meals we enjoyed together.

For obvious geographical reasons, I was seeing mainly American friends at this time, but the transatlantic telephone lines were red hot with calls from my close friends in Britain – Malcolm Pearson, Richard Shepherd, Paul Johnson, Erik Bennett, Alan Duncan, John Aspinall, Wafic Said and others, all of whom kept asking the question, 'Is there anything we can do?' My most frequent reply was, 'Please keep an eye on my mother.' This they generously did by visiting her, taking her out for meals and steering her through the shoals of her own maternal worries and anxieties.

I reflected much on the concept of friendship at this time, not least because one or two journalists back in Britain were suggesting that I had lost all my friends along with the libel case and that there was no sympathy for me in any quarter. As an *Evening Standard* columnist put it, 'Try saying the following sentence out loud: "I feel sorry for Jonathan Aitken" – saying it, that is, without laughing or throwing up. It's impossible of course. The answer to the question, "Should we feel sorry for Jonathan Aitken" is NO in one hundred foot letters of fire.'[15]

This may have been the opinion of one school of thought in the London media, but it was not a universally held view. I knew this not only because of the rock-solid fidelity of my closest friends, but also because of the astonishing flood of mail that came in during the weeks after the case had collapsed.

It is an old axiom of politics that when you win you hear from everybody, but when you lose you hear only from your friends. If that was true, then I had more friends than I had ever dreamt of, because the letters I received were overwhelming both in quantity and in the quality of the sympathy they expressed. Over the next three months I answered well over a thousand of these kind correspondents in my own hand. A small number of these letters were from what I called my 'hoops of steel' group, after Shakespeare's lines:

The friends thou hast, and their adoption tried,
Grapple them to thy soul with hoops of steel.[16]

An infinitely greater number came from that wider circle of friendly acquaintances whom I knew from politics, business or social life. Yet the largest and most surprising category of letter came from complete strangers, or people I had tangentially met perhaps once or twice. Why so many of them should have taken the trouble to write to me was a mystery, but it was a profoundly comforting one. At a time when I was myself starting to believe the media assertions to the effect that I was a disgraced pariah, a ruined exile, a broken man, a complete shit, etc., etc., day after day there arrived in the post these wonderful letters offering sympathy, support, prayers, hope, love, the view that the *Guardian* had gone completely over the top with their propaganda against me, and the hope that, whatever happened, I would find the strength to weather the storm. Those letters helped me greatly in that storm-weathering process.

Although the media noise gradually quietened, I became conscious that some of it had merely gone underground. One sign that I was still being hunted came when American Express called to say that computer hackers had broken into the records of my credit card transactions. Another was the trickle of information that reporters had physically turned up in at least a dozen locations where I had been 'sighted' – among them Jimmy Goldsmith's estate in Mexico, Lucia Santa Cruz's farm in Chile, Henry Kissinger's country house in Connecticut, and Peter Janson's mansion in Melbourne. What these wild-goose chases cost, and whose reliable information initiated them, must have required interesting memorandums of explanation to the accounts departments of the various newspapers concerned.

At first I was amused by the absurdity of these media pursuits, but gradually I grew dismayed by them, especially when it became clear that telephone tapping was part of someone's agenda. One night a pair of British reporters showed up at the apartment block where

William and I were staying, equipped with a record of my calls from my host's telephone number and asking many unpleasant questions. A well-trained concierge ejected them in a cloud of misinformation, but their visit showed that the hounds were hot on my trail, baying for even more of my blood. Maybe I was starting to suffer from paranoia, but I had learned the hard way that some journalists will stop at nothing in pursuit of a story. This time around I had no defences left and no place to hide.

In fact, I did find somewhere to hide, at least for the next couple of weeks. With the help of some ingeniously anonymous travel arrangements made by Larry Strenger, William and I set off to one of the remotest parts of the US: Sonoma County, California. I had been in those parts 12 months earlier as Henry Kissinger's guest at the Bohemian Grove Club in the wilderness of the redwood forests around Monte Rio. This time I picked another Sonoma County wilderness, a 5,000-acre estate on the Pacific coast known as Sea Ranch. Renting a log cabin there overlooking the ocean, I settled down to ponder on the future of my life.

CHAPTER EIGHTEEN

Stirrings of the Soul

To be, or not to be: that is the question...[1]

THE OPENING WORDS OF Hamlet's soliloquy as he contemplates the option of suicide were mirrored in many of my thoughts and emotions as I gazed out over the Pacific Ocean in July 1997, growing increasingly despondent about the disaster that had engulfed me.

One of my negative voices kept proclaiming that life was no longer worth living. There was ample evidence to support this view. My humiliation had already been devastating, but the worst was yet to come. To judge by the tone of their continuing attacks, the *Guardian* and its allies were in a pitiless mood and would stop at nothing until their campaign to put me behind bars had succeeded. My marriage was on the rocks and so were my finances. I had no career or employment prospects. All that lay ahead was an unending vista of media tortures, legal nightmares, money crises, family upheavals and jail. It was hardly surprising that in such circumstances the satanic option of suicide should have boiled once again to the surface of my troubled mind.

A perfect spot for the deed presented itself less than a mile from our rented log cabin, where the Northern California coastline rose into a promontory of high cliffs extending far out into the ocean. Early one morning, after a sleepless night, I climbed to the top of the highest of these cliffs, stared down at the rocks some 200 feet below me, and felt seriously tempted to throw myself into the swirling seas around them. It was a moment of madness which quickly passed, as did other deranged thoughts at this time, such as swimming out into the Pacific never to return, or swallowing all my sleeping pills in one go. Dramatic though these recollections may look in cold print, the episodes themselves were too momentary to be close calls in hot blood. The decent pulls of sanity and commitment to family were always stronger than the fleeting urge to self-destruction. I soon turned away from the suicide scenario, a change of mood attributable to an unlikely quartet of influences – Richard Nixon, William Aitken, King David and C. S. Lewis.

I had known Richard Nixon as well as anyone outside his own family in the last years of his life because of the intimacy that developed between us when I was writing his biography. In March 1992, when the book was completed but still unpublished, I went to see him at his home in New Jersey for a farewell call to thank him for the co-operation he had given me. Having listened to my words of gratitude, Mr Nixon started asking impossible questions. 'How many copies do you think it will sell?' 'Do you think it will get good reviews?'

After trying to deal with these inquiries I finally said to him, 'Well, Mr President, I hope the readers and reviewers will think that my book is a full and fair portrait of you, but, whatever they say, you and I will know that it has been a failure.'

At this point President Nixon became extremely nervous. He crossed and uncrossed his legs several times, shifted around in his chair and looked at me as though I were Woodward or Bernstein.[2] Finally he said, 'Your book a failure? What do you mean, a failure?'[3]

'Well, Mr President,' I replied, 'after working hard for over four years, studying you and your life story, I have come to the conclusion that you are far too complicated a character to be captured by the pen of a mere mortal writer.'

At this, a great, wolfish grin spread over Richard Nixon's face as he said, 'Aha! Now you're really getting somewhere.'

One of the few uncomplicated traits in Nixon's character had been his resilience in adversity. This quality shone through his life, from his childhood brushes with TB (which carried off two of his brothers) to his defeats for the Presidency in 1960 and for the Governorship of California in 1962, and finally during Watergate. At the height of that tragedy, he consoled himself by reciting *The Ballad of Sir Andrew Barton*:

I am hurt but I am not slain
I'll lay me down and bleed awhile
Then I'll rise and fight again.[4]

That was exactly what Nixon himself did, fighting back from the nadir of his resignation to unprecedented eminence as America's most respected foreign policy expert. In my biographer's travels I had come to know other Nixon alumni, who rebuilt their lives to impressive new heights after serving prison sentences, among them H. R. Haldeman, Egil 'Bud' Krogh and Charles Colson. I tried to call Colson from California, but was disappointed to be told by his office that he was 'travelling overseas'. Yet even without being able to make human contact with any of these phoenixes who had risen from the ashes of Watergate, their message was clear: with courage and vision, the man who does not give up can always start up again.

Another strong influence on me for not giving up was the presence at Sea Ranch of my son William. I did my utmost not to let him share in my 'black dog' moods of despair by keeping both of us busily active. So we filled our days with tennis, swimming, long walks, GCSE Latin coaching, television-watching, cookouts, and regular trips to the foodstores, restaurants and video shops of the nearby town of Gualala. Yet even in this ceaseless round of activity, William could not fail to catch glimpses of my distress. One night, as we were consuming our hamburgers and Budweiser beers under a spectacularly clear Milky Way in the heavens above us, I asked him obliquely whether he thought his own life and future career might have rather better prospects if he was not encumbered with the burden of a disgraced father hovering in the background.

'Don't be a chump, Daddy,' he replied. 'Even the *Guardian* can't keep you in the doghouse for ever. You'll find plenty to do. Besides, I need you.'

'Out of the mouth of babes and sucklings hast thou ordained strength' (Psalm 8:2 KJV). Thanks to the advice of the priest in New York, I was now reading through the Psalms of David in my long hours of sleeplessness. The more I studied the Psalms, the more I found them an incomparable treasure-house of hope and encouragement. One of their most compelling messages is that there is nothing new under the sun in the human condition. King David himself appears to have had more than his fair share of dark sins and darker periods of despair, yet his total reliance on God always pulled him through, often with a refreshed and quietened soul.

My starting point in these readings was that great penitential cri de coeur, Psalm 51, which had been recommended by the Manhattan pastor. It became a turning point in my journey because of its clarion call to face up to guilt, repent, and accept God's promise of receiving forgiveness through faith.

The background to the Psalm is that King David had been caught out by Nathan the Prophet committing a series of reprehensible crimes which made mine look like pinching an extra lump of sugar at a vicarage tea party. King David had engaged in an adulterous betrayal of one of his officers, followed by a devious and escalating cover-up which culminated in murder, followed by marriage to the murdered officer's widow. But having been unexpectedly caught out, David faced up to his guilt, confessed all and threw himself on God's mercy in trusting faith.

> *Have mercy on me, O God,*
> *according to your unfailing love;*
> *according to your great compassion*

blot out my transgressions.

Wash away all my iniquity

and cleanse me from my sin

(VV. 1-2 NIV)

begins Psalm 51, going on to acknowledge the burden of guilt and the pain of penitence with lines of confession for having done 'what is evil in your sight' and agony for 'the bones you have crushed'. Eventually King David asks for divine therapy:

Create in me a pure heart, O God,

and renew a steadfast spirit within me.

Do not cast me from your presence

or take your Holy Spirit from me.

Restore to me the joy of your salvation

and grant me a willing spirit, to sustain me.

(VV. 10-12 NIV)

From my childhood years as a choirboy to my middle-aged years as a churchwarden, I must have sung or spoken those verses dozens, if not hundreds, of times, yet never before had they held me in thrall as they did when I read and re-read them in our log cabin at Sea Ranch, California. Somehow or other I absorbed them into my heart and trustingly believed the messages of repentance, forgiveness, change and confidence in God's love which run through this and many other Psalms.

As I went through the Psalter time and again, the one piece of advice which struck home more than any other was this: if you are 'going through the vale of misery *use it for a well*' (Psalm 84:6, *The Book of Common Prayer*). Taking this to mean that the miserable man should dig deep into the causes of his well of unhappiness, I began to think and read intensively about the themes of repentance and redemption. My reading list was not a long one, for there was only one bookshop in the great metropolis of Gualala (population 961, according to its signpost), but I did buy the C. S. Lewis classic *Mere Christianity*, and came across this passage in a chapter headed 'The Perfect Penitent':

Now repentance is no fun at all. It is something much harder than merely eating humble pie. It means unlearning all the self-conceit and self-will that we have been training ourselves into for thousands of years. It means killing part of yourself, undergoing a kind of death. In fact, it needs a good man to repent. And here comes the catch. Only a bad person needs to repent: only a good person can repent perfectly. The worse you are the more you need it and the less you can do it.[5]

That last sentence really caught my attention, even though I was a most imperfect penitent. For my horizons were lengthening far beyond the sins of the libel case. Those had been bad, but they were merely the symptoms of a more fundamental disease which C. S. Lewis diagnosed as 'self-conceit and self-will'. Unlearning those characteristics was going to require a complete change of direction. Was I capable of it?

At about this time in my nocturnal reading activities I came across the term *metanoia*, which is the New Testament Greek word for 'repentance'. Some scholars think this translation is inadequate. They may be right. In the original Greek, *mete* means 'change' and *noia* means 'mind', so a literal rendering would be a 'change of mind' which, if it was achieved, would also mean a change of heart, life and outlook.

The starting point of my *metanoia* was the rock bottom I had hit in terms of despair. Was I going to collapse at this rock bottom and lie there wallowing in thoughts of suicide, self-pity and sadness? Or was I going to get up and change direction in the spirit of *metanoia*? Although the choice looks obvious now, it was a difficult one to make at the time because I was paralysed by depression. The two engines that eventually pulled me out of the slough of despond were the glory of the natural world and the power of prayer.

It is difficult to stay depressed when all nature is rejoicing around you. Northern California in high summer is an extraordinarily beautiful environment with some of the most attractive flora and fauna in the world. Yet for all the eagles, roe deer, songbirds, redwood trees, long grasses, colourful wildflowers, sandy beaches and rolling billows of the Pacific, what touched me most was the stillness and the silence.

'Nothing in all creation is so like God as stillness,' wrote the fourteenth-century German mystic Meister Eckhart. Six centuries on, I was captivated by a similar thought as I spent my early mornings watching the sun rise over the redwood forests with not so much as a murmur from the sounds of man or his machines anywhere near me. In that enormous silence I became more and more still myself, finding peace and humility as I acknowledged my minuscule insignificance compared to the splendour and majesty of God's creation. In one such moment of solitude I thought I could sense the mystery of the divine presence somewhere close at hand. Soon afterwards the gentle electricity of prayerfulness reconnected itself inside me and I was once more able to listen, ask, seek and knock.

After I began praying again there were some interesting developments. On the physical front, I slept better, walked longer distances, laughed more at William's corny jokes, and became increasingly competitive in our tennis matches. In life's spiritual dimension, there seemed to be a calming of my turmoil. I felt the first stirrings of renewal and the healing balm of God's serenity. I read much Scripture, moving from the Psalms to the Gospels and the Epistles. The Gualala bookshop sold me an orange paperback with the title *The Ways of the Spirit*. This was just the sort of publication which in the past I might well have ridiculed at first glance as 'New Age nonsense'. However, it turned out to be a series of beautifully written retreats given in the 1920s by Evelyn Underhill, an Anglican Doctor of Divinity and a former religious affairs editor of the *Spectator*. Some of her retreat themes, particularly those on adoration, penitence and patience, were a great help to my searchings at this time. These were also strengthened by my own simpler efforts at personal prayer.

Such initial manifestations of *metanoia* were disturbed by the arrival at the Sea Ranch Nature Reservation of a new and hitherto unknown species of nature – British journalists. Tipped off that these invaders were knocking on log cabin doors around Gualala hunting for a tall Englishman and his teenage son, William and I bade a hasty farewell to our wilderness retreat and drove down the coast to San Francisco. Reporters and photographers were waiting for us at the airport. Some of them even managed to travel with us on our homeward-bound but separate flights.

With a little help from some kindly airline staff it proved possible to give these tormentors the slip, but the respite was only temporary. When I returned to England, Lord North Street was besieged around the clock by paparazzi. So was my mother's flat and so was our seaside house at Sandwich Bay. For a few days I hid away from these locations, but my invisibility only increased the interest and the number of the media surveillance teams.

Life was clearly unliveable under these conditions, so I took an initiative which resulted in what became known as 'The Battle of College Green'. The initiative consisted of sending a message to the Press Association stating that, although I would be making no statement and giving no interviews, now that I had returned to England I would make life easier for photographers by giving them a silent photocall on College Green – the lawn opposite the Houses of Parliament. My thinking (which turned out to be right) was that once I had given the paparazzi one big omnium-gatherum photo opportunity, their sieges and stakeouts would become pointless.

At the appointed hour, I walked towards College Green accompanied by my solicitor Richard Sykes and my driver Alan Woods. Both are men of large build, which was just as well because, when we were still a good 75 yards away from the rendezvous point, I heard a loud shout, 'It's him!' The cry might just have well have been 'Tally Ho!' because immediately over 150 journalists came charging towards me with lights, ladders, sound booms, microphones, tape recorders, television cameras, still cameras and all the impedimenta of modern mass communication. Within seconds I was engulfed in a frenzied media melee which quickly turned vicious as rival cameramen jostled, kicked and even punched each other as they literally fought for the best snap of the day.

It soon became apparent that I was never going to reach College Green. Indeed, there was some doubt as to whether I was going to be able to remain standing upright. 'If this is how you're going to behave, then I'm going back,' I was reported as saying to no one in particular. Unfortunately, going back was impossible too, because the road behind me, like the route ahead of me, was jammed solid. For the next five minutes my position resembled that of the embattled centurion in Macaulay's *Lays of Ancient Rome*, to whom 'those behind cried "Forward!" And those before cried "Back!"'[6]

The mob was now growing as more journalists, curious spectators, innocent bystanders and even a bemused group of Japanese tourists swelled the throng. As the column lurched unsteadily away from College Green in the direction of Lord North Street, the television camera crews were getting particularly savage with each other. ITN's Political Editor, Michael Brunson, received a blow which sent him crashing backwards onto the pavement of Great Peter Street. I caught a glimpse of him waving his arms and legs in the air like a giant turtle turned the wrong way up. Meanwhile, fists were flying between various paparazzi combatants, many of whom kept bellowing commands such as, 'Turn this way, Jonathan!', 'Give us a big smile!', 'To your right!', 'To your left!', 'Look happy!' or, best of all, 'Snarl please!'

Keeping calm amidst this tumult was not easy, but, with the help of bodyguards Sykes and Woods, I eventually reached my front door. One infuriated reporter shouted, 'So what's been the point of all this?'

'To try and be helpful to you,' I replied.[7]

When I reached the sanctuary of my house, a handful of hardened Aitken-hunters stood on the doorstep for an hour or so intermittently chanting, 'Out, out, out!', 'Goodbye, goodbye!' and other less edifying slogans. But they had their photographs, and after these had been published in the next day's newspapers I was left alone by the media for most of the summer.

I spent the month of August in relative seclusion at Sandwich Bay. Much of my time was spent answering the tidal wave of sympathetic correspondence which continued to flow in through my mailbox. Anyone who ever feels inclined to express some kindness to a fellow human being who is in trouble may like to know how much such letters can help the healing process. I was deeply touched by the compassion of my known and unknown correspondents in this period. Often my daily postbag moved me to tears, and it never failed to uplift my spirits.

If I had to pick out a single letter which helped me more than any other, it would be the one which came from Charles Colson. When I had been trying to reach him by telephone from California, he had been vacationing in London where, like all readers of the British press in late June of 1997, he had been inundated with articles on the awfulness of Aitken. A few days later, having returned to Washington, he wrote me this letter:

Prison Fellowship International
Washington DC
USA

2nd July 1997

Dear Jonathan

I was passing through the UK last week, picked up a newspaper and read of your troubles. I just want you to know that my heart goes out to you, that you're in my prayers and that I consider myself your friend. I hope, therefore, that you will let me know if there is anything I can do to help.

I think I got to know you quite well during our many meetings together. I was greatly impressed with your energy, vision and with your character. I believed then that you were a man destined for greatness in public life. And I still do. It may not be in the areas that you and I thought likely, but it will be in something, perhaps even more significant than you had imagined.

I say that for two reasons. The first is that good men, dare I say great men, are only strengthened when they go through a breaking experience. One has to only look at our mutual friend Richard Nixon for the best evidence of this. And my life certainly stands for that proposition, if it stands for anything.

Greatness is made not in the easy things of life; greatness is made when men of character and strength can respond to and overcome the obstacles that are put before every one of us.

Your greatest test will be right now, Jonathan. You can let circumstances shatter you, as I saw you quoted in the press, or you can decide that adversity will be your greatest blessing.

The second reason I believe you will overcome this, is that through this I believe you will find the great truth of life. It isn't in the things of this world, it is in the human soul. And adversity as the Bible tells us can only strengthen us, God uses these things to chasten whom He loves.

Of course all of this depends upon whether through this experience you come to trust totally and completely in Christ. As you know I have looked back on Watergate and thank God for it. Through that crucible I came to know Christ personally and discovered that in the darkest moments of my life He was working to produce what I would later see as the greatest blessings of my life.

I love what Solzhenitsyn wrote from the gulag. He was in prison for ten years, yet he could say – and this is a paraphrase – bless you prison, bless you, for there lying on the rotting prison straw I came to realise that the object of life is not prosperity as we are made to believe, but the maturing of the human soul.

So I do pray that this terribly difficult experience will be used first to strengthen you and your character and second will be used by our gracious God for His purposes to bring blessings to others. Don't let this break you, this is where everything you hold dear and believe in is being tested most. Talk to the Lord. He knows your heart better than you know it yourself. Trust in Him and you will rise from this stronger than ever.

If I can be of any help or of encouragement, please don't hesitate to get in touch. I've been where you now are. God bless you.

Yours in His service,

Chuck[8]

This letter, especially the arresting phrase in its final paragraph, 'I've been where you now are', made a great impact on me. Colson had also drunk deeply of the cup of political disgrace. Yet his roller-coaster ride from the White House to Holabird Federal Penitentiary had not been the most dramatic event of his life. Far more important, and just as well publicized, had been his conversion to a life of Christian service. His achievements for the Prison Fellowship Ministry which he founded had brought hope and redemption for many thousands of prisoners, both in the USA and in 80 other countries around the world. Moreover, Colson's spiritual journey as described in *Born Again*, *Loving God* and a score of further best-sellers had been a beacon of inspiration to uncountable numbers of his readers who had drawn strength from it in their times of adversity.

As I sat in Sandwich Bay wrestling with my own adversities, I kept reading and re-reading Chuck Colson's letter because several of his challenging phrases nagged away at me with difficult questions. Had I been totally broken by the debacle of the libel case, or could I be strengthened by this severe test? What was Solzhenitsyn getting at in those comments about the blessing of prison? Above all, did I really 'trust totally and completely in Christ'?

There were no quick or easy responses to these questions, but I knew I would like to discover the answers to them. So I thought, prayed and read about these subjects all through the summer. I was helped along the road of my quest by one or two Sandwich friends such as Pip and Patricia Lavers, Maureen Collins, E. W. 'Jim' and Ann Swanton, and especially by my parish priest Mark Roberts and his deaconess wife Jasmine. Mark and Jasmine encouraged me to borrow many challenging books from their rectory library, including *The Imitation of Christ* by Thomas à Kempis (a difficult classic which I came to love); *With Pity Not With Blame* by Robert Llewelyn; *Crossfire* by Richard Holloway; and several works by Archbishop William Temple, among them his *Readings from St John's Gospel* and

Palm Sunday to Easter. In this last book I was much struck by a wonderful Temple passage on penitence:

It is penitence which creates intimacy with our Lord. No one can know Him intimately who has not realised the sickness of his own soul and obtained healing from the physician of souls. Our virtues do not bring us near to Christ – the gulf between them and His holiness remains unbridgeable. Our science does not bring us near Him, nor our art. Our pain may give us a taste of fellowship with Him but it is only a taste unless that great creator of intimacy – penitence – is also there.[9]

By the early autumn I was moving in the direction of this intimacy through penitence. The high-blown pride that in the past had caused me to live in one direction while praying in another had subsided. Prayer life and real life were fusing together in a way that both excited and frightened me by the stirrings of the soul that were going on within. I was excited because the *metanoia* process was clearly working, pulling me by some mysterious power towards the brink of a commitment to Christ which I knew I wanted to make. Yet I was also frightened by the prospect of setting sail into these unknown waters. I was scared of drowning in them because of my own inadequacies of faith and character. I was afraid of the winds of ridicule which were certain to blow in my direction from ill-wishers and even from patronizing well-wishers, whom I could hear saying, 'Poor old Jonathan – lost his marbles, I'm afraid – he's got religion.' Above all, I was terrified of my own unworthiness and unseaworthiness for the voyage ahead.

For some reason or other, I kept using the analogy of the sea as I hesitated over daring to start the next phase of my inner journey. This may have been because I love the sea and so much enjoyed living beside it, watching its moods and changes every day.

One afternoon in September, I took a long walk along the coast towards Dover. The Channel was blowing up rough, and as I climbed up the cliff paths near St Margaret's Bay and the South Foreland I looked out towards the storm-tossed Goodwin Sands. Then there came to me the memory of a local legend about the coxswain of one of the East Kent lifeboats in the nineteenth century.

The story goes that on a night of terrible weather a schooner was wrecked on the Goodwins. Its distress rockets were clearly visible, so the lifeboat prepared to launch. But when the lifeboatmen saw the fury of the tempest, some of them got cold feet. They began to argue whether it was right for them to risk their lives on such a violent night. 'In this storm we won't get back,' they said.

At this point in the story the coxswain of the lifeboat rallied his men with the words, 'We have to get out, we don't have to get back!' The lifeboat was launched and successfully carried out one of the most heroic rescues in the history of the Goodwin Sands.

I do not know why this tale suddenly floated out of my memory on this particular afternoon, but it did. Like the lifeboatmen who faltered, I did not like the look of the storms ahead of me. I was afraid. Yet at the same time I could recognize my own distress signals. So I had to get launched; I had to get out. Whether I drowned or got back would depend on a power far greater than my own.

CHAPTER NINETEEN

Deep Calls to Deep

HAVING DECIDED TO LAUNCH the battered ship of my soul into the deeper waters of the sea of faith, I soon discovered that I was pitifully short of plans for how to navigate in them.

Some fortunate believers evidently find it simple to steer towards salvation. They talk with confidence about how they have 'seen the light', 'formed a personal relationship with Jesus', and 'been saved'. I respected such fast-track conversions, but because of the heavy barnacles of sinfulness still stuck on my conscience, I felt that if I set my compass towards similar havens of redemption the voyage would be a rougher, longer and slower haul. This was frustrating at first because I was impatient to achieve 'results'. I was also under the erroneous impression that such results would be related to the work I put in at the traditional disciplines of prayer, meditation and Bible study. I therefore made the mistake of trying to do too much too soon, until another letter from Chuck Colson calmed me down with these wise words:

I would have to say that the process of metanoia is always a gradual one. Somehow we think of conversions as being instantaneous. The moment when God regenerates us is. There is certainty about the fact that we are now His. But the conversion, that is the transformation from the old man to the new man, sometimes takes us a long while. There are lots of struggles that we inevitably go through. That is particularly true for strong willed,

able individuals like you and me. We have been so accustomed to thinking
that we can do it on our own that it is very hard to release everything and
simply trust God. But that is precisely what we must do. And we only learn
to do that as we stumble and often grope in the dark. Don't be impatient
with yourself...'

Learning to be patient became one of the hardest struggles of my
new journey. Throughout my career I had been in one long, energetic rush to set agendas, achieve targets, make deliveries ahead
of schedule, claim the first-past-the-post winner's bonus, and then
accelerate ahead to the next milestone. This style of existence had
been exciting but ultimately unfulfilling. Long before my world fell
apart I knew that there should be more to life than the onwards-and-
upwards drive of the ambitious careerist. Now that the pace of my life
had slowed from a sprint to an amble, I had the time to discover what
that phrase 'more to life' might mean. Gradually I came to recognize
that if I wanted it to mean anything at all in the spiritual domain of
God's work, that could only be started when the fever of impatience
had been conquered.

The message that I must quell my impatience was reinforced by
what I can only describe as a supernatural experience. It happened on an
early autumn walk along the beach at Sandwich Bay. The weather was
idyllic, for it was an indian summer of an afternoon. The westering sun
was blazing as if it was still July, while on the eastern horizon a pale
September moon was beginning to rise over the Channel. There was
not a cloud in the sky or a breath of wind on the sea. Only the tiniest of
waves were trickling in over the sands, burbling contentedly like babies
at play, reminding me of a line from Keats which describes the sea as 'an
untumultuous line of silver foam'. The beach was totally deserted and I
was a good two miles from the nearest house, so I was able to drink in
this beautiful moment of maritime solitude with deep contentment.

Suddenly, yet quietly, I became aware of someone else's presence
on the beach. For a moment I thought I heard the crunch of footsteps

on the shingle behind me, but when I turned round no one was there. But someone was – I sensed them, strongly at first, and then over-whelmingly. Again I looked around, particularly on my right, for the presence felt as though it had drawn alongside me, but all I could see was the sun, whose rays seemed to be blazing even more intensely.

'Slow down,' said a gentle voice somewhere inside my head. It was not an audible or even a human voice, but I knew it was speaking to me. So I obeyed and slowed my pace.

The next extraordinary happening was that tears started to trickle down my cheeks for no reason at all except that I was feeling blissfully happy. Once again I felt overwhelmed by the invisible presence that was so close to me – in the sun, perhaps, or beside me, or inside me, but undoubtedly right there with me. And then amidst swelling feelings of joy, that gentle voice spoke again, saying words which were very close to this: 'Slow down. The road ahead of you is longer and harder than you think. But keep on it. Keep praying. Keep trying to find the way. Trust, believe, and you will discover the path. Do not worry about your problems. They will test you but I will guide you. I have work for you to do. I will show you the way. I love you.'

Then I shed a few more happy tears, feeling utterly insignificant yet totally protected and loved as this amazing presence gently faded away and I floated back to reality, wondering what on earth had been going on.

When I got back to our house I literally pinched myself to make sure I was still all there and *compos mentis*. The next thing I did was to sit down and write an account of what had happened. Reverting to my most methodical style of record-keeping, I set out every detail I could remember. Getting it all down on paper (including the words spoken to me as best I could recall them) took about three-quarters of an hour. When I read it through I was so astonished that I called Victoria – the only member of the family with me in the house – into my study and read her my description of what had happened. She was almost as amazed as I had been.

'What time was all this?' she asked.

'I noted down the exact time just as I came off the beach and put it down at the top of the page,' I replied. 'It was ten to four.'

'What time is it now?' inquired Victoria.

I looked at my watch, an automatic-winding Platinum Rolex which had never stopped in the 12 or more years I had owned it. On this afternoon it had stopped at precisely 3.50 p.m.

To my rational mind this strange experience was inexplicable. In retrospect I was unnerved by it. Hearing voices and feeling presences were the preserve of saints, surely off-limits for a decidedly unsaintly and worldly ex-politician in disgrace. But I was not mad. Everything else happening in my life was down to earth and normal. Yet on that beach I had heard something, felt something, and my watch had unaccountably stopped. All I could fall back on was the term 'super-natural experience', which gave me little understanding but much food for thought. By the time I returned to London a few days later, I had decided that I must strive to be more patient, recognize that my journey was going to be far longer and more difficult than I had imagined, and pray for guidance.

How to pray was another problem. I was not getting particularly far in solving it until by chance I was brought into a series of prayer partnerships. 'When you start to pray, get yourself some company,' wrote the fifteenth-century mystic St Teresa of Avila. I read her words at about the same time as the latest instalment in our corre-spondence arrived from Chuck Colson, suggesting that I should form a prayer group with Michael Alison, an old friend of his and a former parliamentary colleague of mine.

Although the concept of sharing in oral prayer was alien to me, I felt it might be right. A few weeks earlier I had stumbled into a one-to-one prayer relationship with Mervyn Thomas, the Sales and Marketing Director of Sweet'n'Low plc, the low-calorie sweetener company. On the face of it, Mervyn was an improbable character to become the repository of some of my most intimate confidences of the soul. We came from different social backgrounds, different religious traditions, and had no obvious interests or connections in common. We had corresponded but never met until the late summer of 1997, when he called at my house saying that he had read so much about me in the newspapers that he felt he would like to come and pray with me. I was touched but embarrassed. 'I'll try it once, but I wouldn't like to make this a regular thing,' I told him awkwardly. Yet soon we were meeting two or three times a month, bonding together over prayers and a course of Bible studies.

My Colson-inspired prayer breakfasts were something else again. As Chuck had suggested, I got in touch with Michael Alison. He had been a long-standing friend, though not a particularly close one, in the House of Commons where he had served with distinction as a minister, as Margaret Thatcher's Parliamentary Private Secretary, and as an MP for 33 years until his retirement in 1997. Between us we recruited a further quartet of Christian acquaintances: Alastair Burt, who had been a rising star in the previous Government as Social Security Minister until he lost his seat in the Labour landslide of May 1997; Anthony Cordle, a pastoral adviser with wide-ranging political connections in Westminster and Washington; Tom Benyon, a former MP in the 1980s who now owned an insurance magazine; and Jim Pringle, a retired businessman from Winchester. As we assembled for our first breakfast I was full of misgivings, for I did not feel that we looked like a particularly fraternal or mutually congenial team. How wrong I was.

Over the next few months our Thursday morning prayer break-fasts became a vital and love-giving force in the lives of all six partici-pants.[2] At first we were shy of each other, hesitant at expressing our needs and reluctant to show our feelings – in short, a quintessential group of middle-aged Englishmen. There was initially a tendency to focus the prayers of the group on me as the lame duck so obviously in the worst trouble. But as we gradually opened our hearts to one another in friendship and faith, we not only became a mutual support group for all our respective family and personal problems, we also became increasingly aware of the presence and guidance of God, speaking to us through our prayers and readings of Scripture.

In my case the 30 or so Thursday mornings we spent on an in-depth study of the Sermon on the Mount was a cumulative spiritual experience which I found both humbling and enriching. Coming to realize how little I really knew, understood or practised of this most familiar of Gospel passages, I began to look forward eagerly to the weekly interpretations of whichever verses from it we had reached. Through our combined efforts we could (on our good days) produce an interesting mixture in our discussions of humour, theological scholarship, scriptural knowledge, intellectual argument and personal testimony. As I struggled to try and live the Word as well as hear it, I gradually developed a hunger for seeking God which took me into new territory of the soul.

One of the turning points in this new territory was my participation in a week-long 'Christian Teaching Holiday' at Launde Abbey in Leicestershire. At the last minute I almost dropped out of this gathering on the grounds that it sounded too much like a jolly-hockey-sticks jamboree for retired gentry, only to discover that it was a deeply spiritual gathering of the active intelligentry. The talks we heard from Doctor Graham Scott-Brown, a former medical missionary, the prayers we shared in Launde's sixteenth-century chapel, and the warmth of the friendships I began to build with one or two people who were to become linchpins of my life in the crises of the next few months, were all very deep and very special.

In the afternoons at Launde I went for long walks with Martin Marriott, the recently retired headmaster of Canford School, and his wife Judith. We had never met before, but we struck up a rapport of intimate communication which deepened as both Marriotts intuitively perceived my pain and gently ministered to it.

After one long afternoon of shared confidences walking across the rolling country of the Cottesmore and Pytchley hunts, we came across a sheep caught in a thicket. It turned out to be a ram, trapped in no ordinary tangle, for he had several strands of heavy bramble twisted round his neck which were cutting deep into his flesh. Assuming the role of two RSPCA volunteers, Martin and I tried to free the wounded animal. It would have been a difficult rescue job at the best of times, but without a knife, gloves, or any means of protecting ourselves from the continuous butting and kicking of the far from grateful captive, the task proved almost impossible. Yet after a considerable struggle, and not inconsiderable pain to all three participants, the ram was eventually liberated and bounced joyfully away towards his lambs and his ewes.

'Very symbolic,' said Martin, wiping the blood and thorns from his hands. The symbolism was not lost on Judith either. From that time on, the Aitken–Marriott friendship steadily deepened – so much so that without the growing strength of this relationship with its loving fellowship, laughter, prayer and good companionship, I might well, like that ram, still be trapped in a thicket of unbearable pain.

It was one of the most remarkable aspects of my inner journey that unexpected people kept popping up to offer me their friendship and prayerful support. I jokingly came to call Judith Marriott 'my guardian angel', but I could well have conferred wings on a small galaxy of old and new Christian friends who visited me, wrote letters to me, prayed for me and sustained me in a multitude of visible and invisible ways. Among these supporters and helpers were several priests from different denominations. The clergy often get a bad press in the modern world, yet those who offered me pastoral guidance showed great skill and sensitivity in their compassionate care for a bruised pilgrim, so I have listed their names with gratitude in the notes to this chapter.[3]

One of these good shepherds was Sandy Millar, the Vicar of Holy Trinity, Brompton. Against all my instincts he persuaded me to do an Alpha course at his church.[4] Not my scene at all, I decided in advance. Happy-clappy evangelicals in the congregation listening to

Bible-bashing fundamentalists in the pulpit ... easy-believism and instant salvation ... bringing down the Holy Spirit by turning up the volume of the electric guitars ... I had read all about HTB in magazine articles, which portrayed it as a charismatic circus for the Hooray Henry brigade from SW7, who allegedly swooned in the aisles, confessed their sins in public, put £3 million a year from their City bonuses into the collection plate, and saved the souls of celebrities. If my anti-HTB prejudices were not quite in the category of 'Pass the sick bag, Alice', they were certainly a case of 'Pass by on the other side'.

So how on earth did I find myself walking into a crowded Holy Trinity, Brompton one Wednesday evening in September 1997 to enrol for the first night of the autumn Alpha course? As 800 pairs of eyes swivelled curiously towards me (I was still near the height of my notoriety), I could think of no explanation other than that I had made a bad decision out of good manners to Sandy. I settled uneasily into my seat, firmly resolved to make this first visit to HTB my last attendance at an Alpha course.

My immediate discovery was that the magazine articles on HTB were a travesty. Nobody clapped, confessed, blessed, swooned or even passed round a collection plate. The electric guitar playing was good once you got used to it. As I listened to the sermon, or 'talk', from Nicky Gumbel, the energetic priest in charge of Alpha, I was struck by his sensible, mainstream theology and by his powerful presentation of the Gospel message. 'Everyone can have a second chance through Christ,' was a phrase that I remember from that evening. I needed one myself. So I condescendingly gave Alpha a second chance, then a third, then a fourth, and ended up completing all 15 sessions.

About three weeks into the course there was a certain amount of chatter about 'the Holy Spirit weekend'. Apparently it was being suggested that we should set off in groups for two nights at a seaside hotel where someone would call down the Holy Spirit into our hearts. Never had I heard such codswallop! This part of evangelical Christianity was certainly not for me. Moreover, I knew that the Alpha discussion group of which I was a member contained such obviously sensible people, whose feet were so firmly on the ground, that it just would not be possible for our lot to get into this sort of weird activity.

It was therefore another strange surprise that I found myself, still a Spirit sceptic, turning up in the unpromising venue of the Chatsworth Hotel in Worthing with most of the other members of my Alpha group. Our number included the senior partner in a successful firm of London solicitors and his down-to-earth Australian wife; a photographer from Windsor; the owner of a chain of language schools; a successful young tax barrister and his solicitor wife; a Northamptonshire farmer turned horse equipment importer; a merchant banker; two lady university teachers; and myself – an unemployed ex-Cabinet minister in disgrace.

The early part of the weekend passed peacefully and agreeably. The talks were good and the walks over the South Downs were even better. I did a seven-mile hike on the Saturday afternoon with the Northamptonshire farmer and a Lloyd's insurance broker. As we enjoyed the autumn sunshine of a mellow Sussex afternoon, all three of us agreed that Alpha had been helpful, even at times inspirational, but that this 'summoning up the Holy Spirit' business we were going to hear about at 5 p.m. was just too fanciful for experienced men of the world like us.

The keynote talk on the Holy Spirit was given by the leader of our group, Bruce Streather, the founder and senior partner of the solicitors Streather and Co. As I was to discover on my numerous later visits to his firm's Mayfair offices, Bruce has many sterling qualities and talents. Oratory, however, is not one of them. His talk was as far removed from Bible-thumping or hot-gospelling as the Chatsworth Hotel is from Claridges. When he brought his preaching of Scripture to the climax of an appeal to the Almighty with the words, 'Come

Holy Spirit, come,' his tones sounded so monotonous that he might as well have been reading out the small print of some dry-as-dust contract in a commercial court.

Nevertheless, as Morely said of Gladstone, 'It was not the words but the character breathing through his sentences that counted.' I already knew that Bruce Streather was one of the most attractive Christian characters anyone could meet. So I listened respectfully to his mumblings and obeyed his instruction to stand with hands out-stretched at waist height, palms upwards, praying that the Holy Spirit would come.

Nothing happened. After two or three minutes of standing awkwardly in this posture, the young tax barrister in our group, Tom Adam, came over to me, put his hands on my shoulder and whispered into my ear that he was praying especially hard that the Holy Spirit would descend on me. I cannot now remember exactly what Tom said, but the gist of it was that he knew I needed help, that he and others were grateful that I had contributed to the course from my heart, and that he knew the Lord would now send the Holy Spirit to me.

At this point my palms suddenly began to tingle with a strange physical sensation which strengthened until my hands and wrists became hot and uncomfortable, as though they were being charged with an electric current. Then I began to cry. This should have been deeply embarrassing, for shedding tears in public is anathema to me. I rather pride myself on my stiff-upper-lip stoicism in emotional gatherings, even to the point of trying hard not to cry at the funerals of close friends and relatives. Yet here I was in a room full of people in the lounge of a seaside hotel, letting out not just a trickle but a torrent of tears. To my surprise I felt amazingly warm and good about those tears. The more they flowed, the more I recognized that they were tears of happiness. I smiled, beamed and physically shook with silent laughter. Something extraordinary and uncontrollable was going on inside me.

Meanwhile, the voice of Bruce Streather, still sounding as if it was doing a voice-over in a commercial for dull ditchwater, was reading out more Scripture while Tom Adam kept his hand on my shoulder and continued to pray. Shedding all inhibitions, I hugged both of them with passionate gratitude and joy. It would be difficult to think of three more unlikely characters than these two English lawyers and myself to be taking part in this public spectacle of Holy Spirit calling and receiving, yet that is what was happening.

After about another 10 minutes of high emotion I calmed down, cooled down and reverted to normal. Later that night I was driven back to London by Alphonse Kelly, the language school proprietor. Sitting in bemused silence in his Mercedes, I tried to work out what on earth had gone on. If I could have discovered that the whole episode had been some elaborate conjuring trick, I would have been amused and reassured that my feet were still firmly on worldly ground. But there had been no trick and no conjurors. In all the circumstances there was overwhelming evidence (with two lawyers as my chief witnesses!) that I had received a genuine manifestation of the power of the Holy Spirit.

Despite all the impact that this manifestation had on me, I cannot pretend that my life changed overnight. I did not think I had been 'saved', or that I had seen some blinding light on the road to Damascus. Indeed, in immediate retrospect I felt that my encounter with the force that had shaken me to the core in the Chatsworth Hotel was as much an unnerving experience as an uplifting one. I decided to think about it, pray about it, and ask myself questions about it. Had it been real? Were there any physical or psychic explanations for it? Was I becoming some sort of religious nutter? How could I check it out with the calm and rational thought processes on which I had prided myself in my political career? These thoughts and many others troubled me. So, although I completed the Alpha course, I held myself back from involvement in other HTB services and activities in the following few weeks. I wanted to test my balance and recalculate my bearings.

As part of this process I tried to make daily life as normal as possible. I was looking for a job at this time, so was reasonably busy in talks with companies interested in offering me employment or consultancies. I saw and lunched with worldly friends who had no curiosity about my spiritual dimension. As far as my travels in this realm were concerned, the only progress I made in them at this time was achieved in Christian settings at the opposite end of the spectrum from HTB. In the mornings I kept a daily rule of prayer from 7 a.m. to 8 a.m. in St Faith's Chapel at Westminster Abbey, often breakfasting afterwards with my special friend Canon Donald Gray and his wife Joyce. My evenings were usually given over to reading authors such as C. S. Lewis, Dietrich Bonhoeffer, John Stott, J. I. Packer, Henri J. M. Nouwen, Michael Ramsey, Dallas Willard, Thomas Merton, Richard J. Foster, Evelyn Underhill, Basil Hume, Augustine of Hippo and, last but by no means least, the books of Charles W. Colson.

It was a quotation I read in Colson's *Loving God* that helped to move me towards a new phase of my inner journey. The words came from a conversation between Alexander Solzhenitsyn and Boris Nicholayevich Kornfeld, the doctor who had treated and testified to Solzhenitsyn in a Soviet prison-camp hospital. In that discussion Kornfeld says:

On the whole, you know, I have become convinced that there is no punishment that comes to us in this life on earth which is undeserved. Superficially, it can have nothing to do with what we are guilty of in actual fact, but if you go over your life with a fine-tooth comb and ponder it deeply, you will always be able to hunt down that transgression of yours for which you have now received this blow.[5]

Chuck Colson, with whom I was now corresponding regularly, referred to this quotation in one of his letters and linked it to a personal recommendation for me:

One last piece of advice. Don't look back on the past, the unfairness of the attacks, or the viciousness of the media. That happened. You can't change it. It's part of the travesty of modern life that the press can stereotype a person

– that individual can never escape that stereotype. Believe me, I know. So we have to accept it in the same way that you would have to accept it if you were in an accident and lost an arm. There's nothing you can do to get it back. So you have to learn how to live despite it.[6]

Taking this advice was not easy, but I knew I had to do it. It was soul-destroying to keep looking back in anger on this or that journalistic calumny, or to continue fulminating against particular media tormentors, some of whom were still poisonously active in their writings about me. How much better it would be if I could accept, like Solzhenitsyn's Kornfeld, that I had committed enough general transgressions to deserve all blows, even if some of them had been individually unfair. I prayed for help, and unexpectedly got it from Lolicia. She had been following my spiritual journey through our intermittent telephone conversations, and suddenly she called me from her new flat in France to say, 'I believe you should make a confession.'

'Yes I will,' I heard myself replying, 'but how do I go about it?'

Lolicia suggested going to see Father Norman Brown at Westminster Cathedral, who had been extremely helpful to both of us some years earlier at a difficult stage of our marriage. I duly set off to see Father Norman in his rooms at the Cathedral's clergy house in Francis Street, and after some long preliminary talks with him I came back a few days later and made my confession.

This was far too private and too profound an experience to write about, except to say that the discipline of preparing the confession was agonizing, but the sense of joyful release that flooded over me when I received absolution was glorious. Moreover, when doing the preparation work on what for me (as a non-Catholic) was the difficult and unusual task of formalized penitence, I saw clearly that the whole process would fail unless I first unconditionally cast out all my old demons of the lack of forgiveness I felt towards others. So by prayer and meditation I laid these past burdens of animosity at the foot of the Cross, before coming to kneel there to ask forgiveness for my own sins. When this was granted, as I knew at once it had been from the new surge of joy and peace in my heart, I was sure that a great leap forward in my Christian commitment had happened.

Something that had not happened by the late autumn of 1997, despite the efforts of my just-forgiven media adversaries to make it happen, was any sign of a serious police investigation into the *Guardian*'s allegations of criminal activities by me, Lolicia and Victoria. This complaint had been formally lodged by Alan Rusbridger in June. By December there had not been so much as a murmur from the sleuths of Scotland Yard in my direction, nor, so far as I could discover, in the direction of anyone else connected with the case. The only murmurs we could pick up on the gossip grapevine were to the effect that police officers in the department concerned had made dismissive comments about the whole affair, allegedly calling it 'a victimless crime', 'a nine-day media wonder', and 'very difficult to prove in court'.[7]

Although the six months of silence from Scotland Yard could be taken as an encouraging sign that the *Guardian*'s perjury charge campaign was faltering, I did not myself share the growing optimism of my friends and advisers that I would soon be out of the woods. This was partly through intuition and partly because of a conversation I had with my most expert friend in the world of criminal law. He was John Nutting QC, a top silk at the Old Bailey who until a few months earlier had held the post of Senior Treasury Counsel – the Crown's chief prosecutor.

Johnny Nutting and I had arrived together as new boys in the same house at Eton in 1956. The Suez crisis was at its height at that time, and Johnny's father Sir Anthony Nutting had recently resigned as a Foreign Office Minister. As the opinionated son of a loyal Tory backbencher who disapproved of this resignation, I took it upon myself to express some criticism of Nutting *père* to Nutting *fils*, who promptly and with admirable paternal loyalty punched me on the nose. A vigorous bout of fisticuffs ensued. After the Captain of the

House had pulled the protagonists apart, he was heard to say, 'These new boys are extraordinary. Fighting on their first day here, and then they say it was about *politics*!'

Over 40 years after this initial encounter, Johnny Nutting came round as an old friend to offer me advice. His message was not an encouraging one. He said that the delay might not mean much because it was almost impossible to overestimate the glacier-like slowness of the Crown Prosecution Service. When we went over the outline of the case his reaction was that a perjury charge might be difficult to prove. I said that if one was brought I would certainly plead guilty to it and asked him what the penalty would be.

'Four or five years,' said Johnny.

There was a stunned silence.

'But that's the sort of sentence given to armed bank robbers, rapists, arsonists and so on!' I expostulated, for in my ignorance I had been thinking in terms of a light sentence, perhaps even a suspended one or a community service order.[8]

'I'm afraid the Judges take perjury very seriously,' was the reply, 'and they could decide to make an example of you – although a lot will depend on your mitigation.'

This conversation gave me a nasty shock, an experience which was becoming all too familiar in this saga. But I was not devastated by it. Somehow I had got the message that I was going to be tested in the fire for reasons that were unknown, but surely not unconnected with my deepening faith. Trusting in God does not, except in illusory religion, mean that he will ensure that none of the things you are afraid of will ever happen to you. On the contrary, it means that whatever you fear is quite likely to happen, but that with God's help it will in the end turn out to be nothing to be afraid of.

If my faith had brought me to the point of calm acceptance of God's will, this was real progress. Certainly I had sailed way out into the waters of the deep, far enough to recognize the great truth of St Augustine's words, 'In his will we find our peace.'[9] Yet the dark clouds were gathering and it remained to be seen whether or not I would remain at peace when the storm burst.

CHAPTER TWENTY

Christmas Cheer

As CHRISTMAS 1997 APPROACHED, the storm clouds temporarily rolled away, for when our children came home for the school holidays the excitements of their seasonal festivities soon made my worries fade into insignificance. Their boyfriends, girlfriends, shopping expeditions, skiing trips, football matches, carol-singing and above all the merry-go-round of parties all kept me busy as their chauffeur, romantic counsellor, breakfast cook and cash dispenser. In this last role I could afford to be more generous as my worrying months of unemployment ended when two companies, GEC plc and Westbourne Communications Limited (an international telecommunications group) signed me up in late December as a business consultant.

Also in December I had my first outing as a columnist, writing an article which was to have surprising consequences. The genesis of this piece was a snide and fictitious item in *The Times* diary, which announced in a detailed lead story that, after taking instruction from a Father Michael Seed and having talks on religious doubt with Lord Patten, Aitken the disgraced former Cabinet minister was seeking salvation by converting to Roman Catholicism. I decided to correct this fabrication by writing privately to the Editor, Peter Stothard:

All the facts reported in the article are complete fiction. I have not held any talks with Father Seed who I do not know. I have had no conversations about religion or doubt with John Patten. I am not planning to go to any retreat at a leading Roman Catholic Public School, or to take instruction in the Roman Catholic faith. I am not considering converting to Roman Catholicism.

As these are matters of Holy Writ rather than for libel writs I am not asking you to do anything about them, although when it comes to salvation perhaps you may feel your inventive diarist needs a period of repentance in sackcloth and ashes almost as much as I do!'¹

There was one good consequence from this bad reporting. On the day *The Times* published it the Editor of the *Spectator*, Frank Johnson, telephoned me to ask, 'As you're becoming a Catholic, would you like to write the *Spectator*'s Christmas meditation piece for us this year?' Undeterred by hearing that I was not travelling on the path to Rome, Frank pressed on. 'Well, you're interested in religion, aren't you?'

I said yes, I was interested in religion, but I doubted whether I was ready to take on such a prominent spiritual writing assignment. Could I please think about the *Spectator*'s invitation and let him know?

Qualms and questions welled up as I reflected on the proposed article. Did I want to set myself up as an Aunt Sally of Christian journalism? Surely I would get torn to pieces for hypocrisy by my media critics? Even if I was no longer bothered about the views of the press, should I not concern myself with the views of the perjury charge pressure group? Would they knee-jerk into a new round of campaigning if I put my head above the parapet? Was it reckless to break my self-imposed silence? I shared these thoughts with my circle of prayer partners and friends. Their advice ranged from, 'Yes you should seize this opportunity to proclaim your faith,' to, 'Don't bother – nobody reads the *Spectator* anyway.' In the end the consensus view, echoed by my own instincts, was that I should 'give it a go'. So I did.

I must have written well over a thousand newspaper articles in a lifetime of political and journalistic scribbling, but this one was different for it caused by far the most unexpected reactions. The idea that nobody reads the *Spectator* was negated by the *Daily Telegraph* reprinting the article verbatim in the prime feature slot of its

Saturday op-ed page and by the extensive reporting of it in other papers. That reporting oscillated from the sublime to the ridiculous. In the latter category came stories linking me with Samantha Fox (a former Page Three girl in the *Sun*) because in our different eras we had both attended Alpha courses at Holy Trinity, Brompton. This tabloid coupling was more than compensated for by the flood of serious letters (and even a trickle of sermons) which poured into my postbag – along with a raft of further media invitations, all of which I declined.

So what was the fuss about? Although I would like to believe that my efforts at amateur theology on the Holy Spirit were stimulating to the *Spectator*'s ecclesiastical readers, it became clear that it was the few personal touches I had worked into the article which struck the chord of wider interest.

I had begun the piece by referring to my early Scripture lessons from Sister Mary Finbar when I was on my frame in Cappagh Hospital 50 years ago. After some later allusions to the unfair caricatures of HTB's Alpha course, this was my conclusion:

On the subject of caricatures, I must admit to a worry in recent weeks that I might have been developing one or two caricaturable religious tendencies myself. Belonging as I do to the Church Reticent wing of Anglicanism, I am suspicious of foxhole conversions through 'easy believism', and cautious about accepting adversity as the gateway to a deeper faith. So time and again, in all sorts of very different Christian settings, I have inwardly asked the sceptical question: 'What on earth am I doing here?' The answer, in so far as I can search for one, may be found in a verse from the Psalms which says that if you are going through a vale of misery, then use it *as a well*...

So approaching Christmas 1997 I feel an almost mystical symmetry with my Christmas of 50 years ago. There is a different kind of pain; a different kind of frame; a remorse unknown to childhood; and different equivalents of Sister Mary to pray with. Yet now that I can understand the full meaning of the Christmas story and the role of the Holy Spirit in it I can see far more clearly, as another Psalm puts it, that 'Heaviness may endure for a night but joy cometh in the morning'. If the light I can see distantly at the end of a tunnel turns out to be Christmas joy on Christmas morning – Alleluia! Or if it takes more Christmases before the anguish fades and the healing comes – Alleluia too. So long as faith in Our Lord Jesus Christ is one's companion in life's dark valleys, then even a painful Christmas can still be a joyful Christmas.[2]

A joyful Christmas was exactly what I got, for so many friends and relations rallied round that I could hardly remember a time when I was more enfolded by love. My cup of happiness overflowed on 24 December when Lolicia made a surprise appearance in Britain by flying in for a family Christmas. Her arrival filled me with hope that this might be her first move towards the rekindling of our marriage.

As I looked round at our reunited family after our Christmas Day lunch, I felt a deeper gratitude and love for them than ever before. Because of my pride and foolishness they had been subjected to a firestorm of unpleasant shocks and media onslaughts which in retrospect seemed like a horror movie. Yet for all the emotional batterings of the past, not to mention the legal and financial uncertainties of the future, they had remained uncomplainingly loyal and unconditionally loving.

In some ways the bravest heroine on the battlefield was Victoria. She had suffered from the worst case of filial damage by me and from the most intrusive of pursuits by the paparazzi. She had been unsettled at having been named as an alleged criminal conspirator in the Editor of the *Guardian*'s formal complaint to the DPP. She was also facing the hardest challenge in her academic life, since in order to overcome her dyslexia disadvantages she had decided to change schools and tackle her A levels in one year from a specialist Sixth Form College. Yet, despite all these pressures, she had given her greatest priority to worrying about her father's loneliness and vulnerability. Throughout the autumn term she telephoned me almost every day and came home every Friday (something Alexandra and William could not do from their boarding schools) in order to spend the weekends with me. Looking back on this period, I wonder if I could have come through it without Victoria's help – which, unknown to me at the time, also extended to co-ordinating a 'Looking after Daddy' operation with her siblings and her mother.

No one will ever understand the relationship I had with Lolicia, who perhaps summed it up best by exclaiming, 'That's us!' when she read a sentence in an obituary notice I had written on President Nixon saying that he had loved his wife 'deeply but strangely'. I often thought about those words when suffering from the pain of our separation and eventual divorce – neither of which she should ever be blamed for. On this, our last Christmas together, she was on her inspirational best form, full of life and laughter and family love. These good times of our peace and privacy together after the libel case storms are among the happiest of the matrimonial memories I now cherish.

Although our family life was contented and growing in strength at this time, in the public arena the season of goodwill to all men was marred by a surprising attack on me during the Christmas Adjournment Debate in the House of Commons. This obscure parliamentary occasion is traditionally a minor, 'last day of term' event in which backbenchers raise parochial items about their constituencies. To the astonishment, and in some cases the outrage, of the 15 or so MPs who were taking part in the debate, Mr Gordon Prentice, the Labour Member for Pendle, used the occasion to devote his entire speech to the view that I should be prosecuted for perjury.

Citing the *Guardian*'s recently published book on the libel case, charmingly entitled *The Liar*, Gordon Prentice said that I had a history of arms dealing and sponging off very rich Arabs. He continued, 'The Jonathan Aitken libel action collapsed in June. It is now coming up to Christmas. I asked how much time had been spent by the Commissioner investigating the case and was told last month that it was the equivalent of 39 man days. I do not want the investigation to drag on indefinitely. There is irrefutable proof in court transcripts that Jonathan Aitken lied under oath ... I hope that the police are going to pass the papers to the Crown Prosecution Service just as soon as maybe so that the Aitken affair can be finally settled.'[3]

Although I was sorry to see that an MP felt it appropriate to follow in the prosecutorial footsteps of the Editor of the *Guardian* in this way, my general mood of tranquillity was unruffled by the attack. At a higher level I was finding that my commitment to the acceptance of God's will was strengthened rather than shaken by fresh bad news. On the other hand, when I read in the *Sunday Times* of 7 January 1998 that Metropolitan Police Detectives from the Organized Crime Squad were travelling to Paris to interview employees of Mr Mohamed al Fayed's Ritz Hotel in connection with the perjury investigation on me, I felt a sad sense of fatalism about the end result. I knew enough about the top brass of the Met. (some of whom had been past acquaintances of mine when they were senior officers in the Kent Police) to realize that they were likely to be spurred into action by the latest outbursts of parliamentary and media noise about my case. In that context my *Spectator* article had been counterproductive, so much so that I guessed that Alan Rusbridger's campaign to have me prosecuted might well be on the brink of success.

There was no point fretting about this misfortune. In any case, I was having some unaccustomed good fortune of my own. My new business consultancy for GEC required me to visit Saudi Arabia in order to write a report on a 'repositioning strategy' for the company. Even though it was the middle of the Islamic holy month of Ramadan, I decided to move ahead with this assignment, part of which related to a major contract for communications equipment which had become mysteriously blocked within the Saudi bureaucracy. Saudi bureaucrats have cunning ways of their own for delaying contracts and payments, but they are, if anything, slightly less devious than the equivalent practices in Whitehall. I thought I knew a route to unblock the log jam on this particular project, and I did. Within a week of my negotiations in Riyadh, the big export order the company badly needed was coming through. My stock as a consultant went up.

Before travelling to Riyadh, I had wondered how low my stock as a friend might have fallen among my Saudi contemporaries. Some of them had been dragged with me into the mud, most unfairly in their cases, by the *Guardian*–Granada onslaught. So I set off with some hesitation, and decided not to make direct contact with my former associates. Instead I sent one or two of them faxes to their offices, identifying the hotel where I would be staying and leaving it for them to decide whether or not to get in touch with me. In Ramadan, when Saudi office life slows to a crawl, it would have been easy, in fact normal, for such a message to go unanswered.

My faith in human nature, which had been faltering in some quarters in England, was restored abundantly in Saudi Arabia. From the moment I arrived in the Riyadh Intercontinental my telephone never stopped ringing with welcoming calls from friends. I had so many invitations to *Iftars* (the breaking of the fast at dusk) and *Sohoors* (the big social meal of the night two hours before the dawn prayer) that my nocturnal diary was almost as busy as Jennifer's Diary in her heyday. From minor business contacts to major princes, I was in demand. Everyone who saw me wanted to offer their sympathy. The world and the libel case evidently looked different when viewed from the desert kingdom. 'They only attacked you because you were such a good friend of the Arabs' ... 'Those TV programmes were full of disgusting anti-Arab racism' ... 'We read that the Mossad helped the *Guardian* to get the air ticket evidence' ... 'You're one of our few friends who hasn't liked us just because of our money – and look what they do to you' ... 'The *Guardian* hates us first, and you a long way second' ... 'Why do the British let Mohamed Fayed destroy a good minister?'

Listening to this barrage, some of it from voices far angrier than I had ever been, I found myself explaining that freedom of the press includes the freedom to be unfair; that Granada Television was not staffed by racists; that I had read the 'Mossad did it' articles too but could not believe them; and that I had done more to destroy myself than Mr Fayed had.

Of all my welcoming hosts, Prince Mohammed bin Fahd was the most gracious, even though he had received the worst battering in the British media. At no little inconvenience to himself, he insisted on flying me up to Jeddah where he was in attendance on the King. He gave a dinner for me, to which he invited yet more sympathetic friends, and talked to me with deep emotion about the sadness he had felt over my demise. When I told him I thought I would end up in prison before the year was out, Prince Mohammed replied, shaking his head in bewilderment, 'I just hope someone remembers all the good things you did for your country.'

Such kindness was good for my morale, but my visit to Saudi Arabia was bad for my reputation. Within a few weeks of my return the *Guardian*'s headlines were in overdrive:

'GEC RETAINS DISGRACED POLITICIAN JONATHAN AITKEN'
'AITKEN GETS JOB AS ARMS SALESMAN'
'DIRTY ARMS DEALS'[4]

The accompanying story by David Pallister made vague but sinister references to corruption, defence suppliers secretly handing over 26 per cent commissions, the Al Hakim air-launched missile system being on Saudi Arabia's shopping list, and my own close involvement with the 'notorious Al Yamamah contract'.

This was mild stuff compared to the *Evening Standard*, which, under the headline 'WOULD YOU BUY A MISSILE FROM THIS MAN?' launched a missile attack of its own from the pen of George Walden, a former parliamentary colleague turned columnist who in happier days had not been averse to enjoying my hospitality in Lord North Street.

'Sales representative required. Ability to lie under oath an advantage.

£150,000 a year plus performance related commissions,' was Walden's opening salvo, and 800 words of invective later he concluded:

In defence of GEC it may be said that Mr Aitken has 'suffered enough' and that as a result of his sufferings he has become very religious. We know it to be true that he is now very religious because he wrote an article in a magazine saying so … Yet Mr Aitken appears to have decided that a born again Christian is best employed in helping to sell weapons to Arab regimes. A contemptible man will thus resume his connection with a frequently contemptible trade carried on all too often with contemptible regimes.[5]

I was saddened by this combination of factual nonsense and personal vilification. If George Walden or any other journalist had bothered to contact me to check the story, they would have discovered that I was earning £30,000 (without commission) from GEC, not £150,000 plus commission; that I had never heard of the Al Hakim missile, which I subsequently discovered was neither wanted by, nor being offered to, Saudi Arabia; and that my repositioning strategy report to GEC had been largely about opening up new business activities for the group in areas like telecommunications, hospital equipment, the Aramco oilfields, and the Ministry of the Interior. Inevitably defence equipment was also covered in my report, but on the computer and communications systems side of the business, rather than at the sharp end of 'arms deals'. But, alas, it had become a credo of dogmatic certainty with some journalists that Aitken and arms deals were synonymous. In such an atmosphere any stigma would do to perpetuate a dogma.

Although I was philosophical about my latest wave of hostile publicity, GEC were not. Big company, small bottle. One loquacious director whose responsibilities included public affairs managed to unsettle her commercial colleagues by throwing an anti-Aitken boardroom scene with assertions similar to those made in George Walden's article. Other members of the chattering classes continued to chatter along negative lines. So even though I had brought a £50 million contract back from disaster after one 10-day visit to Saudi Arabia, and even though my friends in the company fought hard to keep me, I was expendable. I had been rather effective as consultants go, but as consultants go, I went.

Despite this reverse – which was probably my fault anyway for failing to predict the backlash from any sort of employment that hostile journalists could link to 'arms deals' – I genuinely did feel that life was looking up. Even on the employment front, no sooner had I lost one job than another came along. After news of my Riyadh visit trickled out on the Saudi-watchers' grapevine, I was signed up for a new and even better consultancy with IHG Healthcare Limited, a company specializing in healthcare and hospital management.

If Mammon was being kind, God was being kinder. From those regular early morning visits to Westminster Abbey I came to understand that my prayers were deepening and my faith was strengthening. I saw glimpses that the testing was going to get worse, but was unshaken because I knew that the trusting was getting better. I found myself in strong agreement with the contemporary Christian writer Hubert van Zeller, who once said, 'If you do not pray everything can disappoint you by going wrong. If you do pray everything can still go wrong but not in a way that will disappoint you.'

I was not disappointed when things went wrong. I had some bad moments, but on the whole I came to believe that with God's help I could cope with any blow. This was just as well, for the biggest blow so far was on its way to me.

CHAPTER TWENTY-ONE

Arrested

THE BLOW FELL ON Monday 16 February 1998 when I walked into my office to hear Lynn Fox, who has been my secretary for 21 years, playing back the answer-machine tape to check my messages. A chill descended on the room as we heard a portentously official voice clearing its throat and saying, 'This is Detective Sergeant Wall of Scotland Yard's Organized Crime Squad. I am ringing because we wish to interview Mr Aitken at a police station in connection with allegations of perjury. Would you please ring me and let me know the name and address of his solicitor as soon as possible?'

Although I had been expecting this telephone equivalent of a policeman's knock on the door in every one of the eight months that had elapsed since the libel case ended, the actual moment of it did create the proverbial sinking feeling in the pit of my stomach.

Worse was to come. Two days later my criminal solicitor Bruce Streather (who had become a close friend in the wake of my Alpha course experiences with him) received a letter from Scotland Yard which made it clear that the police were not merely after me. They were also seeking to question 'Olivera Lolicia Aitken, Victoria Aitken and Said Mohammed Ayas' on suspicion of being part of a conspiracy with me to pervert public justice.

This news rocked me to the core. The police were following to the letter the legal course of action suggested to them by their sole complainant, Alan Rusbridger, when he had written to the Director of Public Prosecutions and the Commissioner of the Metropolitan Police on 20 June 1997. Never in my wildest nightmares had I imagined that Victoria or Lolicia could be in danger of serious criminal charges because of the *Guardian* Editor's anger on the day the libel case collapsed. I had not believed this would happen to Said Ayas either. For the *Guardian* to go for my jugular with the criminal law had seemed rough, but perhaps not totally unexpected given the strong emotions our battle had unleashed among its journalists. Yet as a matter of equity it seemed to me to be a punishment too far for a newspaper, particularly one which had engaged in such questionable and arguably even criminal activity itself, to be taking its revenge to the point of putting my wife and daughter in grave jeopardy.

These thoughts troubled me for a short time, but after having an internal wrestling match with my soul, and getting some external help from a prayer partner, I overcame them. After all, my lies, not Rusbridger's letter, were the root cause of these charges. The *Guardian*'s protagonists were yesterday's adversaries. I could hardly forget them so long as they were still so active in my pursuit, but I could certainly forgive them, and had already done so.

Or had I? The friend who asked me this sharp question was Mervyn Thomas, the Sweet'n'Low sales director. At one of our weekly one-on-one prayer partnership sessions, Mervyn listened to me blaming Alan Rusbridger's letter of complaint for putting Lolicia and Victoria into the frame as my alleged conspirators, and then said, 'I've got a verse of Scripture for you. I read it last night in the Contemporary English Version of the Bible and it spoke to me so strongly that I wrote it down for you.' The verse was Matthew 5:25, which in the CEV translation reads:

Before you are dragged into court, make friends with the person who has accused you of doing wrong. If you don't, you will be handed over to the judge and then to the officer who will put you in jail.

Although officer, judge and jail were certainties so far as I was concerned, Mervyn pressed me on the question of whether I had opened my heart in true forgiveness to those who seemed to be the persecutors of my family. The honest answer was that I was only about halfway there. Going the whole way did not require me to become their friend (which would have been an insincere move and one not suggested by any translation of St Matthew other than the CEV), but I could undoubtedly travel further and more willingly down this road of forgiveness.

'Why don't we pray for the Editor of the *Guardian* and his journalists?' suggested Mervyn. After a gulp and a fleeting moment of hesitation, I bowed my head as he led us in a long and generous prayer for me and my former opponents to receive equal measures of God's love and forgiveness. By the time we said our 'Amens' I felt as though yet another heavy burden had slipped off my shoulders. 'If Alan Rusbridger, David Leigh, Peter Preston and co. had heard all that they would think we'd both lost our marbles completely,' I said to Mervyn with a smile. 'But you will know how much strength I gained from your prayer.'

In fact, I gained so much from it that I repeated similar prayers for my former journalistic opponents and their collaborators innumerable times in the coming weeks and months. This process was not as easy as it may sound. At first I had periods of wobbling and failing, sometimes breaking off my prayers with angry thoughts: 'How can I forgive X or Y if they continue to persecute me in print?' or 'Why should I forgive those whose vindictiveness has put Victoria through her new ordeal?' Yet the strength and sincerity of the effort needed to pray for the forgiveness of old tormentors gradually changed my heart, until all reversals into resentment ceased, and all backslidings into bitterness ended.

In the course of time, even when I was going through my worst hours of anguish about the plights of Victoria and Lolicia, I blamed myself for their troubles and no one else. Recriminations were over.

Vengeance was not mine. The forgiveness was real. These attitudes kept me far more serene, stable and sensible in both mind and spirit during the coming months, even when the going was rough.

The first piece of rough going was breaking the news to the family. By chance we were reuniting again on the weekend of 21–2 February in order to clear out the house in Sandwich Bay, which by this time had been sold. Lolicia came over from France to supervise our mopping-up, throwing-out and furniture-moving operations, together with all the children who had half-term exeats.

After supper on the first day of our labours I called a family conference and told them the bad news. I said that I was now certain I was going to prison and that my strategy was to confess, plead guilty and get the whole thing over as quickly as possible – not least in the hope that such an attitude would persuade the police and prosecutors to leave Victoria, Lolicia and Said Ayas out of the loop. However, I was far from certain whether this could be achieved.

My family's reactions to these bleak announcements were wonderful. Everyone showed courage, especially my two alleged co-conspirators. Victoria said defiantly, 'I'd do it again for you, Daddy.' Lolicia was equally resilient, although on a somewhat mystical level, saying, 'You poked the dark forces. You were a fool to think you would beat them, but your heart was in the right place.' Alexandra was also steady, loving and supportive.

The most visibly upset was William, but he hid it until much later that evening. Although at 15 he had grown into a six-foot-tall young man, at around midnight he crawled into my bed as if he were still a small boy, asking me plaintively, 'How long will you go to prison for, Daddy?'

'My guess is that I'll serve a couple of years,' I said.

After a long pause there was no sound except for tears – from both of us.

Over the weekend prayers replaced tears. We had never before prayed together as a family quintet, but suddenly we did it on impulse.

Our communal prayers over this weekend were not for miraculous escapes or deliverances, but rather for the strength of faith to accept God's will and for the courage to cope with whatever he had in store for us. I felt sure that these seeds were falling on good ground, not least because our children had in recent months been visibly influenced by the spiritual journeys which both Lolicia and I were making. With William just three weeks away from his confirmation at Eton, Alexandra the recently appointed head server at King's Canterbury, and Victoria becoming a regular attender at Holy Trinity, Brompton, we were already a Christian family, but an uncoordinated one. Adversity was now bringing us together in faith and love – another great blessing amidst the turmoil.

The last week in February was lawyers' week. John Nutting QC, my old schoolfriend who had been the first to warn me some months earlier just how serious a perjury charge could be, accepted the brief. With great generosity, knowing more about my financial situation than most people, he refused to accept any fees for it – a truly magnificent gesture when it later became clear how much of his valuable time he would have to donate to the Aitken cause.

At our first conference, John Nutting was more optimistic than I had expected. He explained that on evidential grounds perjury is a difficult charge to prove, and after studying the libel trial transcripts he thought that my chances of not being prosecuted could well be better than 50-50. Against that, conspiracy would be relatively easy to prove, particularly in Victoria's case because her witness statement had been far more specific than Lolicia's. So there were good tactical reasons for the prosecutors to keep Victoria in the frame, despite her youth and innocence.

This analysis gave me the sickening feeling that my alleged conspirators were being used as sprats to catch a mackerel. If this was the game, then why not give the police their big fish quickly?

'Because for a start it could increase the penalties for you,' was the crisp reply.

'What is your latest view of the penalties?' I asked.

'Four years,' responded John Nutting.[1]

I swayed in my seat, but did not duck the issue. 'I'll have to take whatever is coming to me,' I said with an inward wince of fear, 'but my priority is getting the others off the hook.'

My feeling that this must be the right course of action intensified after I received a report on my solicitor's informal discussions with the police, in which Detective Superintendent Hunt had said that his *primary* target in the investigation was me, while the alleged conspirators were of *secondary* importance. Even though this was a statement of the obvious, it was useful to hear it from the horse's mouth. So I sat down and wrote a memorandum to my lawyers on 10 March, whose concluding paragraphs read:

As my legal team already know my passionate concern and priority is to protect Lolicia, Victoria, and also Said Ayas from charges. Would I succeed in doing this if I made an admission in a considered statement handed over at the end of my police interview on March 17th?

I recognise that by doing this I may be putting my head in a noose at a time when the police may not have got quite enough rope to hang me with, but even so I would feel I had responded honourably to the pressure on my family which the *Guardian* have imposed.

So finally let me offer a short paragraph of admission for consideration and discussion by my legal team:

'In view of the pressure of the allegations made by the *Guardian* against innocent members of my family and others, and in the light of implications of the comments made by the police to my solicitor on March 6th, I would like it to be known that if this investigation should end with a charge of perjury being laid against me as a sole defendant, then I would plead guilty to this charge.'

I would feel infinitely more at peace with myself if I took a course of action along the lines of the above. It would be an honourable and decent end to the nightmare, not perhaps for me, but surely in all probability for Victoria, Lolicia and Said Ayas. Advice please.[2]

Criminal lawyers are not used to advising clients who volunteer to put their head in a noose. They had to work hard to persuade me that I should hold back from making any statement of admission or confession to the police at my forthcoming interview. Eventually I was convinced by two of their arguments. The first was that no defendant should incriminate himself or risk incriminating anyone else by providing the police with admissible evidence that may not already be in their possession. The second, and far more important clincher was that the Crown Prosecution Service (CPS) lawyers had agreed in writing to allow all the potential defendants in the case to make further representations after their police interviews and before any decisions on charges were taken.

Despite these reassurances, I was on tenterhooks about the police interviews that were arranged for the week beginning 16 March, not because of my own position but because of Victoria, for whom I engaged her own separate solicitors and counsel. This expensive but essential move was necessary to remove all suspicion of paternal pressure in her case.

Victoria was notified in advance, as I was, that she would be arrested on arrival at the police station before being interrogated. The same went for Said Ayas.³ This new procedure for arresting all suspects prior to being questioned was introduced in the 1991 Criminal Justice Act in order to replace the much disliked 'sus law' and to give defendants more rights. Unfortunately the procedure also gives journalists more headlines, because the word 'arrested' in bold type has the worst of meanings.

It was therefore inevitable that all hell broke loose when the tabloids and television headlines screamed on Monday 16 March: 'JONATHAN AITKEN'S DAUGHTER ARRESTED',⁴ complete with pictures of Victoria leaving Lord North Street for Chelsea Police Station. As usual someone had tipped off the paparazzi.

Inside the police station Victoria was treated with exemplary fairness, as I was when I went for my interview the following day. On legal advice, neither of us said anything of substance beyond the standard 'no comment' in response to each and every question.

Victoria, well supported at the police station by her solicitor, and by my sister Maria in her role of 'accompanying adult', came through her ordeal with head held high. Like most teenagers she lives in the present, so her main concerns were not what had happened in Villars in 1993 when she was 13 years old, but how her hair looked outside Lord North Street at the age of 17 in March 1998 as she ran the gauntlet of the photographers. The police were not unsympathetic to Victoria's priorities. At the end of her interview she was released without charge and granted bail until 20 May, accompanied by a stern warning that failure to turn up at Chelsea Police Station at 12 noon on that date could constitute a serious offence.

'But I can't possibly come to London on 20 May,' said Victoria emphatically.

'Why not?'

'Because it's my A level French oral.'

Collapse of stout policeman, whose frown turned to a smile as he readjusted the law's demands to fit in with the alleged conspirator's examination timetable.

My own 'no comments' at my interview the following day were not the harbingers of 'no prosecution'. I could see clearly from the lines of Detective Sergeant Wall's questions to me that the police had already established that Lolicia could not possibly have been in Paris paying my bill at the Ritz Hotel on the afternoon of 19 September 1993. They had collected evidence from two hotels and a car hire firm in Geneva which showed she was still in Switzerland at the relevant time. So my perjury was, as far as I could see, what policemen call 'bang to rights', subject only to documents being produced officially by a mysterious functionary of the European legal system described by DS Wall as 'the Commissioner Abattoir' (presumably he meant 'Rogatoire'?). The malapropism seemed rather appropriate, since one way or another I was heading for the slaughterhouse.

DS Wall knew this too, for the most testing parts of his interrogation were not about facts but emotions, as this extract from the interview records shows:

You see I am just a Detective Sergeant of the Metropolitan Police. I don't understand the stresses that you must have been under but I imagine that they must have been huge for a man in your position, absolutely immense pressures. Maybe you felt you'd been pushed into a corner here? ... Did you feel that the *Guardian* and others had a conspiracy to bring you down? ... It must have been a dreadful decision to involve your daughter in this matter? ... You see I am a father of a daughter about the same age and I know that daughters will often respond to Dad. They will really want to help Dad ... This is your chance to say you are sorry even if you have told lies Mr Aitken.[5]

It was difficult to keep on saying 'no comment' to such valid arguments, but I maintained the discipline of silence, consoling myself with the thought that at least I would shortly be able to hand in my confession statement.

The word 'shortly' in the context of the English Criminal Justice system does not mean quickly. Like Victoria, I had been released without charge and given unconditional police bail until 21 May. I imagined that I would turn in my confession statement at least a month before that.

Confessional life with lawyers is not so swift or simple, however. When I got into conferences with the various solicitors and barristers on the case, it appeared that we had, as one of them observed, a case of *quot homines, tot sententiae* (so many men, so many opinions). Certainly there were more questions than answers. Did Victoria have a defence on the grounds of very little *mens rea* (a legal term meaning 'guilty knowledge', without which no one can be convicted of a criminal offence) and a lot of dyslexia-based muddle, or should she make an 'I did it for Daddy' confession as soon as possible and hope to be punished only by a caution? Could Lolicia be extradited from

Switzerland (where she had naturalized citizenship), Serbia (where she was born), or France (where she preferred to live)? If she did return voluntarily or involuntarily, would she too have a defence to the conspiracy charge on grounds similar to Victoria's?

As for Said Ayas, he confused everyone by having two teams of lawyers and barristers, both of which at various times had been instructed by him on a civil litigation case he was defending against a Saudi prince, and now on the criminal case he was defending against the English Crown.

In my own case, my lawyers were in favour of me preparing a confession statement but not handing it in. As one criminal practitioner put it, 'In this business you don't cough until you see the colour of the prosecution's evidence.' I rather thought that we had seen it, but my learned friends were of the opinion that, however 'bang to rights' the perjury case might have appeared to a layman, in the eyes of professional lawyers it still looked as though the police might have serious difficulties of evidential sufficiency.

There was only one British witness listed in the police paperwork as having co-operated in giving them evidence – Owen Bowcott, a *Guardian* journalist. All the other potential witnesses were foreign nationals – mainly ex-employees of Mohamed al Fayed, ex-employees of hotels, and ex-employees of credit card and car hire agencies in various parts of Europe. How many of these shadowy figures would turn up in court? And if they did volunteer to appear as witnesses before an English Judge and jury (which no subpoena could compel them to do), how reliable would their memories be under cross-examination, particularly those relating to identifications made some five years earlier?

'All these matters will be revealed in the effluxion of time,' observed John Nutting, 'but in the meantime you must stay mum.'

Staying mum was difficult. I found the concept of evidential insufficiency hard to accept. Even harder was the notion that nonconfession was more appropriate than confession. With the moral imperatives becoming confused by the professional advice, I sought spiritual as well as legal counsel. Prayer partners, retreat tutors, nuns, vicars, canons, fathers, and other common-sense Christian friends were all consulted. Amidst sleepless, asthmatic nights and tense, argumentative days I felt as though I was already in jail, banging my head against the walls of the cell, as I went round and round the question of what was the right thing to do.

The vital issue here was not my own fate. The question was: Would an early and voluntary confession incriminate or exculpate my alleged fellow conspirators? If the prosecutors were offered my head on a platter in the form of a full statement promising a plea of guilty to perjury and *attempted* conspiracy (an offence which can be committed by one defendant alone), surely the public interest would be well served without dragging Victoria, Lolicia and Said Ayas into the dock with me? My own instinctive answer to this question was yes, but the lawyers all said no, leave it to us to play the poker game for you, and also for your wife and daughter. Since my advisers held at least one card, namely the letter from the CPS (now backed up by an oral promise from the Treasury Counsel briefed by the CPS) stating that further representations could be made by all potential defendants before charges were laid, I eventually accepted that my stance should be one of wait and see rather than rush in and confess. Once this decision had been taken, peace of mind returned.

Prayers had been my mainstay in this phase of the ordeal, not so much mine (although they had been plentiful) as those of others. It is an extraordinarily humbling experience to come to realize that you are the undeserved subject of other people's prayers. These were now coming from far wider sources than my familiar circle of intercessors. I knew this from my postbag, which bulged with letters from score upon score of well-wishers concerned at the publicity given to Victoria's arrest. So many of these known and unknown correspondents ended their sympathetic messages with words to the effect of

'I am praying for you' that I began to feel blessed and sustained by new legions of unseen hands.

This phenomenon of growing public sympathy evidently troubled the *Guardian*, which decided to reinforce its pressure for my prosecution with an editorial published a few days after the arrests. 'There is a small swell of sympathy for Mr Jonathan Aitken as the net closes around him,' proclaimed this leader. 'That is understandable and predictable. He rose high in his political career; he made many friends. But for all that it is right that Mr Aitken should be prosecuted.'[6]

I shook my head sadly at this attack, whose secondary purpose seemed to be the suggestion that I particularly deserved to be prosecuted because I had pursued the libel action for motives of personal gain in order to enrich myself with 'loadsamoney' gained by deception.[7]

This was *Guardian* propaganda at its most unfair. As my three libel case barristers and my solicitor were to confirm,[8] I had been advised that as a result of recent Court of Appeal judgements the highest libel damages I could expect to receive under the new physical injury related ceilings were £125,000. This sum was smaller than the deficit between taxed and untaxed costs which I would have had to pay in the event of total victory. Moreover, in the abortive settlement discussions between Charles Gray QC and George Carman QC, I had offered to accept any deal offered by the defendants whose terms would give me an apology and a retraction but little in the way of damages. Those terms were presented to the *Guardian*, but were refused.[9] Against that background it seemed a trifle harsh to be pilloried in the leader columns of the *Guardian* for being an extortionate litigant grasping for 'loadsamoney', but I ignored the slur and turned the other cheek.

In any case, I was too busy with family matters to bother with answering editorials. The most moving event in this department during March was William's confirmation, which – like some other Aitken activities at this time – was not without its own touches of drama.

William had taken his confirmation preparations seriously. About a fortnight before the event he had telephoned me to say, 'Daddy, I think I now see why you go to retreats. The one I've just been on really stirred me.' This was quite a surprise. William had set off to the Eton confirmation weekend complaining that he was being unfairly prevented from attending a home match at Chelsea Football Club, which he thinks of as heaven. He had returned talking about the real heaven, God and the Holy Spirit.

This religious progress was nearly derailed by an attack of bronchitis. Three days before the confirmation service, William was admitted to the school sanatorium with a foghorn of a cough and a temperature of 101°, both of which steadily worsened. Twenty-four hours before the Bishop of Lincoln was due to confer his blessing upon some 200 confirmands, W. S. O. Aitken was voiceless, feverish and had a temperature of almost 103°.

'I'm afraid there is no way William can be confirmed tomorrow evening,' decreed the school doctor. After hearing that judgement I drove back to London in disappointment and stood down the godparents.

The only two people who did not accept the medical diagnosis were William and his school chaplain, who proceeded to perform what in family folklore we later called 'the Mullins Miracle'. The Reverend Tim Mullins visited William's sickbed an hour or two after the school doctor had vetoed his attendance at the confirmation service. 'God may have other ideas,' said the chaplain, placing his hands on William's brow and saying a healing prayer along the lines of, 'Raise up, O Lord, thy suffering servant William. Let him be well enough to attend College Chapel at 5 p.m. tomorrow afternoon...'

An hour or two after this improbable scene had taken place, a chirpy William telephoned from the san to describe it and to deliver the even more improbable news that he was completely better. 'Well, his temperature *is* back to normal,' reported a doubtful school nurse.

Normal it was the following morning, and normal still at lunchtime. Expressing much surprise at the speed of his recovery, the school doctor reluctantly gave permission for William to leave the san to attend the service. The Aitken family and godparents then had to perform a minor miracle of their own by remobilizing at two hours' notice, arriving at College Chapel with minutes to spare.

By chance I was ushered into a seat which turned out to be less than six feet away from the spot where William came to kneel to receive the laying on of hands. I do not think I have ever felt closer to my son than at that moment. With the extended arms of Christ glowing like embers of fire in Evie Hone's famous depiction of the crucifixion in the East Window; with the College Chapel choir singing Mozart's 'Agnus Dei' and the words '*Pace, pace*' soaring away into the transepts just at the moment when the Bishop's hands came down on William's inadequately brushed hair, I prayed that peace might soon come into his life, even if I would not be around to help him find it. When the choir burst into a tumultuously joyful rendering of Haydn's 'The Heavens are telling' a few moments later, I felt, to paraphrase the words of C. S. Lewis, that I had caught for a moment the power to detect shafts from the glory of God as they impinge upon our sensibility. These shafts struck so positively that from this moment onwards I knew I need not worry how William would manage during his next few terms without a father. I had made another surrender, and I had made it with joy.

Over the following days I saw a lot of William, because within hours of his confirmation he was back in bed again recording a high temperature. In the absence of a second Mullins miracle, his bronchial infection was slow to respond to antibiotics, so I found myself making daily visits to the san. Our father-and-son conversations there were among the most intimate we had ever had together.

Inevitably, we spent a fair amount of time discussing the impact of my coming prison sentence. William was concerned about how he should present this little local difficulty to his school contemporaries.

Showing early promise in the art of spin-doctoring, he eventually came up with this formula: 'Daddy, I think the way to handle it is to explain that you're a really interesting Old Etonian,' he mused. 'You see, some OEs start out in the law, and you did that. Some OEs become writers and authors and you've done that. Some OEs go into merchant banking and even become chairmen of merchant banks, and you've done that. Some OEs go into politics and become MPs, or even get into the Cabinet and you did that. One or two, I suppose,' he said rather less confidently, 'go to jail and now you're going to do that. But you must be the only Old Etonian in the world who's done all those things!'

I enjoyed this filial accolade. The only one of my occupations William had omitted was that of amateur schoolmaster. This activity kept me remarkably busy as the Easter holidays arrived, and with them frantic appeals for paternal help with A level and GCSE revision work. An average day's tutorials in this period saw me working for a couple of hours in the morning with Victoria on British and US politics, then an hour or so with William on his GCSE Latin set books – Virgil and Cicero, and then for even longer sessions in the afternoon with Alexandra on her two Religious Studies papers – Ethics and St Luke's Gospel. I am not sure how much all this academic effort helped the children's education, but it did wonders for mine.

After the happiest of family Easters staying with Nicholas and Nadine Bonsor and their five children in Bedfordshire,[10] I made an excursion with Victoria to Washington DC. The purpose of our trip was to try and reach a decision on whether or not she should accept the place she had been offered to read politics at George Washington University. After talking to students and members of the GW faculty, Victoria decided to defer her place for a year, which seemed a sensible move since we then thought that if she had started her US university career as a freshman in September 1998, it would soon have been disrupted by my trial, and possibly hers too, in the criminal courts of Britain.

This springtime visit to Washington was also notable for some high-level practical research on Victoria's A levels, for my last public speech before going to prison, and for a reunion with my friend and mentor Chuck Colson.

The British A level paper on American politics focuses on the powers of the legislative, judicial and executive branches of the US constitution. It is one thing to learn these subjects from textbooks and another to see them in action. Pulling a string or two from my past life in politics, I was able to get House Speaker Newt Gingrich to welcome Victoria to his office on Capitol Hill and to arrange for one of his aides to take her on a private tour of the House and the Senate. Similar arrangements were made for visits to the Supreme Court and the White House. These expeditions gave Victoria new insights into her subject and were worth a few extra marks when she took her A levels in June.[11]

My last public speaking engagement took place by happenstance at a Washington banquet to celebrate the fiftieth anniversary of Regnery Inc., the US publishers of my biography of President Nixon. I had not planned to be there, but having arrived in the Beltway during the week of these festivities, I called Al Regnery and received a last-minute invitation not only for the dinner but also to make a speech on behalf of the firm's many foreign authors. Under the 'A's alone, Regnery had published the works of Marcus Aurelius, St Augustine, Thomas Aquinas, Konrad Adenauer – and, at a respectful distance behind them, J. Aitken. So I was delighted to fill the overseas authors slot – live on C-span television – by telling some light-hearted Nixon anecdotes to an assembly of political and literary luminaries which included Cap Weinberger, Bill Buckley, Ed Meese, Jeanne Kirkpatrick, Bob Tyrrell and many others.[12] My next audience, I reflected, was likely to be the debating society of Wormwood Scrubs Prison.

The morning after this publishing soiree, I went to see Chuck Colson at the Virginia headquarters of the organization he heads,

Prison Fellowship Ministry. We talked alone together for nearly two hours. As had already emerged from our extensive correspondence, I found Colson's life story an inspirational role model for the extraordinarily similar dramas and traumas through which I was now passing. This feeling of a growing bond between us was deepened when at the end of our meeting we prayed together. Chuck's prayers were so moving that from that moment onwards I thought about him every day and for a great deal of time, throughout April and most of May 1998. What I did not realize was that he was also thinking a great deal about me.

CHAPTER TWENTY-TWO

Charged

ON THE FATEFUL DAY of 21 May 1998 when I was charged at Chelsea Police Station with perjury and conspiracy, Charles Colson was my house guest and prayer partner at 8 Lord North Street. The background to this remarkable coincidence deserves some explanation.

Chuck and Patty Colson had been planning for many months to take a spring vacation in the English countryside. Rest, writing and relaxation in rural Gloucestershire were their priorities. London was not on their itinerary until four or five days before departing from Florida, when Chuck said to his protesting wife, 'I have a strong feeling that we should change our schedule on the day we arrive so that we can go and see Jonathan.'

Although I was delighted when I heard that Chuck would like to come and talk on his way to the Cotswolds, I had no sense of urgency or impending crisis surrounding our meeting. So far as the legal news was concerned, I had been told by my QC, John Nutting, that the decisions on whether or not I would be prosecuted were some weeks away. He had been reliably informed that neither the CPS nor the Treasury Counsel, who was advising them, had received the police report and papers on the case. Moreover, John Nutting had also been given assurances in writing from Mr Fuat Emin of the CPS that before any decisions on prosecutions were taken all defendants would have the opportunity to make final representations if they wished to do so. It was on the basis of those assurances that I was preparing my confession statement. The first draft of it had gone to my legal team, who were working on a timetable which suggested that we had at least two or three weeks in hand before it needed to be finished. Said Ayas' lawyers had received similar assurances and indications of this timetable and they too were working on a draft statement by their client.

Against this background of stately progress on all sides of the case, I made leisurely arrangements for my meeting with Chuck Colson. He and Patty were scheduled to arrive at Gatwick at 11.00 a.m. on Wednesday 20 May. I persuaded them to stay overnight, largely because Chuck could then participate in our regular Thursday morning prayer breakfast. A welcoming lunch, an afternoon nap, an hour or two's discussion and a quiet dinner were the intermediate items on our agenda.

On the morning of 20 May I had a message asking me to attend an urgent conference with all my lawyers at 12 noon. When we assembled in John Nutting's chambers at Gray's Inn, the mood was sombre. Only two days earlier John had dismissed some vague rumours that I was about to be charged as 'inconceivable', citing the assurances in the letter from the CPS and the additional promise he had been given of counsel-to-counsel discussions before the authorities made any final decision on the case. Now he was saying something completely different.

'I am afraid that we seem to have been overtaken by events,' he began, going on to explain that the police had apparently come back from a visit to France and Switzerland with important new evidence. This evidence established 'beyond peradventure' that Lolicia had been in a hotel in Geneva on the afternoon of 19 September 1993 when she had supposedly been paying my bill at the Ritz Hotel in Paris.

I was underwhelmed by this news at first hearing. The evidence that Lolicia had clearly been in Geneva on that afternoon had been given to the High Court almost a year earlier in the form of car hire documents. Her stay in a Swiss hotel had been hinted at by the police when they put their questions to me two months ago. So the only development was that the police had brought in the formal evidence to prove what they already knew was the factual position. Why, I asked, should this change what I had been told was the established procedure, whereby the police collect evidence, submit their report on it to the CPS, who then make a decision with Treasury Counsel on whether or not to prosecute, after weighing up not only the evidence but also the wider question of whether or not prosecutions are in the public interest?

My lawyers looked embarrassed. John Nutting said yes, indeed, I had stated the procedural position absolutely correctly. He would telephone senior officials of the CPS immediately.

The CPS legal team appeared to be in even greater turmoil on the afternoon of 20 May than the Aitken legal team. Dame Barbara Mills, the DPP, had resigned that morning because of a report making severe criticisms of her department. Her immediate deputy, who had previously exchanged correspondence and conversations with John Nutting, could not come to the telephone. The Treasury Counsel in charge of the case had been instructed not to have the counsel-to-counsel dialogue he had previously agreed. Finally John Nutting got through to Mr Fuat Emin, the CPS solicitor who had written the letter some weeks earlier giving the assurances that the defendants would have the opportunity to make further representations before prosecution decisions were taken.

The temperature in the basement conference room of No. 2 Raymond Buildings seemed to rise by several degrees as, in tones of exasperated courtesy, John Nutting spoke into the telephone.

'So are you confirming, Mr Emin, that the CPS has not received the papers on the case...?'

'But your letter does say clearly that there would be an opportunity to make further representations...'

'Have you then transferred the responsibility to the police...?'

'Yes, I am most grateful to you for saying that you will review the police's decision, but that is not what your letter said...'

'I am afraid you have put me in a position of some considerable embarrassment with my client...'

The client had grown accustomed to embarrassing surprises. In recent months I had occasionally joked to friends that it felt rather like being in a performance of *Hamlet* in which the lead actor tries to stick to the script but keeps getting blown off course by Rosencrantz, Guildenstern, Ophelia et al. coming on stage to deliver completely unexpected lines which Shakespeare never wrote.

Now Nutting, in the manner of Polonius, was trying to find out what the prosecutors were doing on the other side of the arras. 'I'm afraid the CPS have funked it,' he was saying. 'They don't seem to want to consider the difficult issues involved here. They are washing their hands of the charging decision, leaving it entirely in the hands of the police. This, in my not inconsiderable experience of high-profile cases, is utterly unique and unprecedented.'

In the subsequent discussion of my unique and unprecedented situation, we reached a consensus that I was likely to be charged the next day because the police had got the bit between their teeth and wanted to wrap the case up as quickly as possible. Sensitive to media criticism (most of it from Paul Johnson in the *Spectator*) about the delays and the amount of police time and money which appeared to have been wasted on the investigation of *R v Aitken*, the Met. were bouncing us with a revolt of Detective Sergeants and Superintendents against the Generals of the CPS and the Treasury Counsel's office.

Although in one way I was almost relieved by this news, on the Shakespearean grounds of 'If it were done when 'tis done, then 'twere well it were done quickly',¹ there were some serious disadvantages in these developments. I had planned to give the authorities a considered statement confessing all, telling all, and explaining the complex background to the saga. This would have made no difference to my fate, but I had hoped it might have a major impact on the fates of Victoria, Lolicia and Said Ayas. All three, in my view, were not criminal conspirators, but innocent spear-carriers in a cause which they had blindly supported – out of family love and loyalty in the first two cases.

As far as Said Ayas was concerned, he too had acted out of loyalty, not only to me but to his employers at the material time: the Saudi royal family in general and Prince Mohammed bin Fahd in particular. Moreover, Said Ayas was entitled to argue that his loyalty was closely linked to issues of Saudi national security. For what no one had said in public up till now was that Said Ayas had been the pivotal link man in the 'Prince Mohammed backchannel' of communication between the British and Saudi Governments in the 1993–4 period when I was a Defence Minister dealing directly with King Fahd on a number of sensitive issues.

In his role as administrative fixer of this backchannel, Said Ayas had done both states some considerable service. He had been busy in this cause in Paris and Geneva during the weekend of 18–19 September 1993. He had become even busier over the next three months. The backchannel's finest hour had occurred in December 1993 when, at the request of the SIS, I had flown to see King Fahd (arrangements made by Said Ayas and Prince Mohammed) to brief him on an important security matter.

With my help, and the help of at least three of his lawyers, Said Ayas had prepared a draft witness statement giving chapter and verse of these secret activities. His legal argument, which did not apply to me, was that he should not be prosecuted for covering up the backchannel at the request of his Saudi superiors. Since Said Ayas had not given any evidence on oath in the libel case, he was in the frame for conspiracy not perjury so it might well seem to the prosecuting authorities that the balance of argument lay in not bringing charges against him on grounds of public interest.

These arguments, and the factual information to back them up, were contained in the unfinished draft witness statements which had not been seen by the prosecutors on 20 May. Our meeting ended with the tactical decision that when I saw the police the following day I should offer them my full witness statement, which was now nearly complete and which could be finalized within a matter of days. Opinions at our meeting varied as to whether or not this offer might delay or ultimately avert criminal charges. The barristers seemed confident that my offer would achieve at least a postponement. I had the pessimistic instinct that the police had succumbed to the media pressures and had already decided to press charges, whatever I offered them on Thursday morning.

While all these discussions were going on, Chuck Colson arrived to an empty house at 8 Lord North Street. When I telephoned him soon after 2 p.m., my first words to him were, 'Chuck, you've turned up at a moment of high drama. I've just heard that I'm likely to be indicted tomorrow.'

This was familiar territory to Charles Colson. In his best-seller *Born Again* one of the most moving chapters, 'Accused', tells the story of his own agonized wait for the news of whether or not he would be indicted on criminal charges connected to Watergate. Now here was I, 24 years later, going through a remarkably similar ordeal – and who had suddenly appeared at my side to help and guide me through this dark valley? As my solicitor, Bruce Streather, observed a few hours later, 'Chuck's arrival was no coincidence, it was a God-incidence.'

Chuck Colson could not have been a kinder or more experienced shepherd to help temper the wind to the shorn lamb on the evening before my indictment. Over dinner at The Turf Club he was full of practical wisdom drawn from his own experiences. Later that night he led me through some of the most moving spontaneous prayers I have ever heard. When I tumbled into bed a few moments later, I had a night of deep, peaceful and utterly untroubled sleep.

Next morning, 21 May, was Ascension Day. Chuck and I walked over at 7 a.m. to St Faith's Chapel in Westminster Abbey for the regular Matins service of prayer, Psalm-reading and Scripture. 'Know that I am with you always, yes, to the end of the world' (Matthew 28:20) were the last words of the Gospel for the day. It was a timely reassurance, for when we got back to Lord North Street, the earthly meaning of this particular Ascension Day was that the media balloon had gone up.

'I LIED FOR MY COUNTRY SAYS AITKEN' was the banner headline in the *Daily Telegraph*. The impression given by the front-page lead was that I was about to defend myself in court and to the police by claiming that my dealings with the SIS over the Prince Mohammed backchannel were my justification for the lie I had told in court about the Ritz bill. As I had never made any such suggestion and as I had specifically said in writing to my lawyers that I would not use any sensitive intelligence material to defend myself, my morale fell to a new low as I read and re-read both the headline and the formidable details of the *Telegraph*'s story, which was based on an unauthorized leak of Said Ayas' draft witness statement.

When morale is low, prayer can be wonderfully uplifting. So it proved on this particular morning as Chuck Colson, Alastair Burt, Tom Benyon, Jim Pringle, Bruce Streather, Anthony Cordle and Michael Alison interceded for me with special fervour. Then it was off and away through the gauntlet of paparazzi (who missed a good scoop by failing to recognize Chuck Colson) to Chelsea Police Station, where it immediately became apparent that the atmosphere was sharply different from my previous encounter with the police.

'DS Wall is going to get very aggressive with you, I gather,' murmured one of my lawyers. So it seemed. I was required to hand over all my possessions before entering the custody suite. My solicitor was forbidden to bring in his tape recorder. When asked why the police had permitted the use of our own tape recorder during the previous interrogation and were refusing it now, DS Wall barked like a parade-ground sergeant major bawling out an unwashed recruit, 'Because I'm going to be raising some *very controversial* matters with your client!'

In fact, the matters concerned were neither surprising nor controversial. As expected, all that had happened was that the police were now in possession of documentary evidence that Lolicia had been a guest in the Geneva Hilton on the afternoon of Sunday 19 September when, according to my account in the High Court, she had been paying my bill at the Ritz. So the case against me for perjury could now be proved. But did the police want my full confession statement on this and all other relevant matters?

At this point a slightly surreal discussion took place. As we politely reminded DS Wall and his colleagues, they had themselves said at the last interview that all decisions on charging were in the hands of the CPS, not the police. The CPS had written to us promising an opportunity to make further representations before any charges were brought. Could we please have that opportunity?

'My Superintendent will decide on that matter,' said Wall somewhat defensively. 'I shall play him a copy of this tape and we will see what transpires. In the meantime I shall have to detain you.'

For the next five hours I was locked into a cell at Chelsea Police Station. It was a surprisingly peaceful and comfortable experience. I had no doubt in my mind that I was going to be charged. The first thing I did was to say a few prayers. Then I lay down on the plastic bench, pulled a blanket over my head, and slept for some 90 minutes until I was woken by a police constable in shirt sleeves saying in the dulcet tones of an airline steward, 'Would you like a late lunch, sir? We have a choice of Chicken Risotto, Vegetable Lasagne or Lancashire Hot Pot.' I opted for the lasagne, which was delicious.

After two cups of coffee, I extracted from the collection of possessions I had yielded up earlier a pocket edition of the New Testament. It was the inscribed copy given to me by the Queen on the day I had been sworn in as a member of the Privy Council on 21 July 1994. I thought back to that afternoon at Buckingham Palace with good memories. The ceremony of kneeling, oath-taking, rising to kiss the Queen's hand and kneeling again in a new position to take a second mediaeval oath had been surprisingly complicated. Of the four new Privy Counsellors on that day (Viscounts Cranborne and Ullswater, Jeremy Hanley and myself) it was the Right Honourable Gentleman of true aristocratic lineage, Robert Cranborne, who had made a hash of the choreography by kneeling on the wrong footstool and mixing up the oaths. The Queen took it all in her stride, enjoying the jokes over tea about whether the ceremony had gone any better in 1558 when her ancestor (Elizabeth I) swore in Robert's Cecil ancestor. Oh England, our England! At least I was not where a disgraced politician might have been in the sixteenth century – incarcerated in the Tower of London waiting to have my head chopped off.

In the confines of my twentieth-century cell, I spent the next two hours reading all 16 chapters of St Mark's Gospel, something I had long been meaning to do at one sitting. The compelling power of the narrative was so absorbing that it completely wiped away all thoughts and anxieties I might have had about what could be going on elsewhere in the police station in terms of decisions affecting my future. Almost the only interruption to my reading occurred when an unknown woman was locked into the cell next to mine. She was crying so heartrendingly that I put aside the New Testament for a few minutes to pray for her until gradually her sobbing subsided and all was quiet again. In that stillness St Mark's last four chapters – the account of the Passion – spoke to me as never before. I felt utterly peaceful, totally overwhelmed by the greatness of the story. Nothing else seemed to matter.

Eventually there was a noisy unlocking of the cell door and in came Milton Silverman and Michael Coleman, my two solicitors. Michael said, 'The bottom line, I'm afraid, is that they're going to charge you.'

My immediate reaction to this not unexpected news was to feel a huge sense of relief. This was completely irrational. I had spent the last 11 months hoping that it would not come to this. Now that it had, I was serene in heart and relaxed in body. I made no reply.

'Are you OK? Are you OK?' asked Michael Coleman as if he was trying to wake up an accident victim displaying symptoms of shock.

'I'm perfectly OK, thanks. What happens next?'

The answer appeared to be a long hiatus as police administration lumbered slowly into action. I was told that bail conditions had to be negotiated, charge sheets needed to be typed, and that in due course I would be required to be photographed and fingerprinted. These preparations took time. I was locked up again in the cell and left alone there for the best part of an hour.

It was a time of total tranquillity. As I lay back on the cell bench and gazed at the pale blue ceiling, I saw those five words, 'They're going to charge you', as the announcement of a new life. Suddenly I began to visualize that I was now crossing some turbulent river, but that on the other side of it lay another world. The crossing itself would be painful. More humiliation; more pain; agonizing upheavals; a hefty prison sentence; and all sorts of coming tests, difficulties and readjustments. Yet I had no fear of these things, for I had a sense of God's presence beside me pointing beyond the far bank of the river to a land that looked green and wonderful. I could only see it dimly, but as I looked at it I was filled with positive thoughts, grateful thoughts, trusting thoughts, and above all loving thoughts. In some amazing way, at what should have been just about the worst moment of my life, I felt myself being so enfolded in the wings of God's love and so enriched by his grace that I was profoundly happy, not least because I also sensed some divine reassurance that no harm would come to Victoria and Lolicia from these criminal proceedings. 'Thank you, God,' I said over and over again in the silence of my cell.

It was extraordinary to feel myself suffused by this warm glow of internal contentment when almost everything external that was happening to me was disagreeable, if not disastrous. Yet, when the routines of the charging process ground into action, I found that my own positive energy affected everyone around me. DS Wall, who had seemed to be the hard man earlier in the day, came across as a kindly human being as he explained my lenient bail conditions to me. 'Much better than the Chief Stipe would have given you,' he said gruffly. I thanked him for being more generous than the Chief Stipendiary Magistrate.

'Well, I'm just a professional police officer. Seen it all after 29 years in the job. I don't take things personally. So far as I'm concerned I've done my duty, and from now on, to me it's purely academic what happens to you.'

'I wish I could say the same myself,' I replied. DS Wall had the grace to laugh. For the next few minutes we chatted like a couple of amicable acquaintances about his coming retirement, his wife, my children and my plans for a summer holiday in the Highlands of Scotland.

Then it was off to be fingerprinted, a surprisingly low-tech and rather messy process which reminded me of fiddling around with inky John Bull printing sets in my schooldays. The fingerprint officer had, like me, been born in Dublin and was planning to retire there, so we talked with mutual enthusiasm about our experiences of the delights of that fair city, from the bars on the Liffey to the nuns of Cappagh. As other policemen with titles like 'Duty Sarge', 'Custody Officer' and 'Charging Inspector' joined in the genial flow of conversation, social life with the Chelsea constabulary seemed rather agreeable.

The only sad moment came in a corridor on the way to the fingerprint room when I met Said Ayas, who had been charged with conspiracy. He looked such a woebegone figure that I felt like crumpling to my knees with remorse for having dragged him into this personal tragedy. I hugged him with a strange mixture of painful tears and loving warmth, saying, 'I'm so sorry my dear friend, I'm so sorry.'

Said Ayas returned my embrace, saying gallantly, 'No, Jonathan, I am sorry for *you*.'

As solicitors and police officers bustled about with the paperwork, Jim Pringle emerged from the bowels of the police station garage, having been patiently waiting all day to drive me home. I told him about my spiritual pilgrimage through St Mark's Gospel in the cell and his eyes lit up with a transparent joy that his prayer partner had been sustained by God's Word at a time of trial.

Then it was time to go home, a process made difficult by the platoon of paparazzi blocking the exit of the police station. Jim Pringle, already nicknamed 'Bugsy'[2] from his previous experience of driving me through media stampedes, wanted to put his foot down and accelerate away from the cameramen in Chicago-getaway style. The risk of injuring a photographer was too great, however, as some of them were practically clambering over the car bonnet. So I said, 'Go easy,' and Jim dutifully eased his Rover away from the mob in first gear, giving plentiful photo opportunities to all comers.

The paparazzi were also thick on the ground in Lord North Street, so we drove to the Kennington Road home of my sister Maria, who fuelled us with a sausages and beans supper washed down by multiple glasses of red wine. My mood remained almost too good to be true, but the combination of those celestial forces in the cell, an evening of wonderful telephone calls from the children, and the loving support of Maria and Malcolm Pearson[3] – who, with Jim Pringle's wife Anne, had joined us for supper – all added up to a positive happiness which far transcended the negative experience of being charged with criminal offences.

The best was yet to come. Chuck Colson had been struggling to contact me throughout the evening. Eventually he gave up and instead sent me a late-night fax which was the first piece of correspondence I saw on my arrival back home. It read:

I have been trying to reach you by phone to no avail. Either there was no answer or the lines were constantly busy. I, of course, understand.

In one sense, I am deeply saddened. I really was praying that this cup would pass and that you could avoid all this. On the other hand, I recognise that this is a complete parallel with my case. I should have never gone to prison because I believe I would have won if the case had been tried. But God had something else in mind. He wanted me to go, and I suspect that He wants you to continue to go through this. In fact, it's quite evident that He does because as I watched the television last night, I realised how preposterous it was (or so it seems by our standards in the States these days) that they would bring this kind of a case to trial.

If indeed God has this in store for you, then take it with grace. I was most impressed by your attitude, by your peace and acceptance of all this, and by your realisation that God's will is to be done and you want it done.

What struck me more than anything else on the television last night was the total transformation in your demeanour, bearing, and spirit – evidenced between the film clip of 1995 when you launched the libel suit and today – as if watching two different persons. The old Aitken is just like the old Colson (and like Nixon). The new Aitken shows a conversion – a real and genuine transformation.

I know it's tough going through this, and you have my prayers and my sympathies. On the other hand, I am absolutely, morally certain that this is God's will and that He has a plan for you that will, as I told you in my letters earlier, lead to far greater achievements than you ever imagined possible in politics.

Just remember, He has His hand upon you and will give you whatever grace is needed to sustain you and for what you must endure...

Blessings, dear brother.

Chuck[4]

This moving message from Chuck Colson was to be an important signpost to the new chapters in my life.

CHAPTER TWENTY-THREE

Waiting and Growing

AFTER THE CHARGING CAME the waiting. There was plenty of it, for a succession of court adjournments and other delay factors caused a 13-month gap to drag out between my indictment at Chelsea Police Station in May 1998 and my sentencing at the Old Bailey in June 1999. This was a strange period in which my life resembled one of those car batteries operating on negative and positive flows of electricity. On the negative side, where the current was largely being supplied by the media, the CPS and the *Guardian*'s or Granada's lawyers, I felt like a proverbial example of Murphy's Law – 'If something can go wrong, it will' – because I was continually being struck by shock after shock of disastrous news. Disgrace, divorce, financial disaster and jail were the four horsemen of my apocalypse at this time, and the pain caused by their thundering hooves was often hard to bear.

On the other hand, I was simultaneously being strengthened by positive currents of less visible, but more powerful energy, whose sources included the growing bonds of family relationships, the loving support of friends and prayer partners, and the deepening commitment to my faith. Looked at in the round, these 13 months were a contest between the forces of outer turmoil and inner peace, with peace gradually emerging as the victor.

'The disgraced ex-minister' was a label assiduously promoted by some journalists, but their name-calling activities troubled me less and less as time progressed. A more crippling impact of the disgrace syndrome was that it made it impossible for me to earn my living and to avoid financial disaster. An early indication of the way these particular winds of ill fortune were blowing came on 8 June 1998 when I made my first of many appearances at Bow Street Magistrates Court, asking for a bail variation which would allow me to make a fee-earning business trip to Oman. It was regarded by my legal team as a routine application which would succeed if the precedents were followed.

The world of Bow Street Magistrates Court was a new experience for me. 'Hi, Motherf****r!' boomed a Rastafarian wearing a woolly green hat as I joined him on the seats reserved for bail applicants. He said it so genially that his words might have been a commonplace fraternal greeting among the criminal classes I had now joined.

No such geniality was forthcoming from the CPS solicitor in charge of my case, Mr Fuat Emin, who sternly opposed my application on the grounds that I would be going abroad in order to abscond. 'Mr Aitken is a man incapable of telling the truth ... he regards truth as a matter of expediency ... he has lost his good character ... his assurances are worthless ... we cannot rely on him ... there is no guarantee that he will return from Oman to the United Kingdom,' declared the official voice of the CPS.

This seemed a little harsh in the context of a minor bail variation requested before I had made an appearance before a court to answer any of the charges against me. In vain did my barrister argue that my children, my home and my roots were all in England. In vain did he point out that I had known for months that charges against me were pending, yet I had not made any move to depart from these shores. In vain did he suggest that I was entitled to some recognition of previous good character. Fuat Emin avoided these broadsides by asserting, 'Our view is otherwise,' and then moving to a second line of attack.

'We are concerned about what Mr Aitken will do when he is abroad. We are concerned about the number of foreign witnesses in this case, and that he might interfere with them,' he said. This was a new theory about the criminality of my character. In the manner of Lord Lucan, the defendant Aitken would not merely vanish but would also 'interfere with' the foreign witnesses.

'But the defendant is flying to Oman. The Crown's foreign witnesses are in France and Switzerland,' objected my counsel.

'I'm not prepared to accept that argument,' interjected the Chief Stipendiary Magistrate. 'He could fly to Oman via Geneva.'

Fuat Emin seemed to gather strength from this original observation on airline routes from the bench. 'The vast majority of the foreign witnesses are ordinary humble people employed in hotels, car hire firms and airlines,' he continued. 'There is a danger that these witnesses can be interfered with. Some of them work for companies that have members of the Saudi royal family as big customers. No one can deny that Mr Aitken has got major influence with major Arabs. No doubt some of them are in Oman. We take the view that, with his powerful contacts abroad, this defendant is quite capable of manipulating the evidence. There has already been considerable manipulation of the press, especially the foreign press.'

My barrister replied that his client could possibly not be held responsible for what was said in the foreign press. 'In any case, where is the link between press publicity and this bail application?' he inquired.

'Well, this is the Crown Prosecution Service view,' reiterated Fuat Emin. As he said this, I recalled a meeting I had chaired in the Treasury some three years earlier to discuss the chaotic budgetary failings of the CPS administration. 'Chief Secretary, I am afraid the Crown Prosecution Service is the worst bureaucracy in Britain,' was how an eminent civil servant had opened the proceedings. Now that I was seeing the CPS in action from the more humble perspective of a criminal defendant, that description seemed far from unfair, especially when Mr Emin embarked on a novel conspiracy theory of his own, based on the police findings that Lolicia, Said Ayas and I had all spent the night of 19 September 1993 in the Hilton Hotel in Geneva as the guests of Prince Mohammed. 'This suggests that the defendant's visit to Geneva was a smokescreen for the entire libel case,' he declared.

This bizarre CPS proposition that there had been a Saudi plot in 1993 to cover up the libel case in 1997 seemed to worry the bench. The Chief Stipendiary Magistrate withdrew and came back with his ruling that my bail variation application was refused. This judgement meant that I had lost my last chance of earning an income. The one company, a telecommunications group, who were still willing to employ me as a consultant cancelled my contract when it became clear that I could not travel to help them with their projects in the Gulf.

'Goodbye, Motherf****r,' said my new friend the Rastafarian, giving me another genial Black Power salute as I left the courtroom in dejection. It was the only friendly gesture made towards me all morning.

The worst news of the day from Bow Street had not been the refusal of my application. In the course of the exchanges between the Magistrate and Mr Emin, the latter had announced that the CPS had just issued an international arrest warrant and extradition proceedings against Lolicia. I felt sick when I heard this. Now both wife *and* daughter were well and truly in the firing line. My sadness and remorse knew no bounds, as I later tried to explain to Lolicia when I telephoned her in Paris. Her response was extraordinary.

'I love you,' she said. 'This just shows you are in the right. I've been dreaming that people were chasing me for the last two nights. They were really bad people. Really evil. This is a struggle between light and dark forces. Only the dark forces would try and do this to me and Victoria.'

After these unexpected revelations of love, light, evil and darkness, Lolicia declared that she would fight all the way, although her immediate moves were to consist of flight. 'Even you won't guess where I'm going,' she said, apparently forgetting that many of her travel arrangements had been an unguessable mystery to me in the 18 years of our marriage.

Sadly, Lolicia's upbeat mood did not last. Within a few days of this conversation the unpleasant realities of being a fugitive had unsettled her. She had become understandably depressed. In this frame of mind she had consulted her lawyers, and on their advice she issued proceedings for an immediate divorce.

This was a thunderbolt. I was shattered by it. For I loved Lolicia and was yearning for the chance to rebuild our marriage once the noisy turbulence from journalists and prosecutors had quietened enough to allow us to reunite in tranquillity. Now that chance would never come. I was devastated by the sadness and loneliness which engulfed me as the moves towards our divorce began.

As I reeled from this latest blow in the mounting sequence of disasters that were accumulating around me, I had many poignant flashbacks of memory about life with Lolicia. Ours had been a love-at-first-sight romance, from the moment we were introduced to each other in 1977 by Said Ayas' mother at a cocktail party in a London hotel. I was instantly impressed by this vision from Switzerland, who ran her own textile factory, was a graduate in economics from Lausanne University, and was visiting London to buy and sell works of art. By contrast, Lolicia was underwhelmed by my status in life as she understood it.

'Have you done many arrestings today?' was one of the first questions she asked me in her charming Franco-Balkan English. It emerged that she thought my occupational self-description 'I'm an MP' meant that I was a Military Policeman. Once we had unravelled this little misunderstanding, I invited her out to dinner. Our acquaintanceship was less than three hours old when we stepped onto the dance floor at Annabel's. 'I must tell you something extraordinary, for I am a very intuitive person,' she whispered. 'You are the man I am going to marry.'

Although I spent the next few moments, and indeed many of the next few months, explaining that I was not the marrying type, two years later on 16 November 1979 Lolicia and I walked up the aisle together in the parliamentary church of St Margaret's, Westminster. Our marriage service was a traditional and joyful celebration, with the church crammed with friends from five continents; lessons read by the Speaker George Thomas and the former Prime Minister Ted Heath; the choir and organist of Westminster Abbey at their musical best; and a glittering reception afterwards in the State Apartments of the Palace of Westminster. Yet of all the bittersweet recollections from that day, the one that ran most frequently through my mind in 1998 was a verse from the opening hymn:

> *Through all the changing scenes of life,*
> *In trouble and in joy,*
> *The praises of my God shall still*
> *My heart and tongue employ.*

Now that life's scenes were changing from joy to jail, and from the service of matrimony to the serving of divorce papers, I did not exactly feel in the mood to sing praises, yet somehow I was able to look back on our 18 years of married life with gratitude for the good times and with understanding for the reaction of Lolicia's lawyers to the bad times that had now overwhelmed us.

In this period there was a great deal of fear around in the minds of various lawyers about my dramas, and not only in Switzerland. I thought I had sensed fear in the minds of the authorities at the bail application proceedings in Bow Street Magistrates Court, for why else should they have treated me like a stage villain at the pantomime (nobody had actually hissed at me, but that was the atmosphere) unless they genuinely feared that I was some sort of master criminal, witness threatener and escapologist rolled into one? Both my own and Victoria's lawyers were fearful, too, over the CPS attitudes to the case as we went through a summer-long sequence of conferences, discussions and paperwork. In these deliberations I kept hammering home the point that my greatest priority was to protect my innocent wife and daughter from standing in the dock with me.

Eventually we received some good news on one part of this strategy from Switzerland. To the chagrin of the CPS, it was established that Lolicia was not extraditable because, under the Swiss constitution, their own nationals cannot be handed over to foreign courts for trial. The CPS then considered pursuing Lolicia under a clause in the Anglo-Swiss extradition treaty which permits Swiss nationals to be tried on a British indictment in Switzerland. The problem here for the CPS was that Lolicia had committed no offence known to Swiss law. Signing an unsworn witness statement in a civil law suit is not a crime anywhere else in Europe. 'Madame Aitken is safe if she remains in Switzerland,' said my Geneva lawyer. 'Swiss prosecutors do not go so far as to put on criminal trials of the wife of a minister at the request of a newspaper which is politically hostile to him. So if the British tried such a strategy here it would, as you say, be laughed out of court.'

Although Lolicia was out of reach, Victoria remained in danger. One of my legal advisers took the view that she had only been arrested because of the formal complaint made against her in Alan Rusbridger's letter to the DPP, and that at the end of the day no sensible prosecutor would risk putting Victoria in the dock, as this would be the quickest way to win the jury's sympathy for the defendants and to score the own-goal result of not-guilty verdicts all round. Other members of my team were far less sanguine. 'This is a rough and dirty game in which the CPS will have no scruples about playing the Victoria card to take the trick against you,' advised one of them. 'You should give them your confession statement as quickly as possible. That's the only way to take the heat away from your family.'

This advice was reinforced by a backchannel conversation we had with the authorities, giving me the message that an early admission of guilt from me would get Victoria off the hook. But could we trust this clandestine signal? One of my lawyers thought we could not, and urged me to volunteer nothing on the grounds that the case against me was far from solid. In his view, a jury trial could easily go in my favour and might even collapse before it started, since the Crown could only prove their case by calling a number of foreign witnesses, none of whom could be compelled to testify by an English subpoena.

I rejected this brinkmanship approach on the simple grounds that since I believed I was guilty of perjury, it was right to say so quickly. That had been my position ever since the moment, some four months earlier, when I first heard Detective Sergeant Wall's tones booming over my office answering machine requesting my presence at a police interview. Then and now I wanted to tell the prosecutors the truth and get it over with. Cutting short the debate, I wrote out a full confession statement and delivered it to the police in early June. One important sentence in its final section stated, 'I am willing to answer further questions about all these matters.'

I then sat back and waited for the summons to be interrogated. To my own and to my lawyers' surprise, it never came. Some 10 days later, the police telephoned to say, 'We do not wish to question the first defendant further.' This was good news. My confession statement had been so comprehensive that the sleuths of Scotland Yard were satisfied. The big fish was now in the net. But what was going to happen to the minnows?

John Nutting QC had advised me from the outset of the case that my confession would be the gateway for Victoria's early release. This was the collective strategy for which we were all working. Even though we were hopeful of its eventual success, it was a major worry when the minnow Victoria was duly hauled in for a second police interview. Her lawyers worked long and hard to prepare her for it. When she returned to Chelsea Police Station she admitted no criminal wrongdoing over her original statement in the libel case. She said she had not understood its implications properly; she had not read it thoroughly; she could not remember all the details of what had happened when she was 13 years old; she had simply signed what I had written for her 'to help Daddy'.[1]

From all accounts of this second interview, the officers of Scotland Yard's Organized Crime Squad who conducted it were gentle, restrained in their questioning and thoroughly sympathetic to Victoria. They did not appear to accept Alan Rusbridger's allegation to the DPP that Victoria had been a party to what he had called 'a well-laid and carefully co-ordinated conspiracy to pervert the course of justice'.[2] Once again the impression was created that the police had some degree of distaste for this aspect of the Editor of the *Guardian*'s complaint.

The interview was expected to conclude with one of three results: Victoria being charged with conspiracy to pervert the course of justice; Victoria being cautioned for the same offence; or Victoria being told that no further action would be taken against her. In fact, this latest chapter of Victoria's travails had none of these endings. Contrary to what had been said to various lawyers on an earlier occasion, it emerged that Mr Fuat Emin of the CPS, rather than the police, would decide Victoria's fate. 'You will hear from him within seven days,' said one of the policemen, winking cheerfully at Victoria's solicitor. The wink later translated into backchannel confirmation that the police report to the CPS had recommended no further action.

Despite this encouraging signal, much anxious waiting was to follow. Seven days went by, then another seven, followed by seven more. What was going on? Telephone calls from Victoria's lawyers to the CPS elicited the unwelcome news that Fuat Emin was not entirely satisfied with the results of the police interview and needed more time to think further about the whole matter. Oh, the torture of these prolonged ordeals! Sometimes I wondered if those who administer our lethargic criminal justice system had the imagination to realize what it must be like for an innocent teenage girl to twist slowly in the wind while unnecessary delays piled on unnecessary delays.

Victoria herself was a rock of courage in this waiting period, although often leaning towards fatalism as she made comments such as, 'Whatever happens, I will always be the girl who was front-page news for being arrested, so they might as well put me on trial now.'

Such pessimistic words came close to breaking a guilty father's heart. I was increasingly troubled by the mounting pressures of delay. As I gradually discovered, however, inertia is the natural order in the world of criminal justice. Having been charged on 21 May, my first appearance in court was adjourned until 8 June, then to 6 July, and then to 15 September. This long hot summer was much worse for Victoria, who was kept dangling in suspense throughout June and July until a decision on her case was announced on 12 August, when the CPS at last issued a two-line press release saying that, 'No further action would be taken against Victoria Spasa Aitken.'[3]

The rejoicings within our family over this news were ecstatic and heartfelt. My own relief was so overwhelming that I was on a high of happiness and thanksgiving for several days. Yet even though the agony was over, I still found it hard to forgive myself for the ordeal I had put Victoria through. It took months for my remorse to fade. This happened gradually, as the caravan of Victoria's teenage life moved on. Without spending much time on retrospection, she instinctively understood that the pressures of the libel case had created their own unbearable and uncharacteristic moments of madness.

'We were a family at war and mistakes happen in war,' said Victoria philosophically, adding that the whole experience 'seems like a dream' as she recruited my help towards the achievement of her next dream, which was winning a place at a first-class American university. She had already been offered a place at one, but her heart was still set on gaining entry to her first choice, Georgetown.

In this endeavour, which required the burning of much midnight oil by Victoria as she completed some 15 US university application forms, the most important help came from her unexpectedly good A level results and an excellent 93 per cent mark in her American

SAT examinations.[4] With these credentials, supported by some adept lobbying of her own, Victoria won her 'dream place' at Georgetown University in Washington DC, starting in January 1999. She is now a happy and successful student there, majoring in Russian and Politics and regularly scoring a high percentage of A grades. So Victoria's part in the story has had a happy ending. I have paid her a small but special tribute for the love she has showed to me by dedicating this book to her.

In the wider picture of our family life, all my relationships bonded and strengthened as never before. The interminable delays of the law brought the side benefit of enabling me to spend far more quality time with my children. Although Lolicia did her best to stay in regular touch with Alexandra, Victoria and William, she was unable to visit Britain, so inevitably my single-parenting became the linchpin of our family life. 'We've decided we all love you more than ever, Daddy,' declared William one evening as I dropped him back at school after an exceptionally happy weekend. It was a throwaway line which brought tears to my eyes, not just because he said it, but because it was so obviously genuine and true. The long months of adversity were bringing us all much closer together; we were confiding more in each other and were gaining a far deeper understanding of our mutual needs and emotions. It was a huge blessing.

Confiding and understanding were virtues which enabled us to rise to an extraordinary development within our family in 1998 – the arrival of a new daughter. This chapter of surprises began on the night we gave a party to celebrate Alexandra's and Victoria's eighteenth birthdays. It was an electrifyingly happy evening. Both our daughters looked stunning in their new dresses and hairstyles, radiating their excitement and energy through the assembled company of teenage friends who danced, buzzed, networked and flirted the hours away as the champagne flowed, the weather stayed warm and the band played on.

As a busy host discreetly fussing about matters such as the shortage of ashtrays in the schoolboy smokers' corner, the supply of food from the kitchen, and the meeting and greeting of guests at the front door, I had little opportunity for long conversations. But one strikingly pretty teenage girl seemed to want to talk to me, so we chatted away together for several pleasant minutes. In retrospect, just about my only memory of this talk was that the girl had an unusual name – Petrina.

One evening about three weeks after the birthday party, Alexandra came into my bedroom with a delicate inquiry. 'Is there any possibility, Daddy, that you could be Petrina's father?' she began in a gentle but probing tone of voice. She explained that Petrina herself was obsessed with discovering the identity of her unknown parent and had recently focused her inquiries on me. 'You see, Petrina's found your photograph in some old press cuttings at her home, and she's discovered you had an affair with her mother,' continued Alexandra, 'and she's more and more convinced that you're her father, because Petrina and I keep being mistaken for each other at parties. We really do look alike. So, Daddy, tell me, is it possible that we could be sisters?'

'Steady on,' I said, trying to steady my own equilibrium by sitting bolt upright in my chair and holding on to both sides. 'Everyone knows I went out with Petrina's mother 20 years ago. But neither she nor anyone else has ever said that I'm Petrina's father. Who on earth started this rumour?'

The rumour, it transpired, had been doing the rounds for some time. At first Petrina had concluded, on the basis of ancient nudges and winks in the gossip columns, that her father was a quite different political figure who had conducted a much reported romance with her mother in the late 1970s. But this boyfriend's appearance and subsequent investigations into the precise dates of his affair had ruled him out. I was now being ruled in to the fatherhood role apparently on the basis of the similarity between Petrina's features and those of Alexandra and Victoria.

'Steady on,' I said again, feeling rather weak. 'There's nothing to prove this at all.'

'That's just the point,' said Alexandra. 'You could prove it by taking a DNA test. I think you really should, Daddy – for Petrina's sake.'

A torrent of confused thoughts, most of them defensive, tumbled through my troubled mind. The last thing in the world I needed at this vulnerable moment in my vortex of problems was another round of negative newspaper headlines and sensational stories. In any case, there was no credible evidence of my alleged paternity of Petrina. So far as I knew, the timings were wrong, and after nearly two decades of silence the suddenness of the suggestion seemed distinctly suspicious. I wondered aloud whether it could be some sort of journalistic set-up.

'Oh, don't be ridiculous, Daddy!' said Alexandra crossly. 'Petrina is the sweetest girl you could ever meet. She wouldn't dream of setting you up. She just wants to know who her father is. Don't you understand that this is the most important thing in the world for a girl who hasn't got a father?'

I tried to understand, but I still wanted to shrink away from it. This was a mean-minded and evasive attitude, although it was probably the one I would have adopted without hesitation in my heyday of power and prominence as a Cabinet minister. But now? I told Alexandra I needed time to think and pray about it.

Before I could make much progress with these activities, a letter arrived from Petrina's mother. It was a sensitive and loving communication containing no allegations, accusations or demands. It simply made the point, which I now knew to be true, that Petrina, Alexandra and Victoria were simmering with speculation that they might be sisters. Would I be prepared, for Petrina's sake, to take a joint blood test with her in order to put her mind at rest one way or the other?

I decided to share the question with my closest prayer partners. With their help a strategy emerged. First I should see Petrina in the company of Alexandra and Victoria. If I believed, as a result of our meeting, that the request for a DNA test was being made in good faith, then I should agree to do it. Ducking the issue would be unjust and unkind.

With this plan in mind, I arranged my second meeting with Petrina. It was an encounter which could easily have become tense and uncomfortable, but long before it had ended all thoughts of tension had evaporated because my heart was melting, and almost breaking, for this lovely but anguished child in search of a father.

Petrina tiptoed into the drawing room at Lord North Street like a highly strung gazelle entering unfamiliar territory. She sat down nervously on the sofa alongside Alexandra and Victoria. As I looked across at the three of them I was stupefied, for their physical resemblances were not just similar, they were uncanny. This visual evidence of sisterhood overwhelmed me. Indeed, if there had been a requirement to select, on grounds of appearance, the identical twins from the trio of sibling lookalikes seated on the sofa, any objective observer would have had to pair off Petrina and Alexandra, rather than Alexandra and Victoria. While I was still reeling from this first thunderbolt of identification, a second flash of genetic lightning gave further illumination to the scene.

Alexandra, when talking animatedly, has a trait of touching her neck with her right hand and then moving it away, giving a graceful little feminine twirl to her wrist as she does so. Five minutes into the conversation, what did I see? Petrina touching her neck and gracefully twirling her wrist away to the right. The movement was so natural, and so identical to Alexandra's familiar gesture, that from then onwards I felt in my heart of hearts that Petrina must surely be my daughter.

Over the next two hours I listened with growing compassion to Petrina's life story. She was still only 18, struggling to make a career as a fashion model as she recovered from a recent motorcycle accident. Her mother, Soraya, was the divorced English wife of the international businessman Adnan Khashoggi. He had been a kind stepfather to Petrina, but she was now obsessed with identifying her real father. 'I saw a photograph of you in one of my mother's old scrapbooks,' she told me. 'That's when I started to wonder if you could be my father and I wondered even more after I kept getting mistaken for Ally and Victoria at parties.'

I was doing much more than wondering as the story continued, particularly when my questions about Petrina's birth date indicated that she must have been conceived around the time when I last saw her mother – some weeks before my marriage to Lolicia in 1979.

In the face of such circumstantial and visual evidence, and because of the obvious sincerity of Petrina's motives, I decided it would be right to go ahead with the DNA test. After further talks and meetings, Petrina and I did the test in November 1998 under the auspices of a well-known London GP, Dr Jonathan Hunt, who sent off our blood samples to an Oxfordshire laboratory under the fictitious names of Camille Kay and Graham Edwards.

A DNA paternity test is not a swift procedure. In our case some five weeks elapsed between the giving of the blood samples and the arrival of the test result. It was a time of tension for both of us. There is no right way of navigating through such uncertainty, for how can an embryonic father–daughter relationship be kept on ice in frozen anticipation of news from a laboratory? Petrina was the first to express her fears on this score. 'I don't want to get too close to you right now,' she said one evening as she declined my invitation to supper. 'I'd be too heartbroken if you turned out not to be my father after all this.' I saw her point. All I could tell Petrina was, 'I'm saying lots of prayers for the right result.'

Although I meant it sincerely, I feared that the words must have sounded hollow and over-pious. I need not have worried. Much later I discovered that Petrina had her own methods of prayer. Some weeks afterwards, she showed me a letter she had written to her heavenly Father during the tense weeks of waiting. 'Dear God, please help me to find peace and happiness within myself,' it began, as Petrina set out her reasons for past unhappiness. She continued with this paragraph:

Please let good things come to me and my loved ones but give me the strength and goodness to deserve them. I so want to be a part of Jonathan and his family. Bless them all and please let the DNA tests be positive. If they are not I know that you would have made them that way for a reason so help me to come to terms with such a loss. If they are positive then please let the Aitkens accept me. I feel that you have been a little harsh on me through life and that everything I have had has been taken away from me. I will try and serve you and others better so that I deserve things more in life ... Amen.

The emotions that this 'Dear God' letter revealed in Petrina's heart were no less powerful in mine. Legal and financial storms were battering my external life as 1998 drew to its close, but I could hardly think of anything else except the DNA test and the long-term impact of its result on Petrina and the rest of my family.

An amusing illustration of this preoccupation occurred outside Bow Street Magistrates Court on 7 December. This was the day on which, seven months after being arrested, I was finally committed for trial. When I emerged from the court, the paparazzi rat pack of yappers and snappers surrounded me in exceptional strength. At the front of the pack was a newly promoted member of this elite corps of guardians of the public interest. He was a heavily inebriated Scotsman who looked as though he had neither slept nor shaved for several weeks, yet he was evidently in the mood to engage in a beery dialogue of camaraderie with a fellow member of the fraternity of the fallen.

'Och aye, Mr Aitken, can ye spare a fiver for a puir wee Scotsman who's doon on his luck just as ye are?' he began, in a voice straight from central casting. I was sufficiently well versed in the provocations of the paparazzi to suspect (correctly as it turned out) that this might be a set-up. So, as the drunk and his companion-in-lager weaved round me in ever-decreasing circles thrusting their cans of Fosters in my face, I disciplined myself to remain impassive and silent.

During the three or four minutes it took to push through the crowd of paparazzi and reach my car, the Scotsman decreased his price and increased his insults. 'Can ye no afford even a quid from yer arms dealing millions, yer mean bluidy Sassenach!' was one of his better lines. However, I hardly heard him because my mind was elsewhere, wondering in particular whether the DNA test result could have arrived during the morning while I was in court.

Intuitively, my inebriated interrogator got the message that I was switched to some other wavelength, because his last few plaintive cries were on the lines of: 'What's on yer mind then? Tell us what's on yer mind then if ye've no charity for a puir Scotsman!'

As I got into the car, my friend and driver Alan Woods said to me, 'Thank goodness you had the sense not to talk to that lunatic. I saw the photographers paying him just before you came out of court.'

Put it down to expenses! Thanks to my faraway thoughts on Petrina, the paymasters did not get much value for their money, although the *Evening Standard* solemnly reported my parsimony in this paragraph of their front-page story: 'As he left court former millionaire Aitken was approached by two florid faced men clasping cans of strong lager and asked for money. He declined and turned away smartly...'[5]

I had to wait for another two weeks after this latest 'Carry on Fleet Street' pantomime until, on 21 December, the envelope arrived with the DNA test report. Its wording required translation, for the paragraph headed 'Results' read as follows:

Twenty two fragments are present in the STR profile of Camille Kay. At least half of these fragments must be present in the STR profile of her father.

The STR profile of Graham Edwards contains a match for seventeen of these fragments.

Graham Edwards is not excluded from paternity of the child. The results obtained are sixty four times more likely if Graham Edwards is the true biological father of Camille Kay than if they are unrelated.

I telephoned Dr Jonathan Hunt to ask, 'What exactly does this mean?'

'It means your paternity is certain,' he replied.

Hallelujah! I then telephoned Camille Kay, alias Petrina. 'I have good news,' I told her. 'The DNA test shows you are definitely my daughter.'

'How wonderful!' she said, her voice breaking. It seemed impossible to have a meaningful conversation about such an amazing event on the telephone, so we agreed to have a quiet celebration dinner.

In the hours before we met for the first time as confirmed father and daughter, I sat on my own trying to sort out the latest surge of thoughts and emotions which were coursing through my head. They were a strange mixture of gratitude, contrition, anxiety and joy.

The gratitude, mingled with relief, was enormous. The worry of waiting was over. The DNA result was the one I had prayed for. Petrina need never again suffer the agony of not knowing who her father was or where she had come from. I could rejoice in the glorious gift of a new daughter. So, with a heart overflowing in thanksgiving, my first and strongest reaction was simply to say over and over again, 'Thank you. Thank you, God.'

These outpourings of gratitude were soon pierced by some painful shafts of contrition. Fathering a child should be a deeply serious, responsible and intentional act of love. I now knew that I had fathered Petrina in a moment of irresponsible self-indulgence with consequences, however unintentional, that had imposed unhappy burdens on her for over 18 years. The longer I dwelt on this aspect of the matter, the more remorseful I felt, but at least I knew what to do about it. Within an hour or so of receiving the wonderful news of my fatherhood of Petrina, I was penitently recognizing that her conception had also involved an outrageously selfish act of sinfulness on my part. By it I had betrayed not only Petrina herself, but also my then fiancée Lolicia, Soraya, and above all God, whose forgiveness I now humbly asked.

This contrition was matched by anxiety. In the rosy dawn of discovering my new daughter, the landscape of our relationship looked beautiful. But what about the landscape of my other close relationships which would be affected by it? So far Alexandra, Victoria and William had been sympathetic and understanding about the possibility of acquiring a new sister. Now that the possibility had turned into a reality, would they genuinely open their hearts and welcome her into the family? And how would my wider circle of friends, relatives and outside observers react to the news? Censoriously? Negatively? Half-heartedly? In my worst moments, not least when I started to fret about how the media would react to the news, I could see that there might be several disagreeable scenarios lurking over the horizon.

I need not have worried. The tone of the family's response was set by my 88-year-old mother. She had been in my confidence from the time when the Petrina story first reached me, and she had been characteristically supportive at all stages of it. Yet even I was surprised by my mother's unalloyed joy at the arrival in her life of a new grandchild. 'How absolutely wonderful! Bring Petrina over at once for a celebration drink,' she commanded. 'I want to welcome her properly.'

My mother's idea of a proper welcome included hugs, kisses, champagne, Christmas presents, photographs and introductions of Petrina to various members of the family who had not yet met her. These included my 25-year-old nephew Jack Davenport, who had just finished the shooting of his first feature movie *The Talented Mr Ripley*, in which he co-starred under director Anthony Minghella alongside Matt Damon and Gwyneth Paltrow. Jack the star was in a festive mood, for he had just decided to make an addition to his own family by becoming engaged to his long-standing girlfriend Michelle Gomez. So he brought along his new fiancée just as I brought along my new daughter, while my mother opened up her best champagne and then started distributing her kisses and her presents without initially explaining to everyone quite what was going on. Amidst the popping of corks the two new ladies in the family were, for a few moments, understandably confused – the more so because my mother's mind briefly slipped between generations as she began addressing me as 'Simon' (her brother) and Jack as 'Jonathan'. The scene quickly became comparable to that hilarious sextet in Mozart's *Marriage of Figaro* when the hero's paternity is suddenly revealed and astonished introductions are made, with one bemused relative after the other singing lines such as: 'And this is your father?' 'My father?' 'Your father!' and so on.

We had just about sorted out who was engaged or related to whom when there was a knock on the door. Enter a rustic lady, who seemed well equipped to play the gardener scene in *Figaro* since she was bearing a large Christmas tree from her estate. Peering at Petrina through its branches, she asked, 'Now, is this Victoria or Alexandra?'

Only a few moments earlier my mother had been given firm instructions to keep quiet about the Petrina story for a few more days, so she dissembled ignorance, only to hear her questioner say rather sternly, 'Pempe, surely you can tell your two granddaughters apart by now?'

In the merriment that followed, I made my excuses and left, taking Petrina out for a quiet dinner. Meanwhile, Alexandra and Victoria were fizzing with excitement at the news they had been expecting, so they too embraced their new sibling with great laughter and rejoicing. As for William, after making many jokes about how he had really been hoping to find a soccer-playing brother in his Christmas stocking, he too reacted warmly and lovingly to Petrina at their first meeting. His first gesture of family solidarity was to invite her to join him on a Boxing Day pub crawl. Fortunately Petrina passed this test, earning a further high score of fraternal Brownie points by inviting William to a New Year party hosted by two stars of the Chelsea football team – his supreme sporting heroes.

Over the next few days of seasonal festivities we saw a lot of Petrina. To my joy, I could see that real relationships were starting to form in the expanded family, with my mother once again playing the matriarchal role in this happy process which united and strengthened us even more.

This harmony remained undamaged even after a leak of the DNA test result burst into the press. At first this seemed to be a blow, as our house was once again besieged by paparazzi and our telephone lines were jammed with intrusive calls from journalists. Yet to my amazement the blow turned out to be a blessing in disguise, for the ensuing media coverage was gentle and almost universally sympathetic. Anodyne headlines such as 'FAMILY WELCOMES AITKEN LOVE CHILD',[6] coupled with a long and positive interview from Petrina's mother, Soraya, for once gave the right spin on the story, telling it as it was: a happy and loving discovery of a long-lost father by his daughter.

As the new year of 1999 opened I felt at peace. Looked at from the outside, this claim must have appeared perverse, for I was passing through some of the worst tempests of my life, with even more alarming thunderbolts looming on the horizon from those four apocalyptic horsemen of disgrace, divorce, financial disaster and jail.

Yet at the same time as I was waiting for the new onslaughts, I was inwardly conscious of how much I had changed and grown, particularly in my relationships with my family and in my relationship with God. The mystical channel of prayer was yielding up a rich harvest of increasing surrender and obedience to his will. The more I listened to that channel, the less I feared and the more I trusted. So I counted my blessings, which included a seen and unseen army of prayer-givers, prayer partners, distant well-wishers and intimate supporters. I often told people in this period that I was being magnificently sustained by what I had already come to call my 'three Fs' – faith, family and friends. The greatest of these was faith, and it was about to be subjected to its greatest test.

CHAPTER TWENTY-FOUR

Towards Bankruptcy and Prison

ON TUESDAY 19 JANUARY 1999, I entered the dock of Court No. 1 at the Old Bailey to plead guilty to charges of perjury and intending to pervert the course of justice.

It was a surreal, almost out-of-body experience in which I literally had to pinch myself for two paradoxically opposing reasons. Firstly, I needed to stiffen my mental and physical sinews in order to keep my feet on the ground throughout this nightmare of a courtroom scene which I, the prisoner at the bar, could hardly believe was really happening. Secondly, however, I had to struggle to stop myself smiling at the comic-turn reading performance of the Clerk of the Court.

Demonstrating that there were still some households in Britain where my name was an unknown word, the Clerk stumbled through the indictment as though it were veiled in the obscurity of some distant language. His mispronunciations introduced to the Ritz bill imbroglio a new cast of characters, among them Ludmilla Atkins, Lucilla Atken, Sad Abbas and Johnason Adkeen. For a fleeting second I was tempted to reply to the first charge by saying, 'Not present,' but respect for the solemnity of the occasion asserted itself, and I dutifully recorded my guilty pleas.

After being granted immediate bail to await sentencing in June,[1] I had to go down to the cells below the court for a few minutes in order to recover my house and car keys, which had been taken off me by a sardonic custody officer with the explanation: 'Just in case one of 'em's a skeleton key to the detention area – we do have people here who do that sort of thing.'

I had been in the detention area before. As a young journalist 28 years earlier, I had stood trial at the Old Bailey along with a retired Army Colonel and the Editor of the *Sunday Telegraph*, on charges under Section 2 of the Official Secrets Act 1911.[2] On the opening day of that cause célèbre, which centred on the leak of a British diplomat's report on the Nigerian Civil War, a prison officer had escorted the Editor, the Colonel and myself along the detention cells corridor to our courtroom. 'You're in Court No. 1, gents, that's the famous one,' the warder had declared. 'That's where we had Dr Crippen, Haigh, the Kray brothers, and now you.'

Despite this inauspicious beginning, I had emerged from my 1971 appearance in the dock of the Old Bailey with an honourable acquittal and, in media circles, something of a hero's reputation. This time it was different. Now I was the media's villain, trapped like a wounded animal in the aftermath of my plea of guilty as easy prey for the picadors and matadors of judgemental journalism. Leading the bullfight this time round was my contemporary and former journalistic rival Max Hastings, now the Editor of the *Evening Standard*. On the afternoon of my court appearance his paper devoted six pages to critical articles on my life and times, each one carrying the banner headline 'AITKEN'S DISGRACE'. The morning papers and the television news bulletins were little better, cumulatively turning me into a national hate object. After I had read my way through a gauntlet of headlines, including:

'BENT AND TWISTED'[3]
'HIS LIST OF LOVERS RUNS FROM A PROSTITUTE
TO THE RICH AND FAMOUS'[4]
'A LIAR AND A CHEAT'[5]

'A BROKEN MAN'[6]
'STRING OF GIRLS FELL FOR A RAT'[7]

I said to my friend Richard Shepherd MP, 'I feel as though I'm a war criminal.'

'Oh no,' he replied, 'Goebbels and Himmler would have been far more kindly treated.'

It was good to get a laugh, but deep down I was badly bruised by the media's hostility, some of which even extended to my mother, who was pilloried by the *Daily Mirror* for 'the arrogance which showed on her face' as she accompanied me to court.[8] I had not expected that I, and my family, would be flayed alive all over again with even greater editorial ferocity and with even more fictional reportage than had prevailed at the time of the libel case collapse 18 months earlier.

During these new scourgings, my spirits were crushed by a darker sense of pain than anything I had previously experienced. Some of this pain even manifested itself in physical illness. A bout of winter flu deteriorated into bronchial pneumonia, complete with high fever and severe headaches. A few days later, while I was driving on a motorway, I suddenly lost much of the sight in one eye as a result of a 'retinal occlusion'. In layman's language, this was a miniature stroke which burst most of the veins and blood vessels behind my left pupil. The diagnosis by the surgeons at Moorfields Eye Hospital was that the occlusion was probably caused by stress.

'Very few human bodies could put up with the pressure you've been under without cracking up somewhere,' was the verdict of one sympathetic specialist as he operated on my damaged retina.

I am not normally prone to stress-related illnesses, but with the reduced vision in my eye and a sharp deterioration in my asthma, I think in retrospect that I was teetering on the brink of a mental and physical depression during the month of February 1999. Yet before I could slide into the downward spiral of this condition, my spirits were restored by the constant kindnesses of my prayer partners, and by yet another inspirational letter from Chuck Colson. He had followed the press reports of my pleas of guilty and he felt moved to write to me from Washington with this message of reassurance:

My first reaction was that nothing in those press cuttings in any way altered my love, respect, and admiration for you. If any human being had to have their entire past laid out in bold print – headlines and photos – it would not make a pretty picture.

My second reaction was, 'welcome to the club!' In the midst of Watergate, there were articles like this about me, and what I remember is that half of them were made up. So, I don't take them all at face value. At the same time, I'm sympathetic. I've been there.

My third reaction was that all this makes absolutely no difference. All of those things would have been there were they disclosed or not. The important thing to remember is that God knew them all. But through His sacrifice on the cross of His Son, He has forgiven you, I emphasise 'has'. So you are free, a whole lot freer than the people that read that trash in the press and self-righteously gloat over it.

And my final reaction was that this is simply further confirmation that God is preparing you for a ministry. Only if you are broken, only if you know what it is to be stripped of everything as Jesus was stripped, can you truly then be His representative. Sometimes I worry about my own life because things go so well that I get used to good, easy times and public adulation. The more used to it I get, the harder it becomes for me to identify with the One who lost everything, was mocked, humiliated, disgraced, and driven to a cross to die between two thieves. This is why Mother Teresa used to say the poor are better off than the rich.

You're going to continue to go through things which in a worldly sense could seem like the end of the world. Most people would expect you to be prepared to jump off a bridge. The grace which you now exhibit, not only in the public press but even to friends and to all you come in contact with, will be all the more striking testimony because of what you are going through.

I can remember when I reached this same point in my own spiritual journey. I felt like I was really dragging. I was embarrassed. I was wondering what other people were thinking of me. Let me tell you what I have learned. It doesn't matter. Your friends will think no less of you, and your enemies have already thought ill of you. Keep your trust in Christ and follow His steps moment by moment, day by day, and He will guide your path. Only His reaction counts and His reaction has nothing to do with the stuff that is in the newspapers. It has everything to do with what is in your heart.[9]

My heart was encouraged by these shared experiences, for I could readily identify with Chuck Colson's memories of that low point in his journey when he was 'really dragging'.

My days at this time dragged their slow length along paths signposted 'Hospital', 'Jail' and 'Bankruptcy'. On the latter front, my money worries had been accumulating for months and were now acute. There were ironies here, because my adversaries at the *Guardian* had by their editorial and prosecutorial campaigns made it difficult for me to earn the income from which I might have financed the payment of their costs in the libel case. The bills for these costs had been mysteriously delayed for over 15 months. When they arrived in September 1998 they came to the amazing total of £2.4 million, which for 13 days in court seemed a trifle excessive. Becoming understandably nervous, with their Granada partners, that I might not have sufficient resources to pay such a large sum, the *Guardian's* lawyers, Messrs Olswang, went into overdrive to freeze my assets with a flurry of injunctions and other legal procedures whose tone can be illustrated by an extract from a letter they sent to me on 23 September.

...we require you to serve your Affidavit of assets on or before 1.00pm tomorrow, Thursday 24th September. If you do not ... we put you on notice that we will apply ex-parte on notice to the Queens Bench Judge in Chambers at 2.00pm ... for leave to issue and serve short a Notice of Motion seeking your committal to prison for contempt of Court.

I was surprised by this latest attempt on the part of a great liberal newspaper to have the size of Britain's prison population increased by one. Hoping that a touch of humour might restore equilibrium in the *Guardian's* legal and editorial offices, I replied as follows:

24th September 1998

Dear Ms Proudler

Thank you for your excitable letter of 23rd September.

My solicitor, Mr Michael Coleman of Harkavy's, faxed you a list of my assets two days ago. The affidavit containing the list is now being prepared by him but this is taking a little longer than expected owing to his travels overseas as he has already explained to you. The affidavit will be sworn on Monday soon after Mr Coleman arrives back in Britain and will be presented to the court. So please calm down. I know you and your clients are very anxious to see me locked up in prison, but there is no need to rush!

Yours faithfully

Jonathan Aitken

Needless to say, I was not committed to prison for the heinous crime of being four days late in submitting an affidavit, but a variety of other legal pressures were maintained against me in court hearings and correspondence throughout the winter of 1998/9. Under such pressures I spent approximately £120,000 in legal fees in this period, struggling to find a compromise solution that would enable me to strike a settlement deal with my creditors. This was a difficult exercise because of the English legal profession's peculiar procedural approach to litigation costs. Whereas in other professions, such as medicine or architecture, the bill submitted is the bill that has to be paid reasonably promptly, in litigation a lawyer's bill can be notional for months or even years until it is 'taxed', or umpired, by a High Court Taxing Master. The arcane taxation process is slow and cumbersome, but it invariably results in a substantial reduction of the original bill. Strange though this seems to a layman, legal bills are quite routinely delayed for a year or two and then cut in taxation by amounts of 20, 30 or even 50 per cent.

I was advised by my experienced team of lawyers and costs drafts-men, after various preliminary hearings, that the £2.4 million worth of bills submitted by the *Guardian* and Granada would eventually be reduced in taxation by about 45 per cent. If that estimate was correct, it would mean a taxed costs figure of around £1.3 million. Under the original court order issued at the end of the libel case, I was required to pay only 80 per cent of the defendants' taxed costs. That further reduction would mean that the final amount I would actually have to pay could come down to just over £1 million.

With this target in mind, I made great efforts to raise enough money to make a credible settlement offer to my creditors. It is not easy to borrow large sums when you are in financial trouble and on the verge of going to prison, but with the help of members of my family and a sympathetic banker I put together a package worth £840,000. My advisers thought this was a fair deal for both sides. The *Guardian* and Granada thought otherwise, telling me firmly that the minimum figure for which they would settle was £1.6 million, even if this meant making me bankrupt. The defendants evidently had a quite different view from my advisers as to the result of the tax-ation process, and also about the funds they might eventually be able to extract from my estate in bankruptcy.

Bankruptcy was an outcome I was desperately anxious to avoid. Quite apart from the further disgrace, it seemed the equivalent of having to serve a three-year financial prison sentence during which I could not earn an adequate living. Moreover, the *Guardian* indicated that they would litigate against me as a bankrupt to try to take away my parliamentary pension and my small occupational pension. Both my short- and long-term prospects were beginning to look distinctly uncomfortable, but I was helpless. After one last unsuccessful attempt to raise more money, I bowed to the inevitable and on 10 May 1999 filed my own petition for bankruptcy. This was another grievous blow to me.

While these financial struggles were in progress, the *Guardian* unexpectedly launched a new editorial attack on me. On 5 March 1999, the paper devoted its first three pages to what it claimed were new revelations about a 'business partnership' between Said Ayas and myself to make money out of arms deals through a company known as Marks One. 'If there is a more serious act of corruption in post-war British politics we would be interested to know of it,' screamed the *Guardian's* front page.

All that needs to be said here about this *Guardian* attack by David Leigh and other reporters is that it was untrue and unjustified.[10] For a start the revelations were not new. The *Sunday Times* had published the same Said Ayas–Marks One–arms-deal commissions story nine months earlier without making any allegations of ministerial corruption against me. Moreover, the *Sunday Times* had printed and accepted my statement saying that I had no knowledge of Marks One and its commission arrangements. The *Guardian* omitted that denial.

There was also no evidence in the article or elsewhere to support the *Guardian's* claim that I had been Said Ayas' business partner, nor was there evidence to suggest that I had ever gained or intended to gain from any ministerial support I had given, always in accordance with government policy and civil service advice, to British defence exports.

One other weakness in this latest episode of the *Guardian's* obsessional saga of anti-Aitken journalism was that none of the alleged Marks One business deals between British companies and Saudi interests had materialized, so no commissions or consultancy fees had ever been paid to anyone. The *Sunday Times* had reported these facts nine months earlier. Since the *Guardian's* articles had been noticeably unable to substantiate any knowledge of, or results from, an alleged wrongdoing which never took place, their charges of ministerial corruption did not look entirely convincing.

When I read the *Guardian*'s 'corruption' story, I was sufficiently upset by its unfairness and inaccuracy to file a formal complaint to the Press Complaints Commission,[11] but my reactions were much deeper in their sorrow than in their anger. As I explained in an earlier chapter I had, with the help of Mervyn Thomas, been praying for some months to empty my heart of all past resentments towards those whom I had once regarded as enemies, including some of the libel case journalists and their sources. Now, as these resentments resurfaced, I wondered why I had failed so badly in my supplications for peace and mutual forgiveness. Yet I was wrong to falter in this way, because these very blessings were in the process of arriving from another unexpected but rather more important quarter.

In late January 1999, when I was almost too ill to appreciate the significance of it, I received a letter whose consequences eventually warmed my heart and strengthened my faith. The writer of the letter was Valerie Scott, who had been my secretary from 1973 to 1979, the period when my relationships with Prince Mohammed, Said Ayas and all my other Saudi friends had begun. Present at the creation of those relationships, Valerie Scott had turned up nearly two decades later as the crucial and virtually the only source of a number of unpleasant allegations about them in the Granada programme 'Jonathan of Arabia', and in the defendants' pleadings in the libel action. My alleged recruitment of stewardesses as prostitutes in 1977 for Prince Mohammed's BAC 1-11; sleaze, bribes and corruption in relation to alleged deals such as the GEC–Philips contract for the street lighting of Riyadh; neglect of my parliamentary and constituency duties in order to give priority to Prince Mohammed, and financial dependency on Prince Mohammed were just some of the false charges which had emerged from Valerie Scott's conversations in her home with David Leigh of the *Guardian*. He had made her the star (although played by an actress) of his 'Jonathan of Arabia' programme and as a consequence she became the principal source of many of the defendants' libel case pleadings.

Early in 1999, Valerie Scott had a crisis of conscience about her role in the *Guardian*–Granada campaigns against me. It was triggered by the press reports of my Old Bailey appearance, all of which predicted that I was certain to go to jail. Moved by a commendable combination of courage, compassion and contrition, Val Scott wrote to me and later told me on the telephone of her regret about the part she had played in the saga. She blamed herself as much as anyone for what had happened, and wanted to offer me her regrets and apologies.

After taking time to absorb the impact of this remarkable volte-face, I replied as follows:

25/1/99

Dear Val,

Thank you so much for your kind and thoughtful letter. I rejoiced when I read it, and hope I can respond with equal generosity of spirit. My daughter Victoria said: 'It must have taken a lot of courage to write that letter.' A good comment, because as I too have found it is sometimes extremely difficult to express regret when wrongs have been done.

My regrets are greater than your regrets. It is a good time for mutual forgiveness. Without my wrongs there would have been no Ritz bill, no cover up, and no subsequent dramas. Without your wrongs there would have been no material for the 'Jonathan of Arabia' programme and no subsequent libel battles...

I write these words with no pity for myself and no reproaches to you. As you say, neither of us can change the past. However one can always change the future, which is now my greatest challenge. In the short term, my future is grim. However good your kind thoughts for me may be on the day of my trial, the judge will be compelled by legal precedent and by media demand to impose a severe custodial sentence. This is a certainty. Yet prison is not the end of the world. I have thoughts and beliefs which I hope will make my imprisonment a positive and creative experience, even though it will inevitably also have an uncomfortable and indeed miserable side to it as well.

A few days ago I went to the memorial service in Westminster Abbey for Vere Rothermere. It was a magnificent and moving occasion. Tony Blair read the lesson (Colossians 3:12–17) which included this sentence: 'Be tolerant with one another and forgiving. If any of you has any cause for complaints, you must forgive as the Lord forgave you.'

When I heard these words I pictured you and some of my other leading adversaries of the saga. Then I thought: How good that at least Val and I have reached a state of mutual tolerance and forgiveness. That is one peaceful ending, and I am glad for it.

So thank you for having the courage to write your letter which as you can see really meant a lot to me.

Yours gratefully,

Jonathan

This exchange of correspondence with Val Scott brought some remarkable results. I saw her (for the first time in well over a decade) for a meeting of reconciliation which was self-evidently genuine on both sides. In the course of a long conversation, she told me some extraordinary things about the activities of certain people close to the libel case. One of her disclosures was that she had tried to withdraw from her witness statement and from her commitment to give evidence against me, only to be told that if she did this she would be summoned to the court by subpoena and treated as a hostile witness.

After listening to Val's story, I said to her that if she really wanted to do something to help now, she might like to write to my solicitor with a letter that could be used as part of the mitigation plea on my behalf. She did write such a letter. Then, after further meetings with my solicitors and discussions with me, she wrote directly to the High Court Judge, Mr Justice Scott Baker, who was to sentence me at the Old Bailey on 8 June. In that letter she described how her interviews and witness statement had contained many inaccuracies. She detailed the history of her dealings with the journalists and stated:

So to set the record straight now, I wish to make it clear that Jonathan Aitken was never involved in arms dealing. He was never involved in pimping or procuring. He was never involved in corrupt business practices with Saudi Arabians or in corrupt dependency on Saudi Arabians. The suggestions in the programmes and articles which have made these allegations against Jonathan Aitken are to the best of my knowledge and belief utterly false.'[12]

The letter was read out in full to the judge, in a packed and hushed courtroom.

Valerie Scott's willingness to write this letter to the judge gave my spirits a great lift. It brought alive to me the meaning of the Gospel teachings on forgiveness. I had committed many trespasses myself, but at least I could now know what it felt like to give and receive forgiveness when it came to those who had trespassed against me. I had joyful emotions over the whole episode. It showed courage and grace on the part of Valerie Scott, while on my side it was yet another timely reminder that the power of prayer works in the most unexpected of ways.

A more expected development at around this time was an announcement that the CPS had decided to drop all charges against Said Ayas. I had always believed that this would happen, because I knew that an *R v Ayas* trial would do great damage to the national interest. Getting the

CPS to recognize this was a slow and uphill process. I had done my best to move it along by enlisting the help of Anthony Cavendish, a well-connected former member of the intelligence community. He knew that Said Ayas and I had done the State some service through the Prince Mohammed channel. After some preliminary discussions with Tony Cavendish, I wrote him a three-page letter in November 1998 setting out the reasons why it would be near madness to let an Ayas trial proceed. The concluding paragraphs of my letter read as follows:

I set out these concerns because I seriously doubt whether anyone in establishments like FCO, MOD, SIS, or the Cabinet Office have given them any thought. The CPS is probably largely oblivious of them, for its duty is to take a narrow evidential view of *R v Ayas*.

Against this background, the question which I believe needs to be asked by influential voices such as yours is this: Is the CPS view of the public interest in getting or attempting to get a conviction in *R v Ayas* being balanced by other wider views about the national interest problems attached to this case? If you can persuade anyone in authority to think carefully about these issues, I believe you will be doing a useful service.[13]

Tony Cavendish, an effective and skilful operator behind the scenes, made sure that my letter was read by Sir David Spedding, the Chief of the Secret Intelligence Service, and by Sir Colin McColl, his predecessor. The Attorney General also read it. On 4 March 1999, the Crown announced that all charges against Said Ayas would be withdrawn and that his costs would be paid from public funds.

This was a happy outcome for me privately as well as a wise one in the national interest. For nearly two years I had carried the burden of having involved my friend Said Ayas in my troubles. According to the laws and conventions of his country he had done nothing wrong, yet he had suffered greatly. For many months I had hoped and prayed that he would be honourably released from the clutches of the prosecutors so that I could stand in the dock alone. This was another prayer that had now been granted.

The Crown's decision to drop the charges against Said Ayas meant that they could no longer consider any proceedings against Lolicia. She had never been charged, but in theory she was still wanted for questioning for allegedly conspiring with me and Said Ayas to pervert the course of justice. The evidence for such a conspiracy was doubtful at the best of times, but now that all the Ayas charges had been abandoned, and the conspiracy charge had been dropped against me also, there was clearly no case at all against Lolicia. The Crown did not wish to say this formally until after my sentence had been served, but the position was obvious, as the police privately indicated. Lolicia was now in no danger of facing criminal prosecution.

I was not slow to count these blessings and to give thanks for them. With Easter approaching I could look back on the past 12 months with enormous gratitude, although much more in matters spiritual than matters temporal. Despite all my financial, legal and media batterings, I had enjoyed a year of growing trust and confidence in God's love. It is difficult to explain why I knew this was so real, and not some sort of Pollyanna-ish placebo of soft comfort in adversity. Perhaps it was because I had become conscious of being tested. Why, I had no idea, yet I did sense that there would be a purpose in it all. On the face of events I was sinking so quickly amidst a mass of disasters that I resembled a one-man *Titanic*. Yet on a deeper level I knew I was going to survive and strengthen in my coming ordeals. Why this might be so was the last mystery in this part of my journey.

CHAPTER TWENTY-FIVE

The Final Mystery

'WHAT HAS MY JOURNEY really been about?' This was the question
I asked myself, with many variations, as the day on which I would be
sentenced to prison grew closer. Shortly before I was due to make my
final appearance at the Old Bailey, I treated myself to four days of
solitude at Sandwich Bay, rising each morning on the wings of the dawn
to walk by the sea, to pray, to ponder, and to write this final chapter.

There is something about the combination of sea and stillness
which stirs my soul. Many years ago I was told by a science teacher
that there is precisely the same percentage of salt in a drop of sea
water as there is in a drop of human blood. Ever since absorbing that
biological revelation (accurate or not) I have instinctively felt that
going down to the sea can be a return to the roots of our being and a
renewal of the spirit and substance of which we are made.

In such a mood of self-renewal I spent many hours of the last four
days in May 1999 walking the shoreline between those two somewhat
questionable monuments on the East Kent coast which claim to mark
the exact spots where, in their respective centuries, Julius Caesar and
St Augustine landed. It is an area which in the early morning sunlight
contains some of the loneliest and loveliest littorals in the British
Isles. As I climbed its white cliffs and walked along its shingled
beaches, I felt contented, thankful and at peace.

In that peace there lay a paradox. I was under no illusions about the
ordeal that lay immediately ahead of me, nor about the devastation of

my career and fortunes that lay behind me. Yet even as I surveyed the disaster trail retrospectively, all my past battles with political and media opponents chronicled in the early parts of this book seemed to belong to a bygone era. They had been the superficial part of the story, while the profound part concerned the spiritual sea change within and around me. As I reflected on the depth of that process, I began to understand that there had been three great experiences emerging from my journey – humbling, changing and growing.

The humbling was excruciatingly painful, but if I had not passed through it I could never have moved forward to the other two experiences. Not since the days of Oscar Wilde had any public figure suffered so much vilification and punishment for telling a lie in a libel case. My own Icarus-like fall from Cabinet minister to convicted prisoner had left me with broken bones and battered spirits. The damage felt even worse than it was because most of the humbling took place in public. Yet this noisily enforced humiliation was probably a necessity, for it turned out to be such an effective antidote to the poison of pride.

Pride was the root cause of all my evils. Without pride there would have been no libel action; no attempt to defend the Ritz bill payment with a lie; no will to win the battle in court on an ends-justifies-the-means basis. There would have been no deceit of friends, family and colleagues; no Sword of Truth speech; no involvement of my wife and daughter in the front line of the war with the *Guardian*. If I had been blessed with a small helping of humility instead of possessed by a surfeit of pride, the entire tragedy would have been avoided. The ancient Greeks who prophesied that hubris would always be followed by nemesis were right. So was C. S. Lewis in the twentieth century when he described pride as 'the complete anti-God state of mind'.[1] My pride had been such a powerful, blinding, demonic state of mind that it could only be cured by the severest of lessons.

Today I am grateful for the lessons I have learned. It has taken a long time to recognize the benefits of this chastening. If there was an identifiable moment when the recognition began, it came when I received a letter soon after the libel case from the former Archbishop of Canterbury, Robert Runcie, who quoted a sentence from the Roman Missal: 'May what comes to us in our time be for our healing in the everlasting years.'[2]

Puzzling over what this meant as I nursed my emotional scars, I slowly began to surrender to the severity of what was coming to me in my time and to accept that it might be the essential first step in the process of healing. Soon that healing was starting to work in the present rather than the everlasting years, and with it began a new process – changing.

I may not be the best judge of how much I have changed. All I can say with certainty is that my family, my children, my close friends and several other observers all comment favourably on the changes which they perceive in me. I can, however, identify the areas where I think the process is taking place, for I describe them as *inward* change, *outward* change and *upward* change.

Inward change starts with asking the simple question: Who am I? For me it was an essential self-interrogation after falling from a mountain top of political power into a mine shaft of media opprobrium. That fall was so disorientating that for a time I did not know the answer to my own question. I tried on various stereotype hats, such as the misunderstood maker of a mistake, the resilient recoverer, the wronged victim, the comeback kid, the excessively punished teller of an unimportant lie, the determined career rebuilder, and so on, but none of them fitted. In the end there was only one response to the question 'Who am I?' with which I could live. It was: 'I am a sinner who wants to repent.' This cry for help did not go unheard.

From that starting point of inward change, many outward changes manifested themselves, particularly in the field of human relationships. Within the family all sorts of new and enriching horizons opened up as I had more time and willingness to share my fears, frailties and insecurities. This led to renewed bondings, particularly with my children, who seemed to prefer a father who was vulnerable to a father who was powerful. As if to demonstrate the benefits that flowed from this development, in the autumn of 1998 William wrote a school English essay entitled 'My Father'. When I read it in his exercise book several months later as we were doing revision for his GCSE English Language paper, my heart melted. The first half of the essay portrayed a father who had often been impatient, over-worked, short tempered and unreasonably demanding with his son. Then, after some graphic descriptions of 'the most terrible days of my life' during the period after the libel case collapsed, the essay went on with this passage:

Now my father really listens to me and understands my problems. He has time to come and watch me in all my football matches. He drives me every-where. We talk and laugh together for hours … He is in as good a frame of mind as can be expected. His religion has mainly helped him through it, but I'd like to think I helped a little by helping to save our relationship. My father is extraordinarily resilient in the face of hardships. He is inspirational and I only hope I can be half the man he is. I am proud of him because he's my best friend as well as my father.[3]

Similar breakthroughs into greater trust and intimacy came with some of my oldest friends, and also with a new circle of supporters, prayer partners and counsellors. As these links strengthened I gradu-ally became conscious of loving and being loved by my neighbours on a wider and deeper scale than had ever happened before. As with William, the availability of time was a key factor in the bonding process. Instead of forever rushing to the next meeting or leaping away from conversations at the peal of a division bell, in my dark days of disgraced unemployment I could build friendships with generous expenditures of time, gladly going the extra mile to anyone who needed my help – and finding, to my amazement, that there were scores of friends willing to go an extra seven miles to help me. It was a wonderful experience to be on the receiving end of so much goodness and kindness, which I hope I reciprocated as a gentler, softer and more loving attitude of heart kept welling up from within.

None of these inward or outward changes would have occurred had it not been for the most momentous transformation of all. This was what I call the upward change, the change in my relationship with God. Here I begin to tread on holy ground, for I am still too full of awe and wonder to be able to write clearly about what has happened. I am not even capable of saying when it happened, for I cannot point to a blinding flash of light on the road to Damascus, nor to an instant moment of conversion. Yet somewhere along the painful road of the journey described in this book, after many months of prayer and listening, my eyes opened and I recognized that I had accepted Jesus Christ into my heart as my Lord and my God.

I do not believe that this fundamental change came about because I was seduced at a time of weakness by 'the consolations of religion'. It is a phrase I reject, because what followed my commitment to a deeper faith was not consolation but an almost unbearably testing vocation. This required me to run a course of increasingly painful challenges and obstacles. Yet because I believed that this course was God's testing of me, I was determined to complete it, whatever the cost in temporary suffering might be.

Inevitably, there were days of doubt and faltering as the course became more demanding. The strengthening of prayer usually got me through those bad days, but in the really terrible periods, every time I felt like collapsing something extraordinary happened or someone remarkable appeared by my side to help me keep going.

These signs and companions along the journey were a constant source of wonder. Many of them are referred to in earlier chapters, but those accounts did not include the accumulation of questions which the facts provoked: Why on earth should I keep getting letters day after day, often from virtual or total strangers, telling me they were remembering me in their prayers? Why on earth should a disparate collection of acquaintances such as Michael Alison, Chuck Colson, Jim Pringle, Judith Marriott, Mervyn Thomas and several others have grappled their souls to mine in intimate and prayerful friendship? Why on earth should my stumblings into spiritual readings, retreats and Bible studies have produced such a rich harvest of enjoyment and peace? Why on earth should my chronic asthma suddenly recover to the point of near-normal breathing after an embarrassing (at first) laying on of hands session with my solicitor, doubling up as prayer healer, Bruce Streather? Why on earth should my relationships with my children, my sister and my mother have blossomed into so much happiness at a time when all the outside world could see was a landscape of unhappiness? Why on earth, six months after a devastatingly sad and acrimonious divorce, should my telephone calls from Lolicia have taken on a new dimension of positive, and sometimes loving, communication?

The answers were beyond me until I realized that I was asking the wrong questions by prefacing them with the phrase 'Why on earth...' For the explanations were not earthly, even though the results of them were often down to earth. The mysterious and loving presence of God was there too.

One of the biblical texts about God's presence which several of my correspondents sent me in the weeks before my sentence consisted of these verses from Jeremiah:

'For I know the plans I have for you,' declares the LORD, 'plans to prosper you and not to harm you, plans to give you hope and a future. Then you will call upon me and come and pray to me, and I will listen to you. You will seek me and find me when you seek me with all your heart. I will be found by you,' declares the LORD, 'and will bring you back from captivity.'

(JEREMIAH 29:11–14 NIV)

Although these stirring words from an Old Testament prophet might well give consolation to someone on the verge of going into captivity, I did not initially take too much account of them. That attitude altered during a tempestuous period in May 1999 when the remnants of my own worldly plans were suddenly blown apart, only to be reshaped in a quite different direction by forces and coincidences which seemed utterly astonishing.

As related in the previous chapter, I spent most of the early months of 1999 making strenuous efforts to avoid bankruptcy. When those efforts failed because the *Guardian* rejected my settlement offer, I was plunged into gloom and despondency. My future plans for when I came out of prison to be a provider for my children, a big income earner and an entrepreneurial businessman had all collapsed in disaster. Moreover, the early days of my bankruptcy included some of the worst humiliations of the entire saga. The *Guardian* appointed a Trustee in Bankruptcy whose first actions were to remove my wrist-watch, my cuff links and my son's computer. He also announced that he would take the necessary steps to deprive me of my parliamentary pension, my small occupational pension and my library of books. In a further broadside, he seized nine cases of personal correspondence, none of them related to my financial papers which had been handed over earlier. The personal files consisted largely of intimate corre-spondence, among them letters from close relatives, friends, spiritual companions and priests. The seizure was incomprehensible in finan-cial terms, but it sharply made the point that I was now a helpless bankrupt. Some months later, however, Mr Justice Rattlee in a High Court judgement described the Trustee's action as 'repugnant' and ordered all the personal correspondance to be returned to me.

Stripped bare of all my worldly goods and privacy by the Trustee's initial action, my dependency on God was now total and absolute. So perhaps it was not surprising that at this time of material disaster I should have been granted a spiritual breakthrough.

For some months in 1998/9 I had been shopping around in search of a correspondence or distance learning course to study during my prison sentence, in the field of Bible studies or introductory theology. This quest eventually took me to Wycliffe Hall, Oxford. I arrived there in a pessimistic mood, partly because it was the day after my bankruptcy had become inevitable, and partly because my search for a suitable course had been growing increasingly disappointing. When I walked into Wycliffe to discuss the merits of doing some short-term diploma studies in Theology, therefore, my expectations were not much higher than my despondent spirits.

In a testing interview with the Principal of Wycliffe, the renowned theologian Dr Alister McGrath, and his deputy, Dr Graham Tomlin, I quickly realized that here I was in a different league from some of my previous educational encounters. Wycliffe is a theological college of the highest academic standards with an evangelical mission and reputation that is respected around the world. As the discussion developed, I grew more and more exhilarated at the prospect of studying there, particularly when it became apparent that Wycliffe would be willing to accept me for the full Oxford University Honours degree course in Theology.

I have never had a better illustration in my life of the old adage that as one door closes, another opens. Had I gone to Wycliffe 24 hours earlier, I could not have contemplated the degree course. It required at least two years of full-time study at Oxford, passing examinations in subjects such as New Testament Greek which would be unknown and difficult intellectual territory for me. But in the days immediately before the meeting my plans had been turned upside down. My bankruptcy, which had seemed so devastating because it blocked all hopes of a commercial life for the next three years, had now opened up the new and unexpected freedom of undertaking long-term academic studies. An Oxford degree was therefore a serious and viable option for me.

By the end of what had been an extremely interesting and challenging interview, I was literally quivering with excitement. Suddenly

I knew that a whole new plan was unfolding before my eyes. Was it one of God's plans, as summarized by Jeremiah? All I knew was that I felt a great surge of certainty that I wanted to read Theology at Oxford more than anything else in the world.

Why Theology? I made many attempts during and after my Wycliffe interview to answer that question. The best I could come up with was that I wanted to devote the next phase of my journey to getting to know God better by studying his teachings and his truths. Then by chance a friend, who knew nothing about my moves to study Theology, gave me a book which opened with this arresting paragraph:

Theological truth is the truth of God's relationship with man and it is the fruit not of learning but of experience. In this sense all theology properly so called is written in blood. It is an attempt to communicate what has been discovered at great cost in the deepest places of the heart – by sorrow and joy, frustration and fulfilment, defeat and victory, agony and ecstasy, tragedy and triumph. Theology, properly so called, is the record of man's wrestling with God. Wounded in some way or other by the struggle the man will certainly be, but in the end he will obtain the blessing promised to those who endure.[4]

As soon as I read these remarkable words by H. A. Williams, they inspired and encouraged me with the hope that I might already be travelling along the road of the theology of experience. This very book of mine is 'an attempt to communicate what has been discovered at great cost in the deepest places of the heart'. It may even have been 'written in blood'. It is certainly an integral part in the last element of what I earlier described as the three great experiences of my journey – growing.

Explaining the process of one's own spiritual growth is extremely difficult, because so much of it consists of mystical inner feelings which lie beyond the horizon of words. Yet the disciplines of prayer and study which lead to these intangible changes are themselves tangible, just as the outward symptoms of the growing process are themselves visible.

In my case I have visibly passed through the flames of numerous disasters in the past four years, and I write this last chapter on the edge of the final fiery furnace of prison. By all normal expectations I should be apprehensive, depressed, on the edge of a breakdown, tormented by pressures and turmoils, hating my enemies and despairing of my future. Yet I am in none of these moods. Instead I am calm, contented, tranquil, often joyful, full of love for my family and friends, and brimming with positive hope for the future.

Is there an explanation for this final mystery? It has nothing to do with stoicism or fatalism, for I have never believed in sitting back and letting life's destiny run its course. Throughout these dramas I have been proactive in my search for God. The struggle has been momentous, but in the course of it I have learned much about acceptance, patience and obedience to his commandments. With the companionship of the Holy Spirit I now find it easy to pray. In those prayers I commit my own and other people's situations to God, putting him in the centre of them and accepting that his will, not mine, shall be done. The serenity that has flowed from this surrender is almost indescribable, but the words of St Augustine say it beautifully: 'In his will we find our peace.'[5]

In the first chapter of this book I described an episode at the start of the Parliamentary Retreat of 1995 when Father Gerard Hughes SJ read out a text from Isaiah which mysteriously stirred me. Part of it is worth repeating here:

> *Do not be afraid for I have redeemed you.*
> *I have called you by your name, you are mine.*
> *If you pass through the sea I will be with you.*
> *If you go through rivers they will not swallow you up.*
> *If you pass through the fire you will not be scorched and the flames will*
> *   not burn you...*
> *So do not be afraid, for I am with you.*
>
> (ISAIAH 43:1-2, 5)

With tremblings of wonder and tears of humility, I now accept that these prophetic words have come true for me. Redemption has been granted even though earthly punishment remains. I may have lost the whole world of my previous life, but I have found my own soul in a new life. Where that new life will take me is the next step of the mystery. Yet even if the road that has to be travelled lies through prisons, floods and more fires, I am not afraid. Having made the commitment to God, I now look forward to following him wherever he leads with trust, hope and joyful acceptance.

Epilogue

On 8 June 1999 Jonathan Aitken was sentenced to 18 months imprisonment at The Old Bailey, having pleaded guilty to charges of perjury and attempting to pervert the course of justice. He served his sentence at Belmarsh, Standford Hill and Elmley prisons. He was released on licence on 7 January 2000.

Notes

CHAPTER ONE

1 Benjamin Disraeli, *Sibyl*, 1845.
2 Sir Roger Hurn is now Chairman of GEC Plc.
3 David Omand was promoted again in 1997 to become Permanent Secretary at the Home Office.
4 *Mail on Sunday*, 29 January 1995.
5 Ibid.
6 In this passage St Luke describes two men going up to pray in the temple. One is a Pharisee who congratulates himself on his superiority in matters of religious observance. The other is a publican who lowers his eyes humbly and says, 'God be merciful unto me, a sinner.'
7 Reverend Lister Tonge, interview with author, 24 March 1998.

CHAPTER TWO

1 David Leigh, internal Granada memorandum, 30 January 1995.
2 Ibid.
3 Ibid.
4 Ibid.
5 *Guardian*, 10 April 1995.
6 Ibid.
7 These issues are dealt with in detail in Chapter 12, 'What Really Happened at the Ritz'.
8 Sir Robin is now Lord Butler of Brockwell GCB, CBO.

9   Brian Hitchen is a former Editor of the *Sunday Express*.

10 Alex Allan, memorandum to Sir Robin Butler, 31 August 1994.

11 Lord Justice Scott's report reached no such conclusion, specifically exonerating all ministers of the false charge that they had acted improperly over signing PII certificates in the case.

12 John Bercow is now the Conservative MP for Buckingham.

13 Author's speech at Conservative Central Office, 10 April 1995.

14 Ibid.

CHAPTER THREE

1   Luke Harding, David Leigh and David Pallister, *The Liar*, Penguin Books, 1997, p. 96.

2   Mr C's statement, signed and given to the solicitor Richard Sykes on 17 May 1995.

3   Ibid.

4   *Independent*, 4 April 1995.

5   Ibid.

6   See Gerald James, *In the Public Interest*, Little Brown & Co, 1995.

CHAPTER FOUR

1   Sir Terence Burns to author, 10 June 1995.

2   Author, draft letter to the Prime Minister John Major, 11 June 1995.

3   *The Liar*, p. 105.

4   Author's diary note, 20 June 1995.

5   Ibid.

6   *The Liar*, p. 102.

7   Mr C's statement, signed and given to the solicitor Mr Richard Sykes on 17 May 1995 (see Chapter 3, p. 33).

CHAPTER FIVE

1 Alastair Goodlad, Conservative MP for Eddisbury, was Minister of State for Foreign Affairs in July 1995. After John Major's leadership election victory he was promoted to Chief Whip. Teresa Gorman, Conservative MP for Billericay, was a leading protagonist of John Redwood's leadership campaign. Greville Howard was a businessman with Eurosceptic sympathies who was willing to lend his house to the Michael Portillo leadership campaign if it had materialized.

2 Author's diary note, 20 June 1995.

3 Anna Airy RA was Playford's most famous artist.

4 Reverend Geoffrey Laing to author, 22 June 1995.

5 Stephen Milligan, Conservative MP for Eastleigh, was my Parliamentary Private Secretary. He was found dead in his house in Hammersmith in 1994, apparently having suffocated as a result of a sexual experiment.

6 *Guardian*, 27 June 1995.

7 Author's diary note, 2 July 1995.

8 Ibid., 18 July 1995.

9 Ibid., 26 July 1995.

10 Gerard W. Hughes, *God of Surprises*, Darton Longman & Todd, 1985, pp. 73–4.

CHAPTER SIX

1 Pleadings Bundle, p. 36.

2 Ibid., pp. 37–8.

3 Ibid., p. 36.

4 British Caledonian Airways (BCAL) was Britain's second-largest international airline until it was taken over by British Airways in the early 1980s. BCAL was the operator of Prince Mohammed's aircraft (see Chapter 9).

5 Pleadings Bundle, p. 36.

6 I later wrote President Nixon's biography, *Nixon: A Life*, published in 1993 by Weidenfeld & Nicolson.

7 During my career in the 1960s as a foreign correspondent, I had reported on wars in these and other international trouble spots, mainly for the London *Evening Standard*.

8 Alfred, Lord Tennyson, *Idylls of the King*, 'The Passing of Arthur', 1869.

CHAPTER SEVEN

1 *Private Eye*, 4 November 1994.

2 Author's evidence to the House of Commons Trade and Industry Select Committee, 6 March 1996.

3 Astra Holdings plc – Investigation under s.431(2)(c) of the Companies Act 1985, report by Colin Rimer and John White, HMSO, 1993.

4 For a long read of these incredible theories, see Gerald James, *In the Public Interest*, Little Brown & Co, 1995.

5 *Guardian*, 12 December 1995, and Granada *World in Action*, 11 December 1995.

6 *Daily Mirror*, 27 September 1995.

7 Derek Dubery to author, later reported to the House of Commons Select Committee, with Mr Dubery's permission, 6 March 1996.

8 The Rt Hon. David Heathcoat-Amory MP, Economic Secretary to the Treasury and Minister responsible for HM Customs, private comment to author, 13 April 1996.

9 Granada *World in Action*, 11 December 1995.

10 Ibid.

11 Witness statement of Mr Allan Frederick Heather, retired HM Inspector of Explosives, 19 September 1996.

12 Author, letter to Gerald James, 8 March 1985.

13 Author's evidence to House of Commons Trade and Industry Select Committee, 6 March 1996.

14 Author, letter to Gerald James, 8 March 1985.

15 House of Commons Select Committee for Trade and Industry Report on BMARC, 12 June 1996.

16 Ibid.

CHAPTER EIGHT

1 Author, interview with Sister Madeleine Prendergast, 18 May 1998.

2 Interview with Robin Lustig, BBC Radio 4, 20 June 1995.

CHAPTER NINE

1 Author's diary note, 2 July 1994.

2 Now Lord Keith of Castleacre.

3 Former Presidents of the United States retain the courtesy title after leaving office.

4 The Congressional resolutions on 12 January 1991 authorizing the United States to commit its armed forces to the liberation of Kuwait were carried by 52 to 47 votes in the Senate and by 250 to 183 votes in the House of Representatives.

CHAPTER TEN

1 Author's diary note, 14 April 1992.

2 Ibid.

3 Ibid.

4 Richard Nixon, *Real Peace*, Sidgwick and Jackson, 1983, p. 5.

5 Author's diary note, 6 July 1993.

6 Henry Kissinger, *White House Years*, Little Brown & Co., 1979, p. 12.

7 Author's diary note, 30 January 1993.

CHAPTER ELEVEN

1 Later alleged to have been Michael Heseltine.

2 *The Liar*, p. 67.

3 Witness statement of Wafic Said, 5 July 1996.

4 The *Guardian* published a front-page retraction which included this passage: 'The *Guardian* now accepts that their report was untrue, that no such meeting took place and that no such donation was made. We apologise without reservation to Prince Bandar for the distress and embarrassment this report has caused him and in these circumstances we have agreed to make a substantial contribution to a charity of the Prince's choice.'

5 Witness statement of Said Ayas, 30 November 1996.

CHAPTER TWELVE

1 *The Liar*, p. 186.

2 *Guardian*, 5 March 1999.

3 *Independent*, 22 June 1997.

4 See Chapter 10, pp. 138–44.

5 *Sunday Times*, 5 July 1998.

6 David Pallister, letter to the author, 19 October 1993.

7 Author, letter to David Pallister, 20 October 1993.

8 Peter Preston, letter to the author, 22 October 1993.

9 *The Liar*, p. 68.

10 Ibid.

11 *Guardian*, 10 May 1994.

12 Comment made to the author in Jeddah, 14 December 1993.

13 Witness statement of Said Ayas, 2 May 1998.

14 Lolicia was oblivious to this lie when I wrote it in this letter to Preston. She was in hospital undergoing major surgery.

15 Trial transcripts, 10 June 1997, p. 20.

16 *Guardian*, 10 March 1994.

17 *Independent*, 13 March 1994.

18 Frank J. Klein, letter to the author, 10 May 1994.

19 *Diplomat* magazine, July 1994, et seriatim.

20 Sir Robin Butler, letter to Peter Preston, 18 May 1994.

21 John Major to author, 20 May 1994.

CHAPTER THIRTEEN

1 See Chapter 12, pp. 172–3.

2 *The Liar*, p. 80.

3 See Chapter 2, p. 22.

4 Pleadings Bundle, p. 59.

5 Ibid., p. 63.

6 Ibid., p. 86.

7 Ibid., p. 87.

8 Ibid., p. 94.

9 Ibid., p. 66.

10 Ibid., p. 124.

11 Ibid., p. 41.

12 Witness statement of David Trigger, 11 June 1997.

13 Lord Pearson of Rannoch, my closest friend.

14 Pleadings Bundle, p. 69.

15 *The Liar*, p. 121.

16 Theodore H. White, *Breach of Faith: The Fall of Richard Nixon*, Atheneum, 1975, p. 142.

17 *Washington Post*, 1972–3, *passim*.

18 From C. S. Lewis, *Mere Christianity*, quoted in Charles Colson, *Born Again*, Hodder & Stoughton, 1977, new edition 1995, pp. 123–4.

19 *Born Again*, p. 123.

20 Margaret Hebblethwaite, *Way of St Ignatius*, Fount, 1999, pp. 89–90.

21 Ibid.

22 Ibid.

CHAPTER FOURTEEN

1 *The Liar*, p. 131.

2 Ibid., p. 125.

3 Author, in conversation with Alan Rusbridger at Wiltons, 15 November 1995.

4 See Chapter 3, pp. 34–5.

CHAPTER FIFTEEN

1 Charles Gray QC, opening speech, *Aitken v Guardian*, 4 June 1997.

2 Ibid.

3 Ibid.

4 Ibid.

5 Ibid.

6 *The Liar*, p. 133.

7 Trial transcripts, 5 June 1997, pp. 21–2.

8 Ibid., p. 23.

9 Ibid., 6 June 1997, p. 57.

10 Ibid., 6 June 1997, p. 72.

11 Ibid., p. 62.

12 Ibid., p. 72.

13 Ibid., p. 73.

14 Ibid.

15 *The Liar*, p. 136.

16 The second action arose out of the defendants' publications in December 1995 (see Chapter 7). The first action arose out of their publications in April of that same year (see Chapter 2). Both actions were 'consolidated' into one hearing.

17 *The Liar*, p. 134.

18 Ibid.

19 Trial transcripts, 18 June 1997, pp. 25–6. See also Granada transcripts.

20 *Evening Standard*, 19 January 1999.

21 Trial transcripts, 18 June 1997, p. 65.

22 Ibid., 13 June 1997, p. 65.

23 Witness statement of Victoria Aitken, 17 June 1997.

24 Trial transcripts, 18 June 1997, p. 72.

CHAPTER SIXTEEN

1 *The Liar*, p. ix.

2 Author's diary note, 18 June 1997.

3 Ibid.

4 Ibid.

5 Ibid.

6 Ibid., 19 June 1997.

7 *Guardian*, 19 June 1997.

8 *The Liar*, p. 168.

9 Richard Sykes' figure was an underestimate. When the defendants eventually lodged their bills for taxation at the surprisingly late date of November 1998, their claim for costs was for £2.4 million. At the time of writing this claim has not yet been taxed. My advisers estimate that after taxation it will be reduced to around £1.3 million, which is still a huge figure for a 13-day court hearing.

CHAPTER SEVENTEEN

1 *Daily Mirror*, 20 June 1997.

2 *Evening Standard*, 20 June 1997.

3 *Guardian*, 21 June 1997.

4 Ibid.

5 *Daily Mirror*, 21 June 1997.

6 *Independent on Sunday*, 22 June 1997.

7 Thomas Babington, 1st Baron Macaulay, essay on Lord Byron in the *Edinburgh Review*, 1828.

8 *Star*, *Daily Mirror*, LBC Radio, BBC Radio 5, seriatim, 22–5 June 1997.

9 DS Hunt to Lynn Fox, 26 June 1997.

10 Author's personal papers, 1997.

11 *Guardian*, 25 June 1997.

12 *Guardian*, 21 June 1997.

13 Approximately £1,750.

14 *Daily Express*, 27 June 1997.

15 *Evening Standard*, 23 June 1997.

16 *Hamlet*, Act I, scene iii, l. 62–3.

CHAPTER EIGHTEEN

1 *Hamlet*, Act III, scene i, l. 56.

2 Bob Woodward and Carl Bernstein were the *Washington Post* journalists who led the hunt for the truth about Watergate.

3 My prediction that *Nixon: A Life* (Weidenfeld & Nicolson, 1993) might be a failure was wrong. So far it has sold over 50,000 copies in its US and British hardback editions. It has also had Book of the Month Club, paperback, Readers Digest and audiotape editions, as well as being serialized in more than 100 newspapers and magazines around the world. The reviewers were kind to it too.

4 *Nixon: A Life*, p. 525.

5 C. S. Lewis, *Mere Christianity*, Touchstone, 1996, p. 60.

6 Thomas Babington, 1st Baron Macaulay, *Lays of Ancient Rome*, 1842, 'Horatius', st. 50.

7 *Guardian*, 17 July 1997.

8 Charles Colson, letter to the author, 2 July 1997.

9 William Temple, *Palm Sunday to Easter*, SPCK, 1942.

CHAPTER NINETEEN

1 Charles Colson, letter to the author, 24 October 1997.

2 A year later we were joined by a seventh participant: Derek Foster, MP for Bishop Auckland and a former Labour Chief Whip.

3 The clerical or religious counsellors who helped me in 1997–9 included: my three retreat tutors, Lister Tonge, Madeleine Prendergast and Gerry Hughes; my cousin Stephen Verney, a retired Anglican bishop; Chris Hancock, the Vicar of Holy Trinity, Cambridge; David Mathers, my closest friend at prep school and now Vicar of Thurston; David Stancliffe, the Bishop of Salisbury; Francis Pym, a Parliamentary Chaplain; Roger Holloway, the Preacher of Gray's Inn; Philip Chester of St Matthew's, Westminster; Father James Naters SSJE; Father Felix Stephen OSB; Donald Gray, Robert Wright and Dominic Fenton of Westminster Abbey; Father Norman Brown of Westminster Cathedral; Michael Chantry, Chaplain of Hertford College, Oxford; Colin Dye of Kensington Temple; Canon Bruce Duncan, Principal of Sarum College, Salisbury; Richard Coombs, Vicar of Burford; Dick Lucas, Rector of St Helen's, Bishopsgate; Jeremy Jennings, Nicky Gumbel and Sandy Millar of Holy Trinity, Brompton.

4 Alpha is an informal introductory or refresher course on the basics of Christianity. Pioneered by Holy Trinity, Brompton, the courses now run in churches all round the country.

5 Charles Colson, *Loving God*, Zondervan, 1983, p. 33.

6 Charles Colson, letter to the author, 24 October 1997.

7 Private information given to the author by police sources.

8 The maximum sentence for perjury is seven years. The average sentence for the 200 or so annual perjury convictions in the courts is four months' imprisonment.

9 St Augustine of Hippo, *Confessions*, Oxford University Press, 1992, p. 61.

Notes

CHAPTER TWENTY

1 Author, letter to Peter Stothard, 18 November 1997.

2 *Spectator*, 20–27 December 1997.

3 *Hansard*, 17 December 1997.

4 *Guardian*, 3 March 1998.

5 *Evening Standard*, 3 March 1998.

CHAPTER TWENTY-ONE

1 Later in the conversation John Nutting added that his gloomy forecast might come down if he could put forward a strong plea in mitigation – which 16 months later, on 8 June 1999, he did brilliantly well.

2 Author, memorandum to John Nutting QC, 10 March 1998.

3 Lolicia was not arrested because of her Swiss citizenship and her residence outside the jurisdiction of English law. Her attorney sent Scotland Yard a fax offering to arrange a meeting between his client and officers of the Organized Crime Squad in Belgrade (where Lolicia was then staying), but this was never followed up.

4 *Evening Standard*, 16 March 1998, et seriatim.

5 Transcript of police interview at Chelsea Police Station, 17 March 1998.

6 *Guardian*, 23 March 1998.

7 Ibid.

8 Witness statements of Richard Sykes, 3 June 1999, and Mark Warby, 26 May 1999. Mark Warby's statement was shown to and agreed with by Charles Gray and Justin Rushbrooke (paragraph 11).

9 Mark Warby's statement, paragraph 10.

10 Sir Nicholas Bonsor Bt is one of my oldest friends. We were contemporaries at school, served together in the House of Commons for 23 years, and have seen strong friendships develop between our wives and children. He was Minister of State for Foreign Affairs, 1995–7.

11 Victoria's marks in her A level paper on US politics were 240 out of 300 – a commendable 80 per cent.

12 Caspar Weinberger is a former US Defence Secretary; William Buckley is Editor of the *National Review*; Ed Meese is a former Attorney General; Jeanne

Kirkpatrick is a former Ambassador to the United Nations and a Professor at Georgetown University; Bob Tyrrell is Editor of the *American Spectator*. All are Regnery authors.

CHAPTER TWENTY-TWO

1 *Macbeth*, Act I, scene vii, l.1.

2 Bugsy Malone was Al Capone's driver.

3 Malcolm Pearson, now Lord Pearson of Rannoch, has been my closest friend for over 40 years. In a well-intentioned effort to dissuade the authorities from prosecuting me, he had that morning published a feature article in the *Daily Telegraph* summarizing some of my dealings with the British and Saudi intelligence services while I was a Defence Minister. Through no fault of Malcolm's, this act of friendship was probably counterproductive.

4 Charles Colson, fax to the author, 21 May 1998.

CHAPTER TWENTY-THREE

1 Victoria Aitken, police interview, 29 June 1998.

2 Alan Rusbridger, letter to DPP and Commissioner of Metropolitan Police, 20 June 1997, published in the *Guardian*, 21 June 1997.

3 *Evening Standard*, 13 August 1998.

4 The Standard Assessment Test (SAT) is the examination gateway for all US university admission candidates. Its verbal reasoning and maths tests are generally considered difficult for non-Americans, so Victoria's result was exceptional.

5 *Evening Standard*, 7 December 1998.

6 *Sunday Express*, 10 January 1999.

CHAPTER TWENTY-FOUR

1 This surprisingly long wait was initially caused by Said Ayas' plea of not guilty, which meant that my sentencing date had to be delayed until his contested case could be scheduled for a full trial.

2 My prosecution for 'unauthorized communication of official information' under this outdated and much abused legislation, and my book *Officially Secret* (Weidenfeld & Nicolson, 1971), were instrumental in bringing about a root-

and-branch reform of Britain's Official Secrets Act, including the abolition of the Section 2 offences for which I had been tried.

3 *Daily Mirror*, 20 January 1999.

4 *Evening Standard*, 19 January 1999.

5 *Sun*, 20 January 1999.

6 *Independent*, 20 January 1999.

7 *Sun*, 20 January 1999.

8 *Daily Mirror*, 20 January 1999.

9 Charles Colson, letter to the author, 28 January 1999.

10 The *Guardian* articles of 5 March 1999 were what the Editor Alan Rusbridger later described (in a comment to James Pringle, 9 March 1999) as 'a plausible theory' for my visit to the Ritz Hotel in Paris. The theory was wrong (see Chapter 12, 'What Really Happened at the Ritz').

11 At the time of writing the Press Complaints Commission has not yet ruled on this complaint.

12 Valerie Scott, letter to Mr Justice Scott Baker, 2 June 1999.

13 Author, letter to Anthony Cavendish, 3 November 1998.

CHAPTER TWENTY-FIVE

1 C. S. Lewis, *Mere Christianity*, Touchstone, 1996, p. 103.

2 Robert Runcie, letter to the author, 8 July 1997.

3 William Aitken, Eton English Language essay, October 1998.

4 From the Foreword by H. A. Williams CR in W. H. Vanstone, *Love's Endeavour, Love's Expense*, Darton Longman & Todd, 1977.

5 St Augustine, *Confessions*, p. 61.

Index

Index

Index